W9-APH-373

NO SAFE HAVEN

DATE DUE

MAR 2 1 2001			
MAY 1 4 2001			
APR 3 0 2007			
11/25/09			
GAYLORD			PRINTED IN U.S.A.

Other titles in
THE NORTHEASTERN SERIES ON GENDER, CRIME, AND LAW
edited by Claire Renzetti, *St. Joseph's University*

NO SAFE HAVEN

*Stories
of Women
in Prison*

Lori B. Girshick

Northeastern University Press • Boston

HARPER COLLEGE LIBRARY
PALATINE, ILLINOIS 60067

HV
9475
.N82
B534.
1999

Northeastern University Press

Copyright 1999 by Lori B. Girshick

All rights reserved. Except for the quotation of short passages for the purposes of criticism and review, no part of this book may be reproduced in any form or by any means, electronic or mechanical, including photocopying, recording, or any information storage and retrieval system now known or to be invented, without written permission of the publisher.

Library of Congress Cataloging-in-Publication Data

Girshick, Lori B.
No safe haven : stories of women in prison / Lori B. Girshick.
p.   cm. — (The Northeastern series on gender, crime, and law)
Includes bibliographical references and index.
ISBN 1–55553–373–6 (cloth); ISBN 1–55553–467–8 (paper)
1. Black Mountain Correctional Center for Women (Black
Mountain, N.C.)   2. Women prisoners—North Carolina—Interviews.
3. Women prisoners—North Carolina—Social conditions.   I. Title.
II. Series.
HV9475.N82B534   1999
365'.975688—dc21   98–48852

Designed by Gary Gore

Composed in Electra by Coghill Composition Company in Richmond, Virginia.
Printed and bound by Thomson-Shore, Inc., in Dexter, Michigan.
The paper is Glatfelter Supple Opaque Recycled, an acid-free sheet.

Manufactured in the United States of America
03 02 01 00   5 4 3 2

HARPER COLLEGE LIBRARY
PALATINE, ILLINOIS 60067

This book is dedicated, with love, to my mother, Ruth Rosenblum Girshick

CONTENTS

ACKNOWLEDGMENTS

It was fortuitous that when I moved to North Carolina to join the faculty of Warren Wilson College there was a women's prison five miles up the road. I knew I wanted to work with female inmates and I had a research project in mind. This work would further a long-standing involvement with incarcerated youth and adults as well as my commitment to addressing the structural reasons for societal inequalities and solutions to those problems.

I am indebted to many people for their help and support with this work. I thank Barbara Bloom for her assistance and feedback as the proposal was developing, as well as for her permission to adapt a questionnaire that she and Barbara Owen had administered to women inmates in California. I am grateful to the Appalachian College Association, Inc., for its continued support by granting me two consecutive summer fellowships. This confidence in me and my work is appreciated, and I hope I am a credit to the Association and its goals. I appreciate, as well, the support of Virginia McKinley, Academic Dean of Warren Wilson College, who has encouraged me and taken a genuine interest in my work over the years.

A number of persons at the North Carolina Department of Correction in Raleigh deserve mention. Jenny Lancaster and Stephan Kiefer helped guide me in my work and patiently answered my questions. Mr. Kiefer, in particular, was always available and I appreciate our working relationship. Thanks to Tom Sutton for providing me with North Carolina data.

That my activities at the Black Mountain Correctional Center for Women went so smoothly can only be attributed to the backing and encouragement of the superintendent, Renae Brame. Ms. Brame supported the project from the initial stages and allowed me complete freedom in my work and in access to the inmates. She spent hours with me in discussion, and I appreciate her honesty and willingness to both provide and receive feedback concerning life at the prison. The program director, Debbie Lara, also found countless hours during her busy days to answer my questions. Both of these women are dedicated to their work and their concern for the well-being of the inmates was clear. I also thank the many guards who helped facilitate my interviewing and visiting, and acknowledge that it is not easy to work while you know a study is being conducted and you are under a microscope. Openness and friendliness characterized my experience during the research.

The persons I interviewed—inmates, family members, community volunteers, and program providers—were gracious to let me into their lives, allowing me to probe into their thoughts, feelings, and behaviors. I am in awe that so many were willing to share and reveal, to be vulnerable, and I greatly appreciate my opportunities to be with them.

I thank Russ Immarigeon, Ellen Clarke, Linda Larsen, Brenda Carleton, Wendy Mitschke, and Marielena Paniagua for their technical and emotional support during the writing of this book. I certainly talked nonstop about my work and received encouragement from a great many friends and acquaintances, but these people deserve particular mention.

Special thanks to Claire Renzetti at St. Joseph's University for encouraging me to submit the book proposal and for keeping me calm during the process. Thank you to William Frohlich, Director, Northeastern University Press, and Tara Mantel, Editorial Assistant, for their encouragement and patience. It is a pleasure to work with them and I value our relationships.

Last, I am grateful to have a place in the grand scheme of things to develop these ideas and to be part of a community of people who want to make a difference in this world. I hope this contribution, however small, helps us to overcome our fears and live lives of greater safety, peace, and integrity.

NO SAFE HAVEN

C h a p t e r

Introduction

N*o Safe Haven* takes us into the lives of forty women in a minimum security prison in Western North Carolina. Through examining their experiences as adolescents, as free adults, and as prisoners, and by placing them in their social networks of family, friends, program providers, other inmates, guards, and community volunteers, we will see the women and the criminal justice system with new eyes. These women are not safe, secure, or respected outside or inside prison, and an understanding of gender inequality helps us to realize why this is so.

I argue that we must reconstruct social life so that prison does not remain the dumping ground for women who have no viable options for self-support or the institution to which they must turn for drug treatment, job training, or safety from battering. Once imprisoned, they become scapegoats for our societal failures, intensifying their degradation; we, by contrast, escape responsibility for changing how we treat girls and women in the United States.

This research was undertaken with the explicit objective of examining the gendered nature of women's lives, their options, their crimes, and their time in prison. Patriarchy and its privileges are defining qualities of our culture, and as such have influenced criminology and the criminal justice system. Sex, according to Joanne Belknap (1996, 4; and many others; see, for example, Carlen 1988, Cressey 1964, Faith 1993, Naffine 1996), is the most powerful variable with regard to crime. It has an overwhelming predictive value concerning not only who commits crimes but also who commits what types of crimes. As a feminist, an academic, and an activist, it is my hope that this work will give us insight into what led these women to their crimes and help us to assess whether imprisonment is the appropriate response to them.

Outreach to the Sample

To gain access to the Black Mountain Correctional Center for Women, located in Black Mountain, North Carolina, I first spoke with the head of the Female Command (the women's section) of the state's bureau of prisons, who supported the plan and gave helpful suggestions. I established a relationship with the prison's superintendent, Renae Brame, who enthusiastically received my ideas and helped me all along the way with feedback, access, and encouragement. We met on many occasions to discuss logistics, issues of confidentiality, referrals for the women if the interview content upset them, the interview questionnaire itself, and other issues related to the study. I also went through the community-volunteer training program to learn about the prison's rules and the inmates housed there.

As part of standard procedure, I submitted a research proposal to the Research and Planning Office of the North Carolina Department of Correction. Its review, which includes gaining approval from the Human Subjects Review Committee, deals with issues of confidentiality and consent, outreach to the sample, and the overall objectives of the study. Approval and support from each of these levels, from the prison superintendent to the Department of Correction, were necessary for the study to proceed. I also applied for and received two postdoctoral fellowships from the Appalachian College Association, Inc., for research in summer 1996 and summer 1997.

Between May and September 1996, I interviewed forty women inmates, twelve family members or friends, sixteen community volunteers, and nine program or agency providers. Talking to this range of people who form the networks surrounding the inmates has given me several angles from which to examine the activities of and influences on the women, both before and during incarceration.

Inmates learned about the study in several ways: through a flyer I distributed in early May; by talking with me at two separate dorm meetings, where I explained what the study was about and invited them to participate; through personal suggestion from the superintendent that they might want to be interviewed (which some women saw as coercive); through word of mouth from other inmates; by direct invitation from me when I was on the prison grounds talking with them casually; and through a last open letter to those I had not yet spoken to, pointing out that the study was nearing an end and asking them to please contact me if they wanted to take part.

Since trust is a very big issue for prisoners, I knew that a number of inmates would not talk to me simply because they suspected my motives. Some, for example, wondered if I was involved to make money from publication, or feared that I would break confidence and give the superintendent information about them. According to what inmates told me, some of the women also distrusted me because I was educated and successful. And, finally, there were those who did not know what kind of "doctor" I was and expected tests to be run on them while they were being interviewed.

Still, there were many who did agree to meet with me, some after being reassured by those who had gone before. Such consent does not imply complete confidence; I agree with Robert Emerson (1983), who suggests that trust itself is a situated access to some secrets, but not to all secrets. In their 1995 project report, "Reframing the Needs of Women in Prison," Cynthia Coll and Kathleen Duff describe an innovation in interviewing female inmates. In speaking with prisoners in Massachusetts, they shifted their approach from one emphasizing why the women should talk to them to one in which the inmates would "allow us to listen to them" (16). They also shifted the sense that the only important part of the experience was what the researchers later did with information to one that focused on the process of exchange, which led to authentic group dialog. I followed this approach.

Inmates volunteered for the interviews by filling out a request form and giving it to an administrative secretary. They could also tell me directly that they wanted to be interviewed, and I could sign them up. There were three times each day when I could meet with them, and on some days I spoke with three women. All interviews were held at the prison, either in a small room cleared out for this purpose, a larger meeting room, an administrative office, or outdoors at picnic tables. The small room was tiny and airless, with an echo. It was also located next to the day room. In the evenings, when prisoners watched television, my tape recorder picked up not only the interview but the sound of the television and inmates' voices from the day room and the hallway. The noise was quite disruptive, and this room was my least favorite of the locations.

All interviews lasted from forty-five minutes to two hours, and were taped. The consent form for the inmates was a bit unusual. One section stated that participating in the interview did not affect their sentence, and another referred to my obligation to report to the administration if I learned of plans for a prison escape or for any intended harm. I read the consent form aloud to each inmate and asked if there were any questions before we began.

At the end of the interview I asked each woman if there was a family member I could speak to. Not all of them responded positively; they felt the person would not be interested, or was in ill health. In some cases, the prisoners were no longer in good standing or in contact with any relatives. If the response was positive, however, I handwrote a note on a pre-addressed, stamped postcard to the family member. I asked the inmates to give the postcards to their relatives and to ask them to mail the cards back to me with their phone numbers if they wanted to be interviewed.

The return of the postcard acted as a permission. I did not want to call family members "cold," since that would not only invade their privacy but would most likely lead to many refusals out of distrust. After receiving the postcard, I conducted a phone interview. Initially, I had hoped to do home visits, but the logistics of driving around a large state, finding times convenient for the relatives, and the realization that family members might be uncomfortable having me in their homes changed my mind. I felt the phone interviews were immediate, convenient, and made it easier for some relatives to disclose personal information because of their anonymity. I did meet four of the family members or friends whom I interviewed. Two were seeing inmates during visiting hours (and we set up times to talk on the phone), and I interviewed two others in person after they visited with an inmate.

Although I feel the postcard method was the best way to secure permission before calling a family member at home, there were several problems with it. The inmate might never mail the postcard. The relative or friend might not understand what the study was about (several told me prisoners explained nothing about the study, but just told them to "please do this"). Or family members might decide the situation was too private to talk to a stranger about. There was no way I could explain to them as I had to inmates in dorm meetings and personal encounters what the interview would entail. Several prisoners who wanted simply to give me their mothers' phone numbers (which I declined) finally took postcards, which I never received back. Would there have been more interviews in these cases if I had in fact called directly, since they assured me their mothers would be glad to talk to me? In any event, rather than complicate my task, I dealt with every situation by requiring the postcard.

I also interviewed members of the surrounding community who volunteered at the prison; some of them had been involved since the site for the institution was chosen. Community volunteers (CV) participate in the sponsor program, taking inmates out with CV passes; help plan and staff retreats, such as the overnight ones for prisoners and their children or for women who are substance abusers; hold monthly birthday parties; take inmates out to cultural events; conduct religious services and Bible study; provide transportation on occasion to job interviews or other appointments; and plan other events. Some volunteers are members of the Resource Council, a community council appointed by the governor. Volunteers made a major contribution to raising funds for the chapel and activity building, under construction during the study period and now being used.

I first asked volunteers for their help at an appreciation dinner held for them in early June 1996. There I made an announcement about the study and talked to persons individually. I made appointments with some of these men and women and followed up with others who were recommended to me. The interviews usually took place at the volunteers' homes, but a few were held in my office or at the prison; some were conducted by telephone. They lasted between thirty and ninety minutes, and covered why and how the individuals became involved, what they did with the prisoners, and what impact they felt these activities had on the inmates.

After listening to the inmates talk about them, I determined to learn more about the prison's programs, to see where they were held, and to hear the perspectives of the providers. These persons were from the substance abuse, vocational rehabilitation, and job training programs, and from the local community college; I also spoke to the prison nurse. I called many of them and usually visited their offices, but I also did two interviews in homes, as well as a few over the telephone. The interviews lasted about an hour; they sometimes involved a tour of a facility, and at other times I was given brochures.

Throughout the process of interviewing I was in close contact with the prison administration. This was essentially a matter of checking in, but I could also ask questions about some aspect of the prison or of my continuing effort to reach out to the inmates. For example, I wrote thank-you notes to all the prisoners I had spoken with, and in late August I gave those who had taken a postcard for a relative a second card if I had not heard from the family member. Actions such as these needed to be approved. I also had fairly regular, though brief, interaction with inmates I had interviewed and with those I had not interviewed just by being on the grounds—walking from my car to the main building, waiting for the woman I was going to speak with, and so on. This provided snippets of interactions, small talk, and follow-ups.

This sample of four different groups (female inmates, family members and friends, community volunteers, and program providers) totals seventy-seven persons. It is not a representative sample, however. Family members were referred by inmates, and program providers were contacted due to their direct connection to the prison. Community volunteers were recruited by referral from the program director and through the "snowball" technique (or accumulation of contacts). Recruitment and snowball methods were used for the inmates. Even though the sample is not random, comparisons with other studies show the inmates involved to be remarkably similar to others across the country in their personal attributes and experiences and in their incarceration demographics and experiences. Furthermore, as Marjorie DeVault has written, the goal is not to search for "generalizable differences among categorical groups[;] the aim is to understand how a member of such a group is caught up in the social relations of her context" (1995, 625). My purpose here is to examine the conditions that surround an inmate's choices and how that context influences her life. Similarly, Jill Berrick in *Faces of Poverty* (1995) studied women on welfare and looked at how individual life experiences can be tied to aggregate experiences. This is the connection between personal troubles and social issues that C. Wright Mills labels the "sociological imagination" (1959).

In-Depth Interviewing

The primary method used in this work, feminist interviewing, is not a one-way process. Establishing rapport and practicing researcher self-disclosure are intimately related for feminists. To varying degrees, a researcher's disclosure of herself may minimize power imbalances, increase solidarity between researcher and participant, enhance information gathering, and transform an interview into a dialog.

On the surface I looked quite different from the women I was interviewing. I held a Ph.D., I was middle-class, I was white, and I was not incarcerated. However, the inmates also knew that I had been married to a man in prison at one time and that I had some past connection with the prison system. They also knew that I worked with battered women and was an active proponent of women's rights. During some of the interview "conversations," prisoners also learned that I had spent short stints in jail for civil disobedience, that I had sold drugs while in college, and that I had abused drugs for many years. Disclosure meant risk, but it also meant the potential for relating. As I was learning about these women, I realized that the majority of the interviews felt like mini-therapy sessions for *me* due to the many connections I had with them. Many feelings about the past were triggered, and I was also able to acknowledge personal growth and change. At the same time, some women accorded me a type of insider status with comments such as, "You're one of us."

An outcome of in-depth interviewing, story telling, or narratives does not reflect random actions and reactions, but provides the narrator with coherence and direction. Tellers mention events that have significance for them. Narratives reveal how people define reality and how they make sense of their past, present, and future, as Marjorie DeVault (1995) found in her interviews with African American nutritionists.

Narratives are social products, not some measurable truth. They are a translation of lived life into told life. Memory is selective. Indeed, Mary Gergen stresses that

> people are not capable of revealing their "true selves" or their actual life stories because such things do not exist. People are only able to construe their lives within the confines of linguistic and social conventions. [Self-narratives are] temporary constructions of what seems most appropriate from the perspective of the narrator at that time. (1991, 102)

In discussing feminist in-depth interviewing, Shulamit Reinharz (1992) points out that one of the key questions for feminist interviewers is whose voice we hear when women speak. The dilemma exists because they speak out of a position of oppression and because their voices are mediated through researchers. As researchers, we attempt to interpret what we are hearing, which is already a selective interpretation by the speaker.

In telling our narratives, we continually manage the impressions we make. We perform, in a sense, and we choose to keep some secrets. When a stigma is invisible or the individual thinks it is not known, managing information is crucial. A constant dilemma is "to display or not to display; to tell or not to tell; to let on or not to let on; to lie or not to lie; and in each case, to whom, how, when, and where," as Erving Goffman points out in *Stigma* (1963, 42). Although an individual may try to "pass" and prevent the stigma from becoming known, we are never as anonymous as we think. There is always the possibility of running into someone who *knows*. For women in prison, their criminality is known to their families, other inmates, people from home, guards, community volunteers, service providers, peers at work, and possibly strangers who have seen them on the news. Although inmates are viewed as being those with a "spoiled identity," it is important to keep in mind that *all* individuals use impression management, and *all* individuals have secrets. Inmates are not the only ones who tell narratives from their own perspective.

Evaluating "Truth"

During my summer of interviewing, an officer told me, "You can't trust anything these women say, they all lie." This officer did not take into account that a key factor in social encounters is the acknowledgment of multiple realities, contradictory social locations, fluctuation instead of consistency, and the right of an individual to change her mind. "Truth" is multifaceted and subjective, and it exists within a certain context.

In this study there were several instances where the issue of how to understand what I was hearing was particularly challenging. I was also aware of talking with members of a stigmatized group who had an interest in "saving face." However, everyone is concerned, to some degree, with trying to make a good impression. I also accepted the idea that information was being shared selectively. While it is certainly possible that questions were not answered fully, I did attempt to ask pointed questions rather than only allow a story to unfold on its own. Still, what and how much to disclose is the prerogative of any of us.

Concerning attributions to behaviors, when I asked what led up to certain events, such as dropping out of high school or committing crimes, I also asked the women to give their reasons in order of importance. Keeping in mind that memories are selective and the prisoners were reflecting on actions from years past, still, this helped in *my* not having to interpret at least this segment of the narratives.

More problematic were the instances when inmates and family members gave different accounts of an event or attribution. For example, one mother contradicted an attribution of her daughter's crime. Whereas the daughter told me she needed money for an operation for her son, the mother said there was no operation (though the illness was real) and that she believed her daughter wanted money for drugs for herself and her friends. Another mother revealed that her granddaughter had lived in her home for years, whereas the inmate claimed that the girl lived with her at the time of her arrest. A third contradiction came from a daughter who discounted virtually the entire version of her mother's "passive" role in her crime; she based her assertions on an accumulation of evidence and judgments about her mother's character.

In trying to reconcile these accounts, I did not conclude that one person was telling the "truth" and the other person was lying. Individuals deliver accounts that are relevant to the audience, the time, and their personal understanding and definition of "reality." So, for example—and here my own interpretations, which may differ from those of the narrators, come into play—I felt in the first case that the mother really did not know why her daughter committed her crime, but in her mind "drugs" could be the only reasonable explanation. She had no proof that her daughter took drugs, but she was trying to make sense of her actions. For the daughter's part, perhaps her son did not have the operation; however, her desire for money for his medical needs was real to her and an operation had apparently been an option. Perhaps the inmate did use drugs; even so, in her mind the money she needed was for her son, not for her drugs.

In the second case, I believe that the inmate's daughter did live with the inmate's mother. But the inmate saw her daughter whenever she could, and I conjecture that she was being the best parent she could be under the circumstances of her drug addiction. Perhaps not having her daughter living with her was inconsistent with her definition of being a good parent, and she interpreted the short stays and visits as "living with." In fact, the prisoner's mother mentioned that she could not believe her daughter would abandon her own child as she had. Perhaps these issues also loomed large for the daughter, and she needed to define herself as a caring parent, despite real absences, meaning holding an interpretation that her daughter "lived with" her.

The last instance was the most difficult to reconcile, and in fact I have not done so. I believe the daughter is correct in her information and interpretation, and I also feel that her mother believes in her version. It is the story the inmate has stuck by since her arrest (despite evidence to the contrary), and in order to save face she, possibly for psychological reasons, needs to stick to it. There is the possibility that she truly does believe her version of events, and that to her it *is* the truth that she was coerced into the illegal acts and did not participate voluntarily.

In essence, I will not be the judge of truth; it is impossible to know what purpose a particular version of the truth serves. We are involved in impression management that is subject to the same constraints whether we are imprisoned or "free," and I believe our process of creating social constructions is the same whether they are contradictory or consistent. I accept the versions of understanding each inmate has told me. Narratives to the contrary are also understandings, all to be reinterpreted depending on audience, memory, and redefinitions of the self.

Story telling does not only occur when people are being interviewed. I am seeing several of the women at the prison with some regularity, and I have heard stories about and from inmates who had been paroled. I hear these "continuing stories" at the prison, at a halfway house, and during outings. All of them have involved discrepancies of one sort or another (e.g., women not doing what they said they would do, or having conflicting versions of the truth told to me). I believe this situation reinforces the notion of truth as relative. In the final analysis, there are simply limits to a researcher's ability to determine "truth." However, these limitations are not any different than understanding accounts in our everyday lives outside research. Hence, I do not find that the complexity and relativity of truth pose a dilemma unique to research; rather, such are the facts of social life.

Women Incarcerated in North Carolina

As of June 30, 1996, the country's tenth largest state ranked tenth in prison population and seventeenth in incarceration rate. As of December 31 of that year, 30,924 women and men were incarcerated in North Carolina's prisons. Of these, 1,898 were women (6 percent) and 29,026 were men. Overall, 65 percent of the incarcerated population was African American, 31 percent was white, and 4 percent came from other groups (North Carolina Department of Correction, 1996). According to the department's Office of Research and Planning, 58 percent of female inmates were African American, 38 percent were white, 2 percent were Native American, and another 2 percent were Asian or members of other groups. The Department of Correction has only recently (since 1995) begun documenting ethnicity, and no accurate statistics are available yet. Most incarcerated women (44 percent) were between 30 and 39 years old. Thirty-five percent were between 20 and 29; 15 percent were between 40 and 49; 4 percent were younger than 20; 3 percent were between 50 and 59; and less than 1 percent were 60 and older.

The state has various correctional facilities for women and men. There are eighty-seven prisons in North Carolina, five of them for women. There is one halfway house, which is for women. One of the four substance abuse facilities is for women. There are also eleven county institutions and three out-of-state facilities, all for men.

Following is a list of the women's institutions, with their standard operating capacity (SOC), population count (CNT), and occupancy rate (OCC RATE) as of December 31, 1996. The North Carolina Correctional Institution for Women (NCCIW) in Raleigh is a close custody prison; the other four correctional centers for women are smaller, minimum security facilities.

Women's Facilities in North Carolina as of December 31, 1996

Facility	SOC	CNT	OCC RATE (%)
NCCIW (Raleigh)	754	1059	140
Fountain CCW	393	494	125
Raleigh CCW	104	141	135
Black Mountain CCW	51	68	133
Wilmington RFW	26	34	130
Eco Half-Way House	20	20	100
Mary Frances Center (substance abuse)	100	83	83

SOURCE: North Carolina Department of Correction, Office of Research and Planning.

The Women in This Study

The Black Mountain Correctional Center for Women (hereinafter referred to as Black Mountain) sits off the main road, surrounded by pine trees. There is no security fence around the perimeter. It houses eighty inmates (sixty-eight at the time of the study) and is a minimum security, or honor grade, prison. The campus features two brick buildings. One is a two-story structure holding the inmates. They sleep four to a room, have a clothes closet, and have a day room and bathroom on each floor; they also have access to the canteen and laundry facilities. The other structure, a recently built chapel and activity-office building, contains a library, administrative offices, and a multipurpose room for eating, religious services, and other activities.

All prisoners at Black Mountain either work in a unit job or a job off-site, attend school or vocational training, or take part in an off-site substance abuse program. The privileges associated with being at this honor grade allow inmates to participate in work release; attend drug treatment off-site; go through vocational rehabilitation; be on study leave; have community-volunteer passes to leave the prison for up to six hours to shop, go to church, go to an event, or do other things; and have home passes ranging from six to seventy-two hours. On-site visiting is allowed on Saturdays from 9:30 to 11:30 A.M. and 2:30 to 4:30 P.M., and on Sundays from 9 to 11 A.M. and 2:30 to 4:30 P.M. The women can wear their own clothes or light green prison-issue uniforms.

There are many programs at the prison, run by either community volunteers or contract employees. Among these are Alcoholics Anonymous (AA), Narcotics Anonymous (NA), Drug and Alcohol Rehabilitation Treatment (DART) Aftercare, individual and group psychological counseling, Bible study, monthly birthday parties, a monthly video and discussion program, and occasional programs such as overnight mother-children retreats. All privileges are earned through good behavior, and inmates with rule infractions are sent back to the NCCIW in Raleigh. Prisoners who come to Black Mountain have earned their way there and are usually close to release; some women, however, do stay for years.

The average age of the forty inmates interviewed was 31.9 years, with a range from 18 to 55. Forty percent of the prisoners had never been married. Thirty-three percent were divorced; 10 percent were married; 8 percent were widowed; 8 percent were separated; and 10 percent were in common law marriage. Roughly half of the women were Baptist; 13 percent stated no religious preference; 10 percent were Catholic; 10 percent were Pentecostal Holiness; 8 percent were Methodist; and Muslim, Full Gospel, Lutheran, and African Methodist Episcopal accounted for 3 percent each.

Racially, 38 percent of the prisoners were white, not Hispanic; 35 percent were black, not Hispanic; 5 percent were Native American; 3 percent were white, Hispanic; 15 percent were white and Native American; 3 percent were black and Native American; and 3 percent were mixed (identified with at least three heritages). I decided to name each racial category separately rather than use one larger "mixed" category to allow for more description, as well as to acknowledge the women's backgrounds. In subsequent chapters, the phrase "women of color" refers to all who identified as other than "white, not Hispanic." This means that even those women who declared themselves part white are included in the nonwhite category. I made this decision because in American society mixed-race individuals are generally recognized by that part of their heritage that carries the lowest status (i.e., nonwhite). The person, for example, who has a white parent and an African American parent is generally seen and treated as nonwhite, regardless of the white parentage.

Looking at the arrest and sentence information, for 30 percent of the women this was a first arrest with prison; for 23 percent, a probation violation with a new charge; for 20 percent, a parole violation with a new charge; for 10 percent, a new offense but not their first; for another 10 percent, a probation violation only; for 3 percent, a parole violation only; and for another 3 percent this was a violation of both parole and probation.

There were 17 violent crimes committed, 41 property crimes, 21 drug-related crimes, and 8 vehicular crimes, for a total of 87 charges for 40 women. This is actually an undercount, however; I only noted up to 6 charges per inmate, and some women may have neglected to mention all of their charges.

The average length of sentence was 10 years, 11 months for 38 women. The shortest sentence was 11 months, and the longest sentence was 47 years, 11 months. Two women were serving life sentences with the possibility of parole.

The average time served at the point of the interview was 2 years, 5 months, with the shortest time 4 months and the longest time 16 years.

There are some other significant facts about the women that figure prominently in the chapters to follow. Eighty-five percent of the inmates have children. Between them, these 34 women have 77 children, 61 of whom are 17 or under, and 20 of whom are 6 or under. Fifteen percent of the women gave birth in prison. Rounding out the picture, 65 percent of the inmates had dropped out of high school; 68 percent were abused as children; 52 percent ran away from home as juveniles; 85 percent have been physically battered as adults; 43 percent have been raped as adults; 55 percent have been on welfare at some point in their lives; and 65 percent were working right before their arrest.

This book is organized to take us into the lives of these women from adolescence to adulthood, to listen to the voices of families, friends, program providers, and community volunteers, and to offer alternative responses to and new ways of looking at incarcerated women. I examine the prison environment and offer a critical analysis of societal structures. It is my hope that this exploration will lead us to a new commitment to transform our social context, leading to a transformation in our personal lives.

References

Belknap, J. (1996). *The invisible woman: Gender, crime, and justice.* Belmont, Calif.: Wadsworth Publishing.

Berrick, J. (1995). *Faces of Poverty.* New York: Oxford University Press.

Carlen, P. (1988). *Women, crime, and poverty.* Milton Keynes, U.K.: Open University Press.

Coll, C., and K. Duff. (1995). *Reframing the needs of women in prison: A relational and diversity perspective* (Project Report, no. 4). Wellesley, Mass.: Stone Center.

Cressey, D. (1964). *Delinquency, crime, and differential association.* The Hague: Martinus Nijhoff.

DeVault, M. (1995, October). Ethnicity and expertise: Racial-ethnic knowledge in sociological research. *Gender and Society* 9 (5): 612–31.

Emerson, R., ed. (1983). *Contemporary field research: A collection of readings.* Boston: Little, Brown.

Faith, K. (1993). *Unruly women: The politics of confinement and resistance.* Vancouver, Canada: Press Gang Publishers.

Gergen, M. (1991). Narrative structures in social explanation. In C. Antaki, ed., *Analyzing everyday explanation: A casebook of methods,* 94–112. London: Sage Publications.

Goffman, E. (1963). *Stigma: Notes on the management of spoiled identity.* New York: Simon and Schuster.

Mills, C. Wright. (1959). *The sociological imagination.* New York: Oxford University Press.

Naffine, N. (1996). *Feminism and criminology.* Philadelphia: Temple University Press.

North Carolina Department of Correction. (1996, March). *Research bulletin,* no. 38. Raleigh: Office of Research and Planning.

Reinharz, S. (1992). *Feminist methods in social research.* New York: Oxford University Press.

2

Women
in Prison

The United States imprisons more people today than at any time in our history. It has the highest incarceration rate in the world at 615 inmates per 100,000 population. At midyear 1996, 1 in every 163 U.S. residents was incarcerated (Bureau of Justice Statistics 1997, 2). The number of inmates has increased fivefold between 1970 and 1996, and America is on an "imprisonment binge." Get-tough policies include longer sentences, more austere imprisonment conditions, so-called three-strikes laws, the "war on drugs," and prison chain gangs (see, for example, Irwin and Austin 1994, Mauer 1997, Sentencing Project 1997).

Female prisoners are largely an invisible population, given their small numbers, their involvement in less violent and less serious offenses, and their neglect by criminologists. Women's experiences with crime and the criminal justice system are shaped by social structural constraints, societal gender ideologies, racism, class inequalities, self-esteem and identity problems, and shifts in the political winds.

By year-end 1996, women accounted for 6.3 percent of all state and federal prisoners. During 1996, the number of women under state or federal jurisdiction grew from 68,494 to 74,730, an increase of 9.1 percent. Moreover, since 1985 the annual growth rate for female inmates has averaged 11.2 percent, compared to a 7.9 percent average increase for men (Bureau of Justice Statistics 1997, 5).

Women of color are disproportionately imprisoned. According to the American Correctional Association (1992a), they made up 61 percent of all incarcerated women in state institutions and 65 percent of women in federal prisons as of June 30, 1991. African American women are overrepresented at four times their proportion of the population, and Latinas by about 30 percent; white women are considerably underrepresented. African American women are incarcerated at a rate seven times that of white women (American Correctional Association 1992b), and they represent a higher proportion of all female offenders than black men do of all male offenders.

African American women have been subject to the largest growth in prison, jail, probation, or parole supervision of all demographic groups, experiencing a 78 percent increase from 1989 to 1994. Minority women are trapped in the racism and sexism of the criminal justice system. In particular, according to Marc Mauer and Tracy Huling (1995) of the Sentencing Project, they have been caught up in the harsher treatment of crack cocaine offenders, since women are more likely to use and distribute crack than other drugs.

Most of the increase in women's arrests is due to crimes of shoplifting, check forgery, welfare fraud—nonviolent property offenses—and intoxicated-driving and drug offenses. Of the ten crimes that women are most commonly arrested for, only two, larceny-theft and aggravated assault, are serious felonies. Women continue to commit crimes that have traditionally been associated with them—larceny-theft, prostitution, drunkenness, fraud, and homicides involving intimates or family members. They have been increasingly arrested for fraud, forgery, and embezzlement, crimes that fit into the expected female role of shopping for the household and paying family bills. These common crimes for women do not involve the use of force or confrontation, which are more typical of male crimes. (For further discussion of the crimes women commit, see Feinman 1994, Mann 1995, and Steffensmeier, 1995.)

Drug violations and prostitution are the most frequent causes of arrest for African American women. The number of black women incarcerated in state prisons for drug offenses, according to Mauer and Huling (1995), increased by 828 percent between 1986 and 1991. Alcohol and drug offenses slightly outnumber property crimes, followed by violent crimes, for Latinas. And alcohol and drug crimes, as distinct from violent and property crimes, are the most common offenses for white women.

Profile of Women in Prison

According to the Bureau of Justice Statistics (1994, 1) most female inmates in our nation's prisons are over thirty years of age, are at least high school graduates or hold a general equivalency diploma (GED), are women of color, are unmarried mothers of children under age eighteen, and have grown up in homes without both parents present. More than four in ten report prior physical or sexual abuse.

Among other characteristics, nearly half of the women are currently serving a sentence for a nonviolent offense, two-thirds have at least one child younger than eighteen, almost half report committing their offense under the influence of drugs or alcohol, and most had been unemployed at the time of their arrest. Nearly two-thirds of those who are serving a sentence for a violent crime had victimized a relative, intimate, or someone else they knew. Women imprisoned for homicide are almost twice as likely to have killed an intimate as a relative. Nearly one in three are serving a sentence for drug offenses (Bureau of Justice Statistics 1994, 1–2).

The American Correctional Association survey (1990) found that the average adult female offender is from a minority group, is between the ages of twenty-five and twenty-nine, has never been married, and before incarceration was a single mother living alone, with one to three children. She most likely came from a single parent or broken home; she had run away one to three times. As an adolescent, she was the victim of sexual abuse, used alcohol and drugs, and was a juvenile offender. She dropped out of high school, but has previous work experience. Her highest earnings ranged from $3.36 to $6.50 per hour. She realizes she needs more education and experience. The length of her present sentence is between two and eight years (17–19).

Women in prison share many of the characteristics of men in prison: they are disproportionately from minority groups, are of similar ages, and have little education. However, more women are likely to be the primary parent of minor children, to be serving time for a drug offense than for a violent offense, to have grown up in a one-parent home, to have a greater number of immediate family members incarcerated at some point, to have been on welfare at some time, and to have higher rates of physical and sexual abuse.

A Gendered Analysis

Crime is mediated through the interaction of race, class, and gender. It does not occur in a vacuum. To begin the analysis using gender, we start by examining the images of women in society and what roles they are expected to play. Gender roles are expectations that define acceptable behaviors and attitudes for children and adults of both sexes; deviation may result in a variety of societal sanctions, ranging from ostracism to name calling to violence to incarceration. Maintained through informal and formal mechanisms, these roles are a powerful form of social control.

There is a relationship between gender inequality and being defined as deviant. Men, the dominant group and the standard of normality, maintain inequality through command of deviance defining and of institutions of social control. Women are defined as different from men and, hence, inferior; this stigma denies them their full civil rights and access to societal resources. (For further discussion, see Figueira-McDonough and Sarri 1987, Heidensohn 1985, Naffine 1996, and Schur 1983.)

According to traditional gender roles, a girl or woman should be moral, deferential, passive, dependent, and feminine. She is to be a good wife, mother, and homemaker. If she deviates from these roles, she may be defined as criminal or perhaps mentally ill. Women are reacted to based on their femaleness, which acts as a master status—they will be categorized first and foremost as women, regardless of their role or position. And to their distinct disadvantage womanhood is a devalued status, as evidenced in women's unequal access to societal rewards; by their treatment in ways that do not take them seriously; through language and media images that objectify, trivialize, and demean them; and by the multitude of deviances attributed to women as women.

It is men, not women, who define and enforce appropriate behavior in both public and private settings. To Edwin Schur, in *Labeling Women Deviant* (1983, 187),

> [d]eviance is not simply a function of a person's problematic behavior; rather it emerges as *other people define and react to* a behavior *as being* problematic. The person's sex—much like her or his social class membership and race or ethnicity—may significantly affect what these other people do. [Schur's emphasis]

In her analysis of how sociologists in early studies of deviance constructed differing definitions of male and female deviance, Marcia Millman (1975) points out that the researchers portrayed male deviants as exciting, friendly, and appealing (as with leaders of organized crime), or as sensitive, gifted, and sexy (as with jazz musicians). Women in these worlds remained largely invisible. Female deviants were portrayed as unsympathetic and were rarely even allowed to tell their own stories. For example, one study of prostitutes used the words of the pimps to further our understanding, presenting them as more reliable authorities than the prostitutes themselves.

The criminal justice system punishes women defined as "unruly" for betraying "true womanhood" and stepping outside their prescribed gender roles of femininity and passivity. They have traditionally been imprisoned not for their offenses but because of their need for moral guidance and protection. The madonna/whore duality, the supposed two natures of women, arose in response to how men perceived female sexuality. Women were to produce children, which was good and necessary. Yet they were also temptresses who inflamed men's desires. Women were necessary, but women were dangerous (Belknap 1996, Faith 1993, Feinman 1994, Rafter 1985).

The "depravity" of women offenders often relates to their refusal of the status of being men's sexual property, the ultimate rejection of patriarchal control. Dorie Klein and June Kress (1976) point out the similarity between the exchange in marriage of sexual services for protection and goods, and the exchange in prostitution of sexual services for money. The criminal justice system harshly penalizes both girls and women for providing sexual services of the wrong sort (labeled as prostitution, juvenile promiscuity, and incorrigibility); this can be interpreted as a reaction to the unacceptable "freedom" of girls and women to reject male sexual ownership and control of female reproduction. Coramae Mann (1995) finds that when considering the control of women's sexuality, women of color, particularly unwed mothers, are viewed as having looser morals and as being more sexually carefree than white women. Such gender and racial stereotypes act against women of color in the courtroom and before the parole board.

Understanding the Increase in the Incarceration of Women

Three variables have disproportionately influenced women's imprisonment: economic marginalization, increased formal social control, and the connection between drugs and crime.

Most women are sentenced for nonviolent crimes such as prostitution, fraud, shoplifting, or drug offenses. Most come from poverty, are addicted to drugs or alcohol, and have emotional or mental health problems. Their crimes are often a response to crisis or long-standing disadvantage. The offenses are primarily committed to produce income, with the money being used to support drug or alcohol addictions, buy food or children's clothes, or pay other bills. Such funds may be the primary or only source of family income.

Being the single head of a household is a significant indicator of economic marginalization, where poverty, low education levels, and under- and unemployment are common. Ruth Sidel, in her book *Keeping Women and Children Last* (1996), reports that in 1993, 27 percent of children under eighteen lived with one parent. Eighty-seven percent of these children lived with their mother. By race, 21 percent of white children, 32 percent of Latino children, and 57 percent of African American children lived with one parent. According to the U.S. Bureau of the Census (1993), 65 percent of all African American women giving birth in 1990 were not married; the corresponding number for white women was 20 percent.

The vast majority of poor people in America are women and children. Almost 15 million women eighteen years and older fell below the poverty line in 1993, representing more than 37 percent of all those in poverty. Children constituted 40 percent of those living in poverty (15.7 million boys and girls). Over three-quarters of all Americans living in poverty were, therefore, women and children (Sidel 1996).

In addition, women are still paid significantly less than men, earning an average of 71 cents to the man's dollar in 1995. African American women earned only 64 cents, and Latinas earned 53 cents. Women are also not as highly educated as men (24 percent of men, versus 19 percent of women, have four years of college), and women are not equally represented in most professional fields, according to the U.S. Bureau of the Census (1993).

The typical female offender, being nonwhite, poor, and a single parent, is victimized by society. She is expected to work to support herself and her children and to be a good parent; when she finds these expectations impossible to fulfill and resorts to crime, she is punished. Yet no assistance was forthcoming to help her meet the expectations of family care. She has discovered a Catch-22 (see Merlo 1995, Sarri 1987).

Women in a study undertaken by Pat Carlen (1988, 108–12) viewed poverty not as the sole cause of their lawbreaking but as part of the larger patriarchal oppression they experienced. They saw poverty, powerlessness, boredom, isolation, and an excess of official surveillance as interrelated phenomena. Economic marginalization goes hand in hand with political marginalization. For them, resisting poverty and powerlessness took the form of lawbreaking.

The economic position of women helps to account for their overrepresentation in the money-generating crimes of larceny, theft, check and welfare fraud, and credit card forgery.

Second, increased social control takes many forms. In response to public concern over violent crimes, the criminal justice system has gotten tougher at every level. Although such offenses are committed primarily by men, the change has affected all persons committing every type of crime. Sentencing reform was also developed in response to male offenders and the disparity between their sentences and women's. The result of averaging disparate prison terms meant that women ended up doing more time. Mandatory sentencing has also resulted in longer terms for women because this reform had a particular impact on drug offenses. Meda Chesney-Lind and Jocelyn Pollock have referred to this trend as "equality with a vengeance" (1995).

Other changes, such as modernizations in social control, contribute to apprehending more women involved in criminal activity. These include more-specialized professionals, more-sophisticated computers and record keeping, an increase in formalized procedures, and more police officers (see Feinman 1994, Merlo 1995, Steffensmeier and Streifel 1992).

The third reason women's incarceration rates have skyrocketed is that the "war on drugs" has become a war on women. Female arrestees test positive for drug use at a higher rate than males do, and increased drug use among women translates into more crimes such as possession, sales, and petty theft (see Mann 1995, Merlo 1995, Singer 1995).

Women are more likely to engage in property crimes than in prostitution to support their drug addictions. The use of drugs relates to economic marginalization in that it provides an escape from the depression and powerlessness of poverty. Trafficking provides an opportunity for access to drugs and to money to make life more comfortable. Furthermore, women can get into drug sales with a minimum of investment, and they can act independently. Elaine Lord, superintendent of the Bedford Hills Correctional Facility in New York, points out that women generally sell small quantities of drugs to ensure their own continued supply, or sometimes, as "mules," move larger amounts for men who control larger markets. Women, she says, "are very small cogs in a very large system, not the organizers or the backers of illegal drug empires" (1995, 263).

Probation violations also play a role in women's increased incarceration, since more women are failing random drug tests. Standards and penalties for driving under the influence (DUI) have increased in recent years, and women have been caught up in that shift as well. Their share of DUI prison terms has been increasing, which again reflects a get-tough stance on crime.

Gender Neutrality?

Laws that seem to be equalizing the treatment of men and women are actually unequal in their consequences. The context of women's and men's lives are different, and these circumstances are significant. The growth in incarceration of women has not been due to their greater threat to society. In fact, women's share of violent crimes has been decreasing; by 1986 only 41 percent of women in state prisons were incarcerated for violent offenses.

One problem with "get tough" policies is that nonviolent offenders are treated as if they were violent criminals. The "war on drugs" imprisons both petty dealers and drug lords. Women, who commit more nonviolent crimes, are paying disproportionately for society's response to violent offenders, who are primarily men. The "neutral" standard turns out to be a male standard, and one that is not neutral at all, an issue discussed in the works by Meda Chesney-Lind, Kathleen Daly, and Catharine MacKinnon. Attempts at equal treatment cannot yield fair treatment because women and men are different in their societal resources, degree of economic marginalization, family circumstances, rates of victimization, and gender norms and expectations. When held to a male standard, women will always lose.

Victimization is a major factor in the lives of women, and this is an area where the sexes differ in their experiences and in how they approach life. For women, there is a strong connection between being a victim of crime and being an offender. They are "blamed" for crimes committed against them such as rape, battering, sexual harassment, and prostitution. The harm done to them is trivialized, the police response is inadequate, and women are questioned about their role in prompting the offenses. They are seen as offenders rather than as victims (see Figueira-McDonough and Sarri 1987, Rafter and Stanko 1982).

Awareness of this victimization has been growing since the 1970s. The term "battered woman" did not come into being until 1974, "sexual harassment" was not labeled until 1975, and "date rape" was not viewed as a problem until the 1980s. Chronic underreporting and the internalized shame of the injured affected our understanding and appropriate responses to victims.

The nature of crimes against women is different from that of crimes against men, which creates a different social environment for women. Elizabeth Stanko (1990) sees fear of danger as being so common in women's lives that they simply learn to manage it. This makes the fear invisible, ingraining it along with gender notions of dependency on men. Susan Brownmiller, in her groundbreaking work *Against Our Will* (1975), states that rape and the threat of rape keep all women in a state of fear and that women are constantly reminded of their vulnerability. Crista Brett (1993) finds that people who have been victimized come to see the world negatively; abused women do not feel the same freedom to make decisions or have the same ability for effective problem solving as do those who have not been abused. Most female inmates are coping with histories of childhood physical and sexual abuse, as well as adult victimization from beatings, rapes, and robberies.

A Feminist Perspective

Clearly, a viewpoint grounded in feminism will refuse to accept the male standard as the basis for all of human experience, motivation, or values. It will acknowledge the social context of patriarchy. Maureen Cain (1990, 6) reinforces this view with her statement that "[w]hat happens to girls and women in courts and prisons connects with what happens in the playground, in the family, and at work. We seem to be entangled in or confronted by a hegemonic web which is resistant to every attack." Accordingly, I will begin by stating an explicitly feminist perspective that incorporates theory and practice in its approach to social issues and social problems.

As Catharine MacKinnon (1987, 169) sees it, "Feminism is the first theory, the first practice, the first movement, to take seriously the situation of all women from the point of view of all women, both on our situation and on social life as a whole." However, Marcia Rice (1990, 58) tells us that black women have been caught between a black criminology that focuses on black male offenders and a feminist criminology that has focused on white offenders. "Women" do not have one universal experience of oppression. For example, any realm of social research on the United States must acknowledge the impact of the experience of slavery and how that has affected black women's economic circumstances as well as control over their sexual reproduction, a point Angela Davis makes so clearly in her book *Women, Class, and Race* (1981).

Feminists must embrace the broader conceptual framework. It is not enough to focus on women (as opposed to viewing the male as the universal experience); we need to go beyond the thought that women's experience is not unified to the action that speaks to how the experiences differ. Race and class are key variables that intersect with sex. Race is a crucial variable in understanding crime because of racial discrimination and limited societal opportunities, and because of the racial bias in how offenders are labeled and treated. For its part, class affects one's life chances and opportunities, as well as one's interaction with every step of the criminal justice system, from arrest to bail to legal representation.

In studying female offenders, we begin with women's experiences and work with them to formulate an understanding of their lives, taking into account the social construction of gender and the larger social forces of race and class that are the context of their lives. As we understand more about the social worlds of women, criminal justice policies can take into account the relationships between crime, women's victimization, racism, and economic marginality. Elaine Lord (1995, 261) affirms what I have come to believe: "In sum, our questions need to be about women, not about crime or prisons, and about who the women are and how they become who they are." We begin to learn about the women at Black Mountain by starting with their lives as adolescents.

References

American Correctional Association. (1990). *The female offender: What does the future hold?* Washington: St. Mary's Press.

———. (1992a). *The female offender.* Laurel, Md.: American Correctional Association.

———. (1992b). *Juvenile and adult correctional departments, institutions, agencies, and paroling authorities.* Laurel, Md.: American Correctional Association.

Belknap, J. (1996). *The invisible woman: Gender, crime, and justice.* Belmont, Calif.: Wadsworth Publishing.

Brett, C. (1993). From victim to victimizer. In American Correctional Association. *Female offenders: Meeting needs of a neglected population,* 26–30. Baltimore: United Book Press.

Brownmiller, S. (1975). *Against our will: Men, women, and rape.* New York: Bantam Books.

Bureau of Justice Statistics. (1994, March). *Women in prison.* Washington: U.S. Department of Justice.

————. (1997, June). *Prisoners in 1996.* Washington: U.S. Department of Justice.

Cain, M. (1990). Towards transgression: New directions in feminist criminology. *International Journal of the Sociology of Law* 18: 1–18.

Carlen, P. (1988). *Women, crime, and poverty.* Milton Keynes, U.K.: Open University Press.

Chesney-Lind, M., and J. Pollock. (1995). Women's prisons: Equality with a vengeance. In A. Merlo and J. Pollock, eds., *Women, law, and social control*, 155–75. Boston: Allyn and Bacon.

Davis, A. (1981). *Women, class, and race.* New York: Vintage Books.

Faith, K. (1993). *Unruly women: The politics of confinement and resistance.* Vancouver, Canada: Press Gang Publishers.

Feinman, C. (1994). *Women in the criminal justice system,* 3rd ed. Westport, Conn.: Praeger.

Figueira-McDonough, J., and R. Sarri. (1987). Catch-22 strategies of control and the deprivation of women's rights. In J. Figueira-McDonough and R. Sarri, eds., *The trapped woman: Catch-22 in deviance and control*, 11–33. Newbury Park, Calif.: Sage Publications.

Heidensohn, F. (1985). *Women and crime.* New York: New York University Press.

Irwin, J., and J. Austin. (1994). *It's about time: America's imprisonment binge.* Belmont, Calif.: Wadsworth Publishing.

Klein, D., and J. Kress. (1976). Any woman's blues: A critical overview of women, crime, and the criminal justice system. *Crime and Social Justice* 5: 34–49.

Lord, E. (1995, June). A prison superintendent's perspective on women in prison. *Prison Journal* 75 (2): 257–69.

MacKinnon, C. (1987). *Feminism unmodified: Discourse on life and law.* Cambridge: Harvard University Press.

Mann, C. (1995). Women of color and the criminal justice system. In B. Price and N. Sokoloff, eds., *The criminal justice system and women: Offenders, victims, and workers*, 2nd ed., 118–35. New York: McGraw-Hill.

Mauer, M. (1997, March–April). The U.S. criminal justice system: Realities, statistics, and trends. *Church and Society*, 5–11.

Mauer, M., and T. Huling. (1995, October). *Young black Americans and the criminal justice system: Five years later.* Washington: Sentencing Project.

Merlo, A. (1995). Female criminality in the 1990s. In A. Merlo and J. Pollock, eds., *Women, law, and social control*, 119–33. Boston: Allyn and Bacon.

Millman, M. (1975). She did it all for love: A feminist view of the sociology of deviance. In M. Millman and R. Kanter, eds., *Another voice: Feminist perspectives on social life and social science*, 251–79. Garden City, N.Y.: Anchor Books.

Naffine, N. (1996). *Feminism and criminology.* Philadelphia: Temple University Press.

Rafter, N. (1985). *Partial justice: Women in state prisons, 1800–1935.* Boston: Northeastern University Press.

Rafter, N., and E. Stanko, eds. (1982). *Judge, lawyer, victim, thief: Women, gender roles, and criminal justice.* Boston: Northeastern University Press.

Rice, M. (1990). Challenging orthodoxies in feminist theory: A black feminist critique. In L. Gelsthorpe and A. Morris, eds., *Feminist perspectives in criminology,* 57–69. Philadelphia: Open University Press.

Sarri, R. (1987). Unequal protection under the law: Women and the criminal justice system. In J. Figueira-McDonough and R. Sarri, eds., *The trapped woman: Catch-22 in deviance and control,* 394–426. Newbury Park, Calif.: Sage Publications.

Schur, E. (1983). *Labeling women deviant: Gender, stigma, and social control.* Philadelphia: Temple University Press.

Sentencing Project. (1997, June). *Facts about prisons and prisoners.* Washington: Sentencing Project.

Sidel, R. (1996). *Keeping women and children last: America's war on the poor.* New York: Penguin Books.

Singer, M. (1995, January). The psychological issues of women serving time in jail. *Social Work* 40 (1): 103–13.

Stanko, E. (1990). *Everyday violence: How women and men experience sexual and physical danger.* London: Pandora.

Steffensmeier, D. (1995). Trends in female crime: It's still a man's world. In B. Price and N. Sokoloff, eds., *The criminal justice system and women: Offenders, victims, and workers,* 2nd ed., 89–104. New York: McGraw-Hill.

Steffensmeier, D., and C. Streifel. (1992). Time series analysis of the female percentage of arrests for property crimes, 1960–1985: A test of alternative explanations. *Justice Quarterly* 9 (1): 77–103.

U.S. Bureau of the Census. (1993). *Statistical abstract of the United States: 1993, 113th ed.* Washington: U.S. Government Printing Office.

C h a p t e r

Growing Up

[At age thirteen I started to run away] all the time. My parents separated and I hated my stepfather. My mom used to beat me all the time. I was really physically abused. She beat me every day just about, me and my sister. . . . She beat me one day and she'd told me not to leave the house . . . dragged me in the house by my hair . . . dragged me to the canal at the back of my house, and she pushed me in there. And I tried to climb back over the sea wall and she pushed me back. Then she freaked out and left. I got on my bike and rode twenty miles to one of my friend's house. That was the first time I ever ran away. I was thirteen, and that's what started it. And then I started drinking after that.

an inmate at Black Mountain

Understanding the adolescent experiences of imprisoned women helps shed light on what might be done to help other young females headed toward marginalization. We might be able to prevent the types of rejections and traumas they experience or to mitigate the impact of family dysfunction.

The extent of childhood trauma experienced by women in prison is extraordinary. Although certainly not every abused child ends up as an inmate, the vast majority of incarcerated persons, female and male, have been abused or have faced other serious difficulties, such as drug addiction or failure in school.

I define trauma broadly, to include not only aspects of abuse (physical, psychological, and sexual) but also teen pregnancy, school failure, and such family factors as poverty, alcoholism, interaction with the criminal justice system, disruption (particularly parental separation or divorce, or frequent moving), and death of family members. Such problems result in high rates of running away and dropping out of school, teen marriage to escape bad circumstances at home, and early drug and alcohol use.

Furthermore, females are treated differently than males within the family and by societal institutions. The variable of gender is highly significant in that society holds different expectations for the sexes. Gender is the most important aspect of the lives of females precisely because they live within a patriarchal society. Girls, in particular, have little power, limited options, and few legal rights. They, like women, are seen as dependent and weak on the one hand, and sexually uncontrollable on the other (Gelsthorpe 1989). Due to different gender socialization, females are not responded to in the same ways as males when they are in crisis, and their crises themselves are distinct in type and intensity.

Female crises differ especially in the nature and extent of physical and sexual abuse involved and in how these abuses affect options to stay at home, to succeed in school, and to develop a healthy sense of self. This victimization is gendered, in that young women are more likely to be preyed upon by males and by relatives, and are more likely to be abused repeatedly over a long period, than young men are (Browne and Finkelhor 1986, Chesney-Lind and Shelden 1992). "Society's lack of concern for their victimization— undoubtedly a product partially of their triple or quadruple invisibility (young, female, poor, and nonwhite)—is not lost on them," observes Meda Chesney-Lind (1986, 87).

Furthermore, abused females are the least likely to have been affected in a positive way by the challenge of the women's movement to traditional gender roles and expectations. A pattern often develops where, as Jane Huntington (1982, 36) expresses it, "Unwanted girls will put up with a lot of abuse in order to try to satisfy the 'terrible need' to have someone close at any price." Even as they cling to dreams of an ideal marriage, their search for the perfect man generally meets with rejection, disappointment, and continued abuse.

In the pages that follow I will address aspects of the lives of the women in the study when they were girls. I will touch on such topics as family disruption, family members' interaction with the criminal justice system, physical, sexual, and emotional abuse, alcohol and drug use, school issues, and juvenile delinquency, among other traumas.

Family Disruption

Instability at home had a tremendous impact on the lives of the women in the survey. Parental absence or alcoholism, poverty, neglect and abuse, and other problems contributed to their low self-esteem, need for escape, difficulty in school, and poor judgment. Regina Arnold (1994) discusses structural dislocation from family and school as two major factors in the lives of young black females who turn to deviance and criminal behavior. Two women had this to say about family disruption during their early years:

> When I was a baby, my mother gave me to my aunt because my father left and went to D——. And so she gave me to my aunt and went to D—— trying to find him, and my granddaddy took me from my aunt and my granddaddy raised me 'til I was in the third grade. And then I went home to live with my brothers and sisters. [My mother] didn't want to tote me along. I got a sister and brother older than me. I guess she took them, I never asked her about it.

And,

> I was raised with my grandmother and my father. My mom left us in O—— when I was five years old. She left me with a broke nose and seven kids sitting in the house with no food but peanut butter and jelly and tomato soup. My dad found us about two months later. He was trying to get on the railroad in O—— and she wasn't answering his calls. . . . They took my two stepsisters to foster homes. My dad tried to fight for them. . . . That left five of us.

For several women, childhood was so traumatic and disorganized that they have forgotten much of it.

> My dad was a really bad alcoholic. My mom was working two jobs to support me and my two sisters. Somebody said something about the house was nasty. They would see us three little girls with my dad, sitting up in the car while he was in the beer joint drinking, or we'd be in the bar, and they took us away. [I was] three or four. At that time we went to stay with my grandma and grandpa. And after my daddy got remarried, we went and stayed with him and the wicked stepmother, which beated me all the time. . . . We were took away from the stepmother and my daddy to the foster home and then from there my mom got us back. I probably was fourteen or fifteen when my mom got me back. A lot of things I can't remember. I talked to the psychiatrist about it. She thinks I'm normal.

Another woman's father died six weeks before she was born:

> [Around age six, I] was in a foster home because my mom didn't want to take care of me. I don't remember much about my childhood. I ran away at fifteen because I

didn't want to live with my mother because of the mental abuse. . . . I haven't been
back.

The absence of their mother or father created confusion and anxiety for
these women in their childhoods. Usually, the agent of emotional abuse or
neglect was the mother. However, rejection by either parent was not easily
handled, as excerpts from these four women's remarks demonstrate:

[I lived with my grandmother.] I had material things, but I didn't have much of a
childhood. When my mother had my sister, she brought her to live with us. She was
around a little bit. I remember her a little bit. Then she left us again, so . . .

Dad left home. Mom, she was a heavy drinker. I got along with her, but she was most
of the time passed out. We always had a place to live and food to eat and things like
that, but it was her attention we didn't have.

Being without my father, that was emotionally painful. Because I loved him so much.
And for him and my mother to fuss and fight. And then finally, my mother just said,
"Well, I'm not gonna put up with it." . . . He left when I was four and he came back
when I was six. And when he left that last time I was seven. And he didn't come back
until I was like eleven or twelve.

I have my mother, and I have my father, which is C——. Well, at a certain age, I was
what, six or seven, I find out that C—— isn't my father, that I have another father,
H——. [After a certain incident] my mom sat me down and said, "Look, C——
doesn't really want anything to do with you because he's not your father." Just like
that. And I was, like, "Okay." And then the next thing I know, my mom's getting
married again, to my stepfather. So I have three people trying to rule this little
person. . . . And then I have the rejection of C—— not wanting me. And so then I
had to go through the search for a couple of years about my father.

For another woman, who was abandoned by both parents and raised by a
strict and sickly grandmother, a carefree childhood was nonexistent. She
stayed inside and ran the household.

My grandmother was the candy lady. A lot of neighborhoods, an older lady, she has
candy or snowcones or a big jar of pickles. Well, she was the candy lady. So a lot of
people knew me as "candy lady granddaughter." Some knew me like that, coming
over to my house. But me going out to play with them, there wasn't. That really

wasn't done 'cause I was always more mature. [My grandmother] started getting sick, I started taking over the house, the chores. And my sister was so small, I wanted to protect her. I didn't want her hurting, feel like I felt.

Family Members' Interaction with the Criminal Justice System

Another significant aspect of the family environment for the women in the study is the number of members of their immediate and extended family who were involved with the criminal justice system. Such high rates of arrest and incarceration lead to the assumption that criminal justice involvement is "normal," a part of everyday family experience, and weakens the negative sanctions against their own involvement. Seventy-three percent of the forty inmates had experienced family members being arrested; 63 percent had experienced having a family member incarcerated. By race, 60 percent of the white women and 64 percent of the women of color knew of a family member being incarcerated.

Family members (usually brothers and fathers) of twenty-nine inmates had been arrested. One or more brothers (two, three, or even four; twenty-nine in all) of 52 percent of the inmates had been taken into custody. Forty-one percent had endured the arrest of their father (twelve fathers in all). Additional family members arrested included other relatives (one or more), among them cousins, uncles, aunts, and nephews, for 38 percent of the inmates; sister (21 percent); mother (10 percent); and son (3 percent). Ten of the inmates had experienced having one family member arrested; thirteen inmates, two or three arrested; and six inmates, four or more family members arrested.

Family members—again, usually brothers and fathers—of twenty-five inmates (63 percent) had been incarcerated. Forty-four percent of the inmates had seen one or more brothers (a total of nineteen) imprisoned; 40 percent of the inmates had experienced having a father incarcerated. Additional family members imprisoned included one or more other relatives (36 percent), sister (12 percent), and son (4 percent). Furthermore, 20 percent of the inmates once had or now have a partner who at some time had been incarcerated, and another 20 percent have a partner who is presently in prison. Although none of the women spoke about visiting at a prison, there is no doubt that the separation, visitation, diversion of family resources, and societal stigma involved had to have an impact on them.

Physical, Sexual, and Emotional Abuse

Interpersonal violence and abuse can play a major role in the lives of all girls and women, and the Black Mountain inmates are no exception. McCormack, Janus, and Burgess (1986), in their study of runaway adolescents, found a relationship between sexual abuse and delinquent or criminal activities. Sexually abused females were more likely to become delinquents, were more likely to have conflicts with school officials and employers, had more trouble with the law, participated in more acts of physical violence, and were more likely to have been arrested. The investigators also point to the growing documentation that sexual abuse of females at home is related to high rates of running away (390–91; see also Widom 1995).

Before they turned eighteen, 68 percent of the inmates had been abused physically, sexually, or emotionally. Surprisingly, many more white inmates (53 percent) had been subjected to physical and sexual abuse than their nonwhite counterparts (32 percent). Forty-seven percent of the white prisoners had been sexually abused or assaulted, as compared with 28 percent of the nonwhite inmates. When African Americans were looked at separately among the nonwhite inmates, I found that 33 percent of them had been sexually abused or assaulted. Before considering how abuse affected the inmates, we will look at the types, frequency, and perpetrators of abuse.

Slightly less than half (42.5 percent) of the women in the study witnessed abuse between their primary caretakers (parents or other guardians). Forty percent experienced physical abuse themselves. (Physical discipline was not counted as abuse.) Sixty-nine percent claimed their abuse was ongoing; 32 percent said it happened more than once; and no one said the abuse occurred only one time. The most common perpetrators were fathers, mothers, and stepfathers; others (mentioned one time) included an aunt, cousins, stepmother, brother, brother-in-law, and grandfather.

Thirteen percent of the inmates had been sexually abused (touched, fondled, "played with"), and 23 percent had been sexually assaulted (subjected to rape or attempted rape). For 20 percent of the women, sexual abuse had been continual; for 40 percent, it had occurred more than once; and for another 40 percent, the abuse had happened only one time. The most frequent perpetrators had been a male peer, male neighbor, father, or stepfather.

Nine women had been sexually assaulted as children or adolescents. Twenty percent of them had been assaulted regularly; 30 percent had been assaulted more than once; and 50 percent of them had been assaulted one time only. The perpetrators, all males, included neighbors, father, father's stepfather, nephew, cousin, baby-sitter, brother, brother-in-law and his friends, and, in one case, kidnappers.

More than half of the inmates (53 percent) reported being emotionally abused as children or adolescents; for 95 percent, such abuse was ongoing. Mothers most often were the perpetrators, followed by fathers; mentioned only once were stepfather, stepmother, uncles, grandmother, and brother-in-law.

In assessing the impact of this overwhelming abuse, it is crucial to keep in mind the lack of resources young people have for coping or escaping. Also, children and adolescents are expected to function in school, participate in peer groups, have friends, and help out at home. If their domestic life is fraught with conflict and if their self-esteem is undermined, it should come as no surprise that running away, poor school performance, quitting school, drug and alcohol use and abuse, teen pregnancy, early marriage, and other desperate responses result. Still, as Huntington (1982) points out, it is ironic that when girls leave home to escape sexual or physical abuse it is they who are labeled as the problem, as "runaways." Sexual abuse at home is the most common experience of girls who run away (Chesney-Lind and Shelden 1992, 35). As young girls, the Black Mountain inmates faced complex family situations with few resources and little assistance. The two accounts that follow are examples of abuse by stepfathers and fathers:

> My stepfather was real abusive and stuff and I just left. He kind of like wanted to make sexual passes at me. And I tried to talk to my mom about it and she typically, she didn't comprehend it. So I just left. I left when I was fourteen and never went back. Then when I was fourteen, they busted me for being out of school. They sent me to training school. They told me I had one day to a year and I ended up doing a year and one day because I got in a fight with this counselor.

And,

> [My dad] would make us stand and strip, literally, strip naked. Then he would whup us with switches, I mean, until blood would run out of our legs, or wherever, on us. He did it until I was sixteen years old and then I finally told him "no." He started beating me with his fists, and I started hitting him back, which that left no respect for neither one of us for either one of us. I take that as it was sort of not right in the head. Because a normal person wouldn't stand and make a child that's not a child

anymore, that's already been turned into a woman, stand naked and gloat and whup 'em and stuff. So, yeah, I see that as not right.

Another woman was gang-raped when she was sixteen:

[I was] handcuffed to a bed. They messed up my pelvic, dislocated my shoulder, blacked both my eyes, broke my nose, four fingers, broke my leg in two places. Then they took me to the hospital. [My brother-in-law] didn't get arrested until '90 when he killed my sister's baby [when he was also charged with my assault].

And this prisoner was raped by a neighbor:

I was raped when I was twelve by a boy who lived up the road. I called him my "boyfriend." After that he used to harass me. He cut both my wrists. I've never told my parents. . . . I was also raped as an adult. I didn't tell my parents. My daddy would have killed him.

Two women mentioned violence in their homes apart from parental fighting. One woman recalled, "[As a child] I used to see my uncles jump on my aunts and stuff all the time. I used to run and hide and cry." The other inmate spoke of her brothers' constant fighting:

My mom and daddy never got into it with each other, but my four brothers, they fight a lot. They used to fight my sister, and I'm talking about fight fight, won't stop 'til the blood comes. And to me, when I was younger, that's all I seen was my brothers fighting. And so, that was kind of exciting to me. And then I looked forward to every time I saw one of them drink a beer. I knew there was going to be a fight.

For some, running away was rebellion against parental authority:

[I ran away at eleven because] things were bad at home. Discipline, control. That, and not wanting to answer to someone who is no kin to you. Like a live-in, somebody else who lives in. Why should I have to answer to you? You're nobody to me. Just something like that.

Another woman left home at fourteen.

I was withdrawing from my parents a lot, and my mom came in from work one day and we got into an argument. She had ripped all my clothes off me; me and her got into a fight. She done it to keep from hittin' me. When I went to get up, she pushed me. She was really trying to get me to stay, but it was all over with. It just got to the point where I just couldn't look at them in the eye no more. I was lying to them all the time. I was hurtin'. And I just wanted to leave so I wouldn't have to see 'em. And when she pushed me down, [I fell back on the bed] and it broke my nose. And I left, and my grandfather, he supported me . . . and then I left there when I was fifteen.

But, more common is the adolescent who desperately wants out of her home because her needs are not being met.

My daddy was drinking a lot. He and my mom were separated and my mom was always working. So, she didn't have time to sit down and talk to me. Dad, if he wasn't at work, he was drinking, so. I just left. I thought I'd have it better by myself. I could do it. I was thirteen when I done it. . . . I called my mom and told her to come and get me. 'Cause it wasn't what I thought it would be.

Running away is one type of escape, but so is early marriage:

My mom always worked. There was seven of us kids, and my dad, he worked, too, but he never contributed to rent, power bill, or anything like that. He always blowed his money. Mom had one hell of a time raising the seven kids. When she wasn't working, she was sleeping, so. As far as being abused mentally, no. I was neglected, but I can't blame her for it. She had to do what she had to do. . . . I got married at fourteen to escape the whole thing.

One inmate married at sixteen to get away from her family, thinking, "I'd have my own place, then, like the fairy tale, get married, maybe have a baby, live happily every after and all this stuff. It didn't work like that." Another woman recalled:

I got married at fifteen with my mother's permission. What I did was I ran away from home and told my mother that if she would sign, I would come back. So, she agreed to it. . . . After we were married seven months I found out I was pregnant.

Thirteen inmates out of the forty (33 percent) were teen mothers; overall, thirty-four had children, so 38 percent of the prisoners with children bore them as adolescents. In one woman's case:

[After I had been raped, they put me on medication] for a long time. I didn't like it. It kept me calm. It kept me from thinking about it. And then, a sixteen-, seventeen-year-old trying to go to school and with everything, and medication was slowing me down, and so I stopped taking it. Then I found out I was pregnant and I had my little boy.

Another woman remarks, "I just felt like I wanted to get out. I didn't have any problems [at home]. I got pregnant at sixteen. I was depressed."

Childhood victims of sexual abuse, physical abuse, neglect, and other traumas are at increased risk for criminal involvement. Sexually abused youngsters are at increased risk of becoming juvenile runaways (Widom 1995, 7). This knowledge should help guide our prevention and intervention strategies for reducing juvenile and adult criminal behavior.

Alcohol and Drug Use

Thirty-eight of the forty inmates reported that they drank alcohol; on average, they began drinking at fifteen. Thirty-two of the inmates reported that they used drugs (marijuana, speed, heroin, LSD, crack and powder cocaine, and pills); their average age when they began was sixteen. Using and abusing alcohol and drugs for these women related primarily to escaping from their problems, but it was also a matter of fitting in with their peers.

> [I got into trouble at seventeen due to] drugs, friends, family problems. That's why I wanted the drugs. And the drugs is the reason for the breaking and entering. Trying to please somebody, trying to make them like me, that would be friends. To be accepted and to please them.

Starting around age thirteen, this inmate drank alcohol and smoked tobacco and marijuana to be accepted:

> I can actually say the first couple of times I did it, I was scared and I didn't really want to. But I did want to fit in with the crowd. It was like, in school, the people I would hang around with, if you didn't smoke cigarettes and smoke marijuana and drink beer every now and then, you didn't fit in. So, that's what started it. So then I got hooked on it.

For another woman, her parents' drug use influenced her own.

> I think [my childhood emotional abuse is] where my drug and alcohol problem comes from. And it really bothers me. I figure that if I was loved more and paid more attention to, instead of my parents running around doing their own thing. Of course, they were hooked on drugs, too. My parents were hippies and stuff, and they were just, they ran crazy, I guess. Not so much my dad, but after my mother left him he did find a girlfriend. But he was always there. It was my mother. She drug-overdosed when I was eight years old. . . . But I can remember her. She'd be under the table,

eating pills. I remember her being on the telephone, lying on the floor. She was out there.

And one woman discusses the influence of her older sister:

I was just wild. I started doing drugs when I was about thirteen and I was just out of control. My sister was on drugs very bad and she turned me on to drugs when I was thirteen. I started using IV drugs before I turned fourteen, and she was killed when I was fifteen. And I stopped using drugs intravenously but I had kept up some form of drug abuse.

Although involvement with alcohol and other drugs began early for many of the women in the study, use and abuse as adults figured more prominently in the lifestyles that led to crime and incarceration. I discuss this issue in more depth in Chapter four.

School Issues

There is consistent bias against girls and women in the schools, whether they are in the elementary grades or working toward doctorates (Sadker and Sadker 1994). Girls generally do better than boys during childhood, but this edge erodes during adolescence (Pipher 1984). According to Allison Morris (1987, 6), "This seems due partly to pressure on girls to adhere to traditional role definitions and partly to the internalization of the low expectations which our culture holds for them." Rather than being a place of safety and growth for girls, "loss of self-esteem, decline in achievement, and elimination of career options are at the heart of the educational system" (Sadker and Sadker 1994, 1).

School can also be stressful for girls due to sexual harassment that takes place in hallways, stairwells, classrooms, the cafeteria, or on the school bus. They have a near-impossible time getting teachers or administrators to take their complaints seriously, and they learn quickly to endure their humiliations in silence. In addition to having an impact on self-esteem, these actions make school a place many girls do not want to be in. They may be withdrawn and afraid; they may transfer or drop out (Pipher 1984, Sadker and Sadker 1994).

According to Sadker and Sadker (1994), girls drop out of school for many reasons—they are doing poorly, they need to work, or they need to help out at home. The biggest factor, however, is pregnancy. Many girls are ignored in school at a time when they need guidance, academic bolstering, and support through the process of sexual maturing. Even though dropping out only exacerbates their problems by reducing their earnings potential, it may be seen as a relief, and motherhood may be viewed as a significant "rite of passage" (116–19).

According to the U.S. Census Bureau, in 1992 the average dropout earned $12,809, compared with $18,737 for those who had a high school diploma. In 1995, more than 40 percent of high school dropouts did not hold a job. Many end up on public assistance or in jail or prison (Barrett 1997, A9).

Sixty-five percent of the inmates in this study had dropped out of junior high or high school (64 percent of the nonwhite women and 60 percent of the white women). When asked for the three main reasons for leaving school, the leading response was left home (cited 9 times), followed closely by pregnant (8). These two overlapped somewhat, in that some girls who were pregnant also left home. The next most commonly cited reason for quitting school was drug and alcohol problems (6). Started to cut and didn't return (4), didn't care (4), and expelled (4) were next. A few inmates mentioned started to work (3), bored (2), involved in crime (2), and felt they didn't belong (2). Other reasons included too hard, fighting with others, and got a GED (General Equivalency Diploma).

For some of the women, school was not as important as other aspects of their lives. The rewards for conformity and working hard in school were not clearly defined, and the future payoff was not understood (Shannon 1982), as shown in the comments of these two prisoners:

> I ran away from home. I was using alcohol. I don't think I understood the importance of school, does that make sense? When you're young you don't understand the importance of it. It's like, I'm here, I'm doing this every day and nothing's coming out of it.

And,

> I was in C——, going to H—— High. My sister got me working at night time. And I'd go home at lunch and smoke a joint and not go back to school. I was with my sister because I had gotten pregnant. My dad made me have an abortion. So, I started running away.

Juvenile delinquency

Studies of the relationship between adolescent and adult criminality have been inconclusive. We know that females commit fewer and less serious crimes than males. Studies from the 1970s showed females commit fewer offenses when on parole and that there are many women offenders who did not have juvenile records (Warren and Rosenbaum 1986). Shannon (1982, v) points out that

> [a]lthough a variety of analytical techniques and measures of continuity and seriousness of careers have generated [a] conclusion that there is some relationship between juvenile delinquency and adult criminality, the relationship is not sufficient to permit prediction from juvenile misbehavior of who will become adult criminals.

However, a study by Cathy Widom (1991) found that childhood delinquency was more significant than childhood victimization or placement in foster care as a contributing factor in adult criminal behavior. Marguerite Warren and Jill Rosenbaum (1986, 410) also found evidence of female "criminal careers," with a large majority of their sample in a longitudinal study of California female juvenile offenders having arrests continuing into adulthood as well as high conviction and incarceration rates. Still, they caution, more longitudinal studies need to be done, and a great deal remains unknown about the lives of female offenders.

The courts define whether a child is disobedient or incorrigible, a standard clearly subjective in its determination and, as it turns out, uneven in its application (Naffine 1989). Compared to boys, girls are overrepresented in courts with noncriminal status offenses, such as truancy or running away—activities that are not illegal if done by adults. Further, they are treated more harshly (held for longer periods in detention, and sent more often to training schools and detention centers) than their female or male counterparts who are charged with crimes (Chesney-Lind 1986, Huntington 1982). Jane Huntington (1982, 37) claims that "[n]ot only do they stay longer for less harmful acts, in many cases they are confined because there are no other places for them—either because they are not wanted by their families . . . or because no other intervention possibilities exist."

Parents will turn in their own daughters to authorities for status offenses. The sexual double standard played out in families results in parents enlisting authorities to maintain control over their daughters in a way not done with their sons. Parents may use the courts to deal with family problems or to deal with sexually active daughters, which is not the case with sexually active sons (Bergsmann 1989, 74; Chesney-Lind and Shelden 1992).

Huntington (1982, 40) sees the "bullying and patronizing" of girls as an "expression of [their] marginality, both to society and to the juvenile justice system." Sexual activity may become part of a girl's record for officials' consideration regardless of the offense for which she is being tried. It is no surprise, then, that the juvenile justice system is used to control the sexual conduct of girls in a society that stigmatizes female sexual activity before marriage. Hence, female defiance is nearly always seen in sexual terms (Bergsmann 1989, Chesney-Lind 1978).

In particular, boys are rarely punished for sexual behavior (exceptions are rape or molestation); the "problem" of adolescent sexuality is seen as pertaining to girls. As a status offender, a young woman will be labeled "promiscuous," "incapable of control," "incorrigible," or, alternatively, as a "good girl." This perpetuates the sexual double standard while making it difficult for adolescent girls so labeled to get the information they need to deal with their biological maturation. Lack of information, excitement, fear, and guilt combine powerfully to ill equip girls for dealing with their sexuality and to create enormous stress (Huntington 1982, Naffine 1989).

With regard to the types of crimes the sexes commit, in Carlen's view (1988, 127) the emphasis on motherhood and female "caring" roles deters girls and women from committing serious offenses, since they are "taught to consider themselves the guardians of domestic morality." Furthermore, as girls they are supervised more closely than boys and they have less opportunity to commit serious crimes. According to Hagan, Simpson, and Gillis (1979), a patriarchal system emphasizing female nurturance and other-orientation, along with male agency, relegates girls and women to private space (the home, taking care of children, and doing unpaid domestic chores), subjecting them to more informal modes of social control. Boys and men, on the other hand, who are socialized to expect to occupy public space, are disproportionately governed by formal mechanisms of social control, which operate outside the home. Hence, the investigators argue, gendered roles are one significant aspect in the involvement of disproportionate numbers of males as compared to females in the criminal justice system. Gender accounts for difference not only in opportunity to commit crime, detection of crimes, but also formal response to crimes committed.

In addition to being socialized into a caring role within the family, adolescent girls are more peer oriented and group oriented than boys. Concerns about being liked and being popular often override interest in academic success (Chesney-Lind and Shelden 1992, Pipher 1984). As noted earlier, this attitude becomes significant when girls do not see the value of education and lose interest in doing well, despite their abilities. If they do not find popularity through success in school or are too poor to have good clothes, many girls attempt to gain status and recognition through partying, fighting, and taking drugs with their peers (Chesney-Lind and Shelden 1992, 211). At the same time, girls generally have a greater stake in conformity and feel more visible than do boys. Sexism is also found in the criminal world. Adolescent female offenders experience greater social disapproval than do boys for their delinquent acts, not only from their law-abiding peers but from other delinquents as well (Morris 1965).

Uniform Crime Report data indicate that the overall juvenile male-female arrest ratio is four to one. The biggest gender gap is in serious property crimes (eleven to one) and violent crimes (nine to one). Males are arrested for shoplifting more than females, at a rate of three to one. One-fifth of boys' arrests and one-fourth of girls' arrests are for shoplifting. Still, the status offense of running away plays a much larger part in arrests of girls (one-fifth) than of boys (one-twentieth). Running away and larceny-theft account for approximately half of all girls' arrests (Chesney-Lind and Shelden 1992, 52–53).

Black girls are not much more delinquent than white girls, according to Meda Chesney-Lind and Randall Shelden (1992, 209–10). Official statistics also support this view, but they are contradicted in self-report studies. There are, however, differences in victimization, as black girls are more likely to be the targets of violence than are white girls.

A negative attitude toward school, along with leaving high school before graduation, are related to both juvenile and adult deviance (Shannon 1982). Meda Chesney-Lind (1986, 85) reports that negative attitudes toward school and poor academic performance were significant predictors of delinquency in both males and females, with a stronger relationship found for girls (see also Rankin 1980).

In addition to running away, promiscuity, disobeying parents, dropping out of school, drug and alcohol use, teen pregnancy, and early marriage, status offenses figured prominently in the lives of the women at Black Mountain. Over half of the inmates (55 percent) had been in trouble as adolescents. The average age of a first offense of some kind was fourteen years. Overall, 38 percent of them (44 percent of the nonwhite women and 27 percent of the white women) had been arrested as juveniles. Eighteen percent had been on juvenile probation. Another 18 percent had been incarcerated in North Carolina's Juvenile Evaluation Center (JEC) or placed in juvenile detention. Once again, 18 percent had been sent to a foster home or group home for some period. Fifty-two percent (52 percent of the nonwhite and 53 percent of the white women) had run away from home at least once.

One woman, for example, was arrested for running away and for not going to school. She started getting into trouble when she was eleven, and she was placed in the JEC at age twelve. She lived in a foster home for one year, which was a positive experience for her. In an echo of her story, another prisoner said, "They got me for not going to school. That's what they locked me up for." A third inmate recalled:

I don't know what it is but I've always had a thing for older men. So I left home and I had some friends of mine get me a motel room. I think I was about fifteen, I was a minor. And I had my little friend, older, not much older than me, but older, to come down there with me. And my mom and dad found out that I was down there and they called the police. I don't know why I got arrested. They took me to the juvenile hold for overnight or two days or something, I don't remember. But that was the first time it happened. And I had to go to court. They tried to get him for contributing to delinquency. They were trying to say that he had raped me. But I couldn't let them do that to him. 'Cause he didn't.

Other adolescents were taken into custody for crimes.

I was arrested for breaking and entering. We were partying in an abandoned trailer, but the charges were dropped. . . . I was sixteen. The guys got charged with statutory rape.

And a woman who was arrested at sixteen for passing bad checks remarks:

I tried to blame it on my family being too strict. That's what I always try to blame it on. I don't really know. I think probably it's wanting to be different from everybody else, to be on my own, so I could do what I wanted to do. And not being told I couldn't. [Bad checks] became an addiction, I think.

Overall, girls in juvenile institutions suffer under a sexual double standard in their treatment and in expectations about their behavior, compounded by racism, class bias, and socialized powerlessness (Huntington 1982). Options must be created to build healthy self-esteem in these young women—offering positive role models, sex education, and scholastic opportunities—and changes must be made in larger institutional structures to move them away from gender discrimination.

Other Traumas

In addition to what has already been mentioned, these inmates faced other misfortunes. The death of a sibling, witnessing a murder, and attempted suicide are some of the traumas that added to their already burdened adolescence.

> [When I was sixteen] they kidnapped us and kept us naked for two months in a house, handcuffed and shackled. And then they were taking us to the desert to kill us. . . . The guy eventually ended up killing this other guy instead of killing us two. Then he let us go.

Another woman experienced multiple traumas:

> My grandmother is an alcoholic, and I seen that. My dad did drugs, and I seen that. My brother, before he died, I seen him doing drugs. He was killed. He was dating a white girl and we lived in a small town in T——, and her father didn't like it. So he caught my brother outside one day, he was getting off third shift, and he hit him across the back with a shovel and threw him in a quarry hole. They said that my brother jumped, but my brother didn't swim.

And this inmate remains confused about what she went through:

> [I was healthy up until the fifth grade, and] I don't know what happened. I tried to kill myself. There's a lot of unanswered questions there. I had anything I wanted as far as material things go. But, something was wrong. It doesn't make sense to me. I had a counselor who told me that she thought that I was sexually abused as a child and that she wanted me to undergo some therapy for that. And I wouldn't do that because I felt like if there was something that I could not remember, then that was a safe thing for me . . . if somebody in my family did do something to me then I don't know that I would want to know.

Looking back on her adolescence, she wonders if

> [t]here was something in my life that was missing or that was there that shouldn't have been there. It's so strange to try to put into words. But I can't imagine a thirteen-year-old child who's just developing breasts putting needles in her arms. There's something wrong there.

Comparisons with Other Studies

Research by the American Correctional Association Task Force on the Female Offender (Crawford 1988) found among adolescents high rates of physical abuse (62 percent) and sexual abuse (54 percent), a connection between these abuses and running away (84 percent), frequent alcohol and drug use, school failure, and high rates of family member incarceration (64 percent). Low self-esteem is a serious problem, played out in suicide attempts, distrust, anger, and depression. This profile of adolescent offenders has been highly consistent for several decades.

The findings of this investigation are consistent with other accounts of the adolescent lives of incarcerated women. A study of inmates in Oregon prisons, for example, showed that the women

> have generally low education levels, and a background of family and other difficulties during childhood. . . . The women's teenage behavior (especially criminality, substance abuse, and running away) correlates with sexual or physical abuse, household instability, and family violence . . . . Other common factors in this population, such as high proportion of relatives who are criminal, frequent family structure disruptions, and poor education, intermingle with childhood abuse in the overall mix of factors influencing adult behavior. (Ireson et al. 1993, i)

Another study, this one of women incarcerated in California, conducted by Barbara Owen and Barbara Bloom (1995), also gives us points of comparison between the North Carolina women and the Oregon and California inmates, as presented in the following table. It is striking how similar the adolescent lives of incarcerated women are.

Concluding Remarks

Chesney-Lind and Shelden (1992, 5) tell us, "Typically, when a boy is arrested or detained, his parents may be upset with him, but will generally support him in court. In contrast, girls charged with status offenses have been in court precisely because circumstances at home led them to try the streets." It is problematic that girls in trouble often do not have the important resource of parental support to help them.

Demographics of Women in North Carolina, Oregon, and California Prison Samples

Feature	NC (1996)	OR (1992)	CA (1993)
sample size	n = 40	n = 89	n = 294
median age	32	32	33
have children	85%	80%	80%
family member arrested	73	66	71
family member incarcerated	63	28	64
As a juvenile			
high school dropout	65	72	40
ever run away	52	66	54
arrested	38	52	45
physical abuse	40	45	29
sexual abuse	13		31
sexual assault	23	64 (combined abuse and assault)	17
emotional abuse	53	—	40

SOURCES: R. Ireson, L. Nebon, K. Kenaston, and C. Brinkerhoff, *Childhood abuse and the female inmate: A study of the teenage history of women in Oregon prisons*, 1993; B. Owen and B. Bloom, *Profiling the needs of California's female prisoners: A needs assessment*, 1995.

Studies of girls in America show a dramatic decline in self-esteem from elementary school to high school. According to a major investigation commissioned by the American Association of University Women, girls lose confidence in their overall abilities, like themselves less, wish they were someone else, and do not feel they are capable of doing things. This holds for all girls, though the fall in self-esteem for African Americans is the smallest (Greenberg-Lake Analysis Group 1990). Ilene Bergsmann (1989, 74) points out that if this holds for girls across varying circumstances, then "it is not difficult to understand how young women from broken homes, urban ghettos, poor schools, and abusive families develop feelings of despair and hopelessness about themselves and their chances for success."

Low self-esteem among girls and the fact that girls and women have not achieved societal equality with boys and men are two major factors contradicting theories that the women's movement has created more opportunity for females to commit crimes or has influenced girls to reject law-abiding behavior.

Jennifer James and William Thornton (1980) point out, rather, that feminism has had little impact in encouraging girls' delinquency; if anything, it has had a negative influence. Girls who approve of equal rights have less involvement in delinquency than do those with more traditional gender notions. This conclusion is supported by Josefina Figueira-McDonough (1984), who finds that "[g]irls with a more feminist view of family roles are, on the average, less involved in delinquency than girls supporting more traditional roles" (337). She states that girls with a strong feminist orientation tend to have higher career aspirations, do better in school, and be less involved with sex (339). She suggests that we need to be more supportive of girls in school and reinforce their career aspirations.

The experiences of the women at Black Mountain illustrate the struggles of girls as they attempt to cope with traumatic family life, peer pressures, school problems, and sexual maturing. Alice Miller, an expert on the impact of abuse in childhood, speaks to the dynamics of repressing trauma and the need for an outlet for these pains. When such outlets are lacking, says Miller, "[E]nter addiction, psychosis, criminality" (1997, 130).

Of prisoners, Miller (1997, 83) remarks: "Life failed them—something, that is, I suspect, true of all prison inmates. One should try to show them that they had the right to respect, love, and encouragement in their childhood and that this right was denied them, but that this does not give them the right to destroy the lives of others." Listening to the women in this study, we hear that family and society had, indeed, failed them, and that their choices could have been quite different under other circumstances. These circumstances that need to change, however, are not discrete aspects of life. Rather, the whole patriarchal framework must change. As long as females are valued less than males, treated as sexual objects, demeaned, and denied opportunity—within families, at school, in relationships, on the job—we cannot eliminate abuse. No child is born a delinquent, and we can do something to stop creating her.

References

Arnold, R. (1994). Black women in prison: The price of resistance. In M. Baca Zinn and B. Dill, eds., *Women of color in U.S. society*, 171–84. Philadelphia: Temple University Press.

Barrett, M. (1997, June 22). Dropout rates steadily rising. *Asheville Citizen-Times,* A1, A9.

Bergsmann, I. (1989, March). The forgotten few: Juvenile female offenders. *Federal Probation* 53: 73–78.

Browne, A., and D. Finkelhor. (1986). Impact of child sexual abuse: A review of research. *Psychological Bulletin* 99: 66–77.

Carlen, P. (1988). *Women, crime, and poverty.* Philadelphia: Open University Press.

Chesney-Lind, M. (1978). Young women in the arms of the law. In L. H. Bowker, ed., *Women, crime, and the criminal justice system,* 171–96. Lexington, Mass.: Lexington Books.

————. (1986, Autumn). Women and crime: The female offender. *Signs: Journal of Women in Culture and Society* 12 (1): 78–96.

Chesney-Lind, M., and R. Shelden. (1992). *Girls, delinquency, and juvenile justice.* Pacific Grove, Calif.: Brooks/Cole Publishing.

Crawford, J. (1988). *Tabulation of a nationwide survey of female inmates.* Phoenix: Research Advisory Services.

Figueira-McDonough, J. (1984, October). Feminism and delinquency. *British Journal of Criminology* 24 (4): 325–42.

Gelsthorpe, L. (1989). *Sexism and the female offender: An organizational analysis.* Aldershot, U.K.: Gower.

Greenberg-Lake Analysis Group. (1990). *Shortchanging girls, shortchanging America.* Washington: American Association of University Women.

Hagan, J., J. H. Simpson, and A. R. Gillis. (1979, March). The sexual stratification of social control: A gender-based perspective on crime and delinquency. *British Journal of Sociology* 30 (1): 25–38.

Huntington, J. F. (1982, May). Powerless and vulnerable: The social experiences of imprisoned girls. *Juvenile and Family Court Journal* 33: 33–44.

Ireson, R., L. Nebon, K. Kenaston, and C. Brinkerhoff. (1993, July). *Childhood abuse and the female inmate: A study of the teenage history of women in Oregon prisons.* Salem: Oregon Department of Corrections, Information Services Division, Research and Analysis Unit.

James, J., and W. Thornton. (1980, July). Women's liberation and the female delinquent. *Journal of Research in Crime and Delinquency* 17: 230–44.

McCormack, A., M. Janus, and A. W. Burgess. (1986). Runaway youths and sexual victimization: Gender differences in an adolescent runaway population. *Child Abuse and Neglect* 10: 387–95.

Miller, A. (1997). *Breaking down the wall of silence: The liberating experience of facing painful truth.* New York: Meridian.

Morris, A. (1987). *Women, crime, and criminal justice.* New York: Basil Blackwell.

Morris, R. (1965). Attitudes toward delinquency by delinquents, non-delinquents, and their friends. *British Journal of Criminology* 5: 249–65.

Naffine, N. (1989). Towards justice for girls: Rhetoric and practice in the treatment of status offenders. *Women and Criminal Justice* 1 (1): 3–19.

Owen, B., and B. Bloom. (1995, February). *Profiling the needs of California's female prisoners: A needs assessment.* Washington: National Institute of Corrections, U.S. Department of Justice.

Pipher, M. (1984). *Reviving Ophelia: Saving the selves of adolescent girls.* New York: G. P. Putnam's Sons.

Rankin, J. (1980). School factors and delinquency: Interaction by age and sex. *Sociology and Social Research* 64 (3): 420–34.

Sadker, M., and D. Sadker. (1994). *Failing at fairness: How our schools cheat girls.* New York: Simon and Schuster.

Shannon, L. (1982, June). *Assessing the relationship of adult criminal careers to juvenile careers.* Washington: U.S. Department of Justice, Office of Juvenile Justice and Delinquency Prevention.

Warren, M., and J. Rosenbaum. (1986, December). Criminal careers of female offenders. *Criminal Justice and Behavior* 13 (4): 393–418.

Widom, C. (1991). The role of placement experiences in mediating the criminal consequences of early childhood victimization. *American Journal of Orthopsychiatry* 61 (2): 195–209.

———. (1995, March). *Victims of childhood sexual abuse—Later criminal consequences.* Research in Brief. Washington: U.S. Government Printing Office, U.S. Department of Justice.

C h a p t e r

Adult Lives
and the Crimes

After adolescence, the Black Mountain women's lives were disorganized. Although there may have been calm stretches, at other times life was chaotic. There may have been probation or parole conditions to meet, work or school to attend, children to take care of, bills to pay, and abusive behaviors to deflect. Low-paying jobs resulting from deficient schooling, low self-esteem from childhood abuse and lessons learned in school, drug addiction encouraged by peers, and abusive adult relationships all combined to limit their life options. Most were the primary caregivers for their children. And although several women had been in fairly stable relationships at some point in their lives, there was not one who was in a relationship in the year before incarceration that did not involve drug use or abuse.

Beth Richie (1996, 1–2) has this to say of women in jail at Rikers Island in New York:

> Their everyday existence has been shaped by very threatening circumstances, many deferred dreams, tremendous unmet needs, and exceptionally hard choices. And yet, their stories represent only the most extreme version of that which is a very common experience for women: being controlled and feeling constrained by tense intimate relationships within a hostile social world. The extent to which some women experience this predicament is directly related to the degree of stigma, isolation, and marginalization imposed by their social position.

Richie employs the concept of "gender entrapment"—holding that the women's position is socially constructed based on limited options due to their gender—to focus on the extreme extent to which the inmates' lives are marginalized and stigmatized. Even as these women attempt to conform—to have relationships, to raise their children, to provide income—they are met with persistent and unyielding constraints. They try to meet life's demands, yet, possessed of few choices, they end up being blamed and "entrapped" (Richie 1996).

The experiences of women are not all the same. Poor women, women of color, and women who are teen mothers, for example, face harder choices than do others (Richie 1996). And the socialization of white women and black women differs in views of the family, of intimate relationships, and of the experience of struggling against racism (Rice 1990).

In the following sections we turn to the life context in which the Black Mountain women committed their crimes. When examining these prisoners' adult lives, it is important to keep in mind that there is generally a time lag between arrest and incarceration. The women faced different circumstances. Some violated probation or parole and may have already served months or years of their time. Some had such violations, and had committed new crimes as well. Some were on the run from police for periods ranging from days to up to ten months. In one case, the time between arrest and incarceration was a year, in another, a year and a half. A few women had just recently been released from prison, only to be arrested again; they were not even free for a year, the time frame I consider in looking at their lives before imprisonment. Finally, those inmates who had already served eight years or sixteen years of a long sentence were looking back quite a ways to recall their last year of freedom.

Housing and Employment

Four women out of the forty interviewed lived with a boyfriend or husband, seven lived with a boyfriend or husband with their children, and eleven lived with a partner. Another eleven inmates lived alone with their children. Six women lived with their children at their mothers' houses, and four others lived with their mothers. One prisoner lived alone, another had run away from home, and six women lived with roommates. Three of the forty women were on the run from the authorities; I counted them by where they had lived most recently.

Eight of the prisoners had children living apart from them. There were various reasons for these arrangements.

[M]y six-year-old, I had him in '90 when I was in Raleigh, and [my cousin] came and got him. And he was about a year old when I finally got home. And I tried to work with him. She had him rotten. So he is right there with her. Now the three-year-old. . . . When I was pregnant with him I was using drugs and gettin' high. And when I had him they detected that and they said, "Well, he's not leavin' with you. You got someone in your family or someone to come by here and pick him up?" And that's what happened. My cousin.

Another woman was divorced from her children's father and had given up custody of them to foster parents.

We separated and he was strung out and I was strung out. I had started doing cocaine and heroin. We both got strung out. I didn't want him to have 'em, and I was going through a treatment. I had had a stroke and I was goin' through a treatment center thing. And so I put them in protective custody with the welfare. Welfare didn't take them from me, I asked them to keep them. I think it was a ninety-day thing, and then after that ninety days, they put me on a probationary period where they got to come home on the weekends for six months. And then after that they just kept delaying it and delaying it and delaying it, and then eventually by then I done got into trouble and that was like I was fixin' to go to prison or they told me I was. I ended up not going, but in the process I gave the foster parents that had them, I gave her rights to 'em. How she got them, my ex-mother-in-law, how she got 'em, I still to this day don't know how. 'Cause I gave all of my rights up to the foster parents.

The maternal grandmother most commonly had care of the children if they were not with their mother. Sometimes this was a result of drug addiction (one woman said, "I was on drugs too bad to take care of them"). At other times the situation resulted from keeping the father from getting custody ("His daddy, he ain't shit. . . . Mama went done and got custody of him"). And in some cases it arose because of the mother's many incarcerations.

My first time in prison I gave my mom and my kids' father's mother temporary custody of my girls, and I went back to prison and I didn't change it. I got out and I didn't change it, so it's been that way ever since. And then, my third time in prison, I had my son in prison. And my mom came and got him. She been had him ever since.

Fifty-five percent of the inmates had been on welfare at some point, usually after the birth of a child or the end of a relationship. Only 13 percent had been on welfare during the year before entering prison. Sixty-three percent were working (58 percent full-time and 5 percent part-time) when they were arrested. The work experience of the women is overwhelmingly in unskilled jobs, particularly factory and mill work and restaurant and fast-food work. Other common jobs include office worker, cashier, clerk, certified nursing assistant (CNA) or other health worker, housekeeper, and construction or other laborer. A few had at one time been strippers, topless dancers, or an escort. A small number of women had held jobs requiring training, such as Department of Social Services eligibility worker or legal secretary, and one prisoner owned an electronics business with her father. Other work included telemarketing, selling drugs, day care provider, bank teller, and bartender.

The women's highest hourly wages ranged from $4.25 to $15.75. The inmate who worked for the escort service made $250 an hour. Those on salary mentioned earnings of $19,000 a year and, for the self-employed woman (whose business went bankrupt), $90,000 a year. Excluding these last three prisoners, the highest hourly salaries of the others looked liked this: sixteen women had earned between $4.25 and $7 an hour; twelve had earned between $7.10 and $9.99 an hour; and nine had earned more than $10 an hour. These sums represent the highest amounts the inmates had ever earned, not necessarily what they were making just before incarceration. In fact, fifteen women were not working at the time of their arrests; five of them were on welfare. These numbers reveal the economic marginalization of the majority of the prisoners throughout their adult lives. Furthermore, employment has an impact on self-esteem, rates of depression, and general well-being. Having work not only enhances the ability to take care of one's family but it creates opportunities for social interaction and support (Fletcher, Shaver, and Moon 1993, 30–31).

Drug addiction ruptured normal working life for many of the women. Said one, "I hadn't been working maybe a month and a half. I never kept jobs long because of my addiction." Another did not want to work. She had a drug problem and made more money from dealing than what her ninth-grade education could provide. Another inmate said she was not physically able to work due to her drug addiction; she and her boyfriend lived off drug dealing and his gambling. As one woman sums up her case,

I didn't have time to work. I was mainly focused on getting high. That was the only thing I had on my mind, was getting high. How I was going to continue to get high, how I was going to get money.

For some of the inmates, adjusting to a recent release from prison was a challenge:

I was living with my mama. I just got out of prison in August and I was looking for a job then, but I got up with some old friends and went back in the same rut. Getting high. So I never did find a job.

Another woman, out of prison two months before being arrested again, was enrolled in Aid to Families with Dependent Children (AFDC), trying to stay clean. She had gotten a job at a mill, but she started using again and got busted before the job actually started.

Most of the prisoners, however, were working. Many found their income was not enough to support themselves and their families.

My husband and I both were working and I was on parole, and I was having to pay for parole fees and all this. And then he didn't want to work half the time. So we were short of money and I would write the [bad] checks for the groceries and stuff like that, write checks to get money to pay bills with.

And,

[I was in college paying out-of-state tuition and my son was in a private school.] I was working part-time at [a bank] and full-time at McDonald's. Then my son's father stopped paying money and I had a certain lifestyle I had to keep. So everything collapsed in.

Another woman, who quit school in the seventh grade, had worked for the same restaurant chain for eleven years. Still, after two prison terms she realizes her limitations:

I'm as further as I'm gonna go 'cause I'm sorta limited as far as my felony. I've got, it's not just one, it's multiple, so it limits me 'cause a lot of places won't hire you 'cause you got a felony. And on top of being a felony, it involves money and all that kind of stuff. So whether I'm trustable or not, they won't trust me, so. It limits me.

Violence against Women

Women have a sense of ever present physical and sexual danger wherever they are in society. They have been socialized to behave submissively toward men and to believe that anger or fighting back are unladylike (Russell 1975, 268–69). Their safety negotiations include not looking men directly in the eyes, not going certain places at night, not going out alone, and not living alone. Women who reject these limitations on their freedoms find they pay the price of increasing their risk of rape (Russell 1984, 161). Whereas race, class, sexual orientation, and physical ability affect women's specific experiences, Elizabeth Stanko (1990, 85) tells us that regardless of circumstance all women reach adulthood with a shared awareness of a common vulnerability.

Women's fear of victimization is greater than men's, yet men have more violence perpetrated against them than do women (Young 1992). However, Vernetta Young suggests that this disparity arises from the number of crimes against men involving strangers, whereas women tend to be victimized by people they know. She urges that data gathering reflect this relationship between women's fear and the source of that fear—actual victimization by intimates. In fact, the National Crime Victimization Survey has used a new design since January 1992 to produce more accurate official reports of rape and sexual assaults committed by intimates (Bureau of Justice Statistics 1995).

Although television news focuses on violence from strangers, women know of violence from intimates. According to a National Crime Victimization Survey, women were about six times more likely than men to experience violence committed by an intimate. Women of all races and Hispanic and non-Hispanic women were about equally vulnerable to such violence. Women aged nineteen to twenty-nine and those in families with incomes below $10,000 were more likely than other women to be victims of violence at the hands of an intimate (Bureau of Justice Statistics 1995, 1).

Women twelve and over were subjected to almost five million incidents of violence in 1992 and 1993 (Bureau of Justice Statistics 1995). Women *know* this. This knowledge comes from a childhood where over a third of girls are sexually abused, where there is great likelihood of many girls having seen their mothers beaten by their fathers or boyfriends, and where as adolescents and as adults millions experience date rape and battering. One major difference between victimization of the sexes is that males generally experience sexual abuse before adulthood, whereas for females sexual and physical abuse begins in childhood and continues into later life (Chesney-Lind 1997).

According to the American Medical Association (1992, 6), nearly one-quarter of women in the United States will be abused by a current or former partner at some time during their lives. Battering is the single most serious cause of injury to women, more so than auto accidents, muggings, and rapes combined. Fourteen percent of ever-married women report being raped by their current or former husbands. Rape is a frequent form of abuse in 54 percent of violent marriages. Koppel (1987) estimates that three out of four women (aged twelve and older) will be the victim of a violent crime (rape, assault, or robbery) in their lifetime. Friends or acquaintances commit over half of all rapes; strangers are responsible for about one in five (Bureau of Justice Statistics 1995). The FBI reports that 30 percent of women who were murdered in 1990 were killed by current or former husbands or boyfriends (American Medical Association 1992), and a full 60 percent were killed by someone they knew (Smith 1997).

Who they live with is significant in women's lives. Their male partners are usually larger than they are, and women may depend on them financially and emotionally (Stanko 1990). Women are at an additional disadvantage in that they are blamed for much of their own victimization and they carry shame due to the sexual double standard. Men who abuse their partners are generally possessive and jealous, hold traditional notions of women's place in the home, feel they are right to punish them for perceived wrongdoing, and feel entitled to the superior role (Dobash and Dobash 1992). Women in prison have suffered unusually high rates of physical and sexual victimization, especially in intimate relationships (Belknap 1996). For the inmates, as for all women, the abuse took place in a gendered context. Their male partners were possessive and controlling, and the police did not take the threats to their lives seriously. Alcohol and drug use, economic desperation, and limited life options heightened male aggression and female resignation.

Overall, thirty-six of the Black Mountain inmates (90 percent) had been abused as adults. Four women said they had not been abused as adults in any form. Eighty-five percent of the women in the study had been physically battered by an intimate, 83 percent had been emotionally abused, and 43 percent had been raped. Every one of the white women in the study had been battered. Ninety-three percent had been physically abused, another 93 percent had been emotionally abused, and 53 percent had been raped. Contrary to the findings of other studies, the women of color were abused less frequently than the white women. Their abuse rates are still very high, however. Eighty percent of them had been physically abused, 76 percent had been emotionally abused, and 36 percent had been raped.

In all, seventeen of the inmates had been raped. Twenty-four assailants were involved, and each rape was committed by a single perpetrator. The women raped by their partners were often faced with ongoing assault. Ten prisoners were raped by boyfriends, and five were raped by their husbands. Seven women were raped by strangers, one by an acquaintance, and one by a john.

> I prostituted myself for drugs a lot. Not standing on a street corner. I worked in a tit bar and pulled tricks for a couple of hundred dollars for about ten or fifteen minutes. That's the kind of whore I was. . . . I wanted money for drugs. I went to bed with a guy. He forced me to have anal sex, raped me from behind. I tried to get away and he wouldn't let me go.

This prisoner was raped by her boyfriend:

> [He] had me locked up for three days. And he took it when he wanted it, I guess. Had me tied up. He came in about twice a day for three days. The fourth day his mom came in the house and I screamed.

Another inmate, who was forced by her husband to have sex, recalls that he "would want to [have sex] and I didn't want to and he would make me. Say things and get all hot and bothered. And if he was drunk, just do it."

Beth Richie's view is that the battered women in Rikers Island who she interviewed were trapped by gender identity, socially constructed loyalty to their partners, and by violence itself (1996, 70) and that this combination made incarceration inevitable. However, all women are trapped by sexism, not just battered women and not just female prisoners. The main difference between those who are inmates and those who are not is the accumulation of life circumstances from adolescence to adulthood, where battering is one crucial aspect, and total life options are very limited. Most battered women feel the lack of societal resources available to help them flee a violent home; they feel the societal lack (involving overall attitudes and the criminal justice system) of will to hold the batterer accountable for the crimes he commits even more.

> I remember the last time that I called the sheriff's department and told them to please come out, that I was afraid he was going to kill me, he was that bad. And they came out and told me that they could not make him leave, that it was his house also. And I said, "His father lives up the road, please take him away." Well, they take him and ten minutes later he's back. He says there's nobody at home. I said, "Well, just drop him off, take him to jail, do something!" "Well, we can't do that, it's snowing

outside." And I said, "I'm sorry, but if you don't get rid of him I'm afraid he's going to kill me." He handed me his business card and said, "I live five minutes away from here. Call me if he gets any worse." Well, he had already ripped the phone out of the wall. I had to go across the road to a neighbor's house to use their phone. I said, "In five minutes he can kill me." He said, "Well, there's nothing we can do." And I said, "There's something I can do." And he said, "And what's that?" And I said, "I can take that shotgun off that gun rack right there, ram it up his ass and pull that trigger." He said, "No, you can't do that." I said, "Why not?" He said, "First of all, I can take you to jail for communicating a threat." And I said, "He's beating me, he's chasing me around the house, I think he's gonna kill me and you're gonna run me into jail for communicating a threat?" He said, "Well, that's the way it works." I said, "Fine, I won't be calling you anymore." And I never called them again.

The danger to battered women is very real. Some of the prisoners almost died.

The first time he beat me, he nearly killed me. He had struck me so hard I had six concussions. I had a broke nose, he knocked out my tooth. I had stitches all the way across my body on the inside of my body. I looked like something from the monsters club 'cause my face was all swelled. He beat me and I took a warrant out on him and he came and broke in my house the next night. They didn't even keep him in jail. And when he raped me and left, I felt so nasty. I felt so dirty. And now, I have no choice but to go back to him. They weren't keeping him in jail. I was scared to death. I would either commit murder or live with it. And so, I lived with it for about another four months.

Another woman's boyfriend would not let go of her:

He killed his daddy when he was sixteen. And he used to say before he'd see me with anybody else, he'd kill me. He'd be glad to go to prison then because he know where I'd be, six feet under. The first time he ever jumped on me he almost beat me to death.

Drugs and alcohol are often associated with domestic violence, not as a cause but as an accompanying factor.

[My boyfriend's] daddy was a big-time drug dealer, so we started out selling marijuana, then we went to selling cocaine. The more stuff we would sell, the more we would use. Then finally, I couldn't take no more, I just had to get away from him because he was so abusive. He was a bad alcoholic and he would get drunk and he would beat me up. And then the next day he would ask me how I got bruises on me and stuff, it was that bad.

This inmate's abusive husband had hidden his alcoholism from her:

[My second husband] was an alcoholic and I didn't know that he drank when I married him. He had been dry, or whatever they call it. I had never had any dealings with this. . . . Then after we got married, well, on our honeymoon, he sets this bottle on the table and he said, "Let's have a toast," and I said, "But I don't drink," and he said, "But I do." I hated him, he had tricked me. [I did not seek help for seven years, and I got out] at the last when he almost killed me. I had to go and take out warrants.

Women do leave abusive partners, but the process can take months or years (Dobash, Dobash, and Cavanagh 1985, Gelles and Straus 1988, Gondolf and Fisher 1988, NiCarthy 1987, Rouse 1986). Fear is the main block to leaving, but low self-esteem and lack of options are close behind. This woman and her boyfriend partied and got high for eight months. He also controlled her and beat her.

He said, "You're going to be with me or I'll beat your ass." I was scared of him. "You ain't nothing, you a tramp," he told me. I despised him but I couldn't get rid of him. Finally he went to jail. He wrote me, "Bitch, I'm locked up, if you don't take care of me while I'm here, I'll kill you." I sent him thirty dollars. Then I got my courage up and wrote him, "Fuck you. I hate you, I never liked you. I want you out of my life. I hope somebody beats you down."

Economic dependence and love kept this woman with her husband— that is, until she killed him.

I wasn't the type that thought that I, if anybody was to leave, you leave, 'cause I've got the children. I knew somebody had to work and pay the bills. I just stuck around and took it. He had me where he wanted me. [The police were called] plenty of times but I never took a warrant out. . . . I even went to the emergency room, but I never took a warrant out. Loved that man.

Emotional abuse is the most common form of abuse, and many women felt it affected their behavior. One young prisoner said,

I think because my mama was telling me that nobody would have me, it hurt. She kept nagging and that made me want to leave. And then my mama and daddy even told me that I wouldn't be their daughter anymore if I kept on seeing black guys. And so, that even made me do more drugs.

Another inmate remarked:

> But at one point I prostituted just for the purpose of it. It weren't for the money necessarily, it was for the purpose of control. . . . I told my mama about it and she said, "Why are you doing that?" I said, "Because I like to sit and watch all those damn goats sit and squirm and beg '[her name].' " And that's awful to say, that's what I told my mom, and she's just like, looked at me and said, "That's sick," and I said, "I know it's sick." I told her, "I know I'm sick, don't you know that. I'm sick in the head and it ain't all my fault. There's things around me, people [who] make me sick." I seen it as, I don't know, a control. Where I done been controlled all my life and beaten and misused and abused, I just, I seen it as, "Well, if you done get it, you're gonna pay for it and I'm gonna be in control."

Drug and Alcohol Abuse

Their dependency plays a complex part in the decision making of addicts. There are many motivations for drug and alcohol use, such as peer pressure, fitting in with the group, escape from problems, and the fun of being high. However, once physically addicted, the need for the drug can replace all other concerns and lead to criminal activity (Chesney-Lind and Rodriguez 1983). The amount of money needed to feed the dependency will depend on the drug of choice and the severity of the addiction. A woman may need many hundreds of dollars a week. Because of addiction, she may not be able to take care of her children, go to work, or hold a job for very long. Her thinking will be impaired as she tries to come up with options for daily living. Drug-related crimes may produce not only the drugs needed but extra money as well, providing an additional incentive. Overall, "her engagement in further criminal activity becomes based less on choice and more on need" (Fletcher, Shaver, and Moon 1993, 48).

Ninety-five percent of the prisoners at Black Mountain had used alcohol at least once, and 80 percent had tried other drugs. One-third had injected drugs.

Seventy-three percent of the women claimed they drank alcohol in the year before arrest; one-half identified alcohol as a problem for them, and only one had quit drinking. Of the inmates who drank in the last year, fifteen drank daily, twelve drank every week, and two drank rarely. Marijuana use was not quite as widespread. Eighty percent of the women had smoked marijuana, 45 percent in the last year. Seven smoked daily, another seven smoked weekly, and four smoked rarely.

The next most frequently used drug was cocaine, both powder and crack; it was addiction to this drug that created the strongest reasons for committing crimes to get money. Sixty percent of the women had tried powder cocaine or crack, and 40 percent used one or the other or both in the last year. Of these sixteen prisoners, eleven used daily; five used weekly, rarely, or on a binge. Fifteen of the sixteen women saw use as a problem, usually a major problem, in their lives.

The women rarely used heroin; only ten (25 percent) had ever tried it. Four inmates had used it in the last year, two of them more than once. Another ten prisoners had abused prescription drugs in the last year; three did so daily, four occasionally, one on a binge, and two rarely. Four women had used methamphetamine ("speed") in the last year, and one woman each mentioned use of LSD and a heroin-cocaine mix ("speedballs").

It seemed clear to a number of the prisoners that drugs were ruining their lives. Many talked of the need to quit, of how using drugs was interfering with getting ahead or taking care of their children. Seventeen women (43 percent) had been in some form of drug treatment before entering prison this term, most commonly an in-patient residential hospital (for seven) or a recovery home (for six). Nine inmates had attended group or individual therapy as outpatients, six had gone to twelve-step programs, and four had gone to detox. One woman had tried methadone. This represents thirty-three treatment attempts for the seventeen prisoners. Only a few had gotten off drugs.

At the time of the interview, for example, this woman was still doing drugs after fifteen years:

> See, my mom was the first one to ever turn me on to drugs. When I was fifteen she turned me on to cocaine and drinking, which I don't care nothing about drinking to this day. If they had just been more supportive towards me, tried to help me get help, not just tell me, "You got to straighten up," I mean tried to help, I think that would've helped a whole lot to keep me out of here.

For others, having fun, being physically addicted, and not having the will-power to resist the temptation of drugs had an impact on their use. The uncertainty of the addict's lifestyle makes routine living, with the daily habit of work, nearly impossible. Maintaining stable relationships with family is also difficult, as women may disappear for days or weeks at a time. Dislocation from both work and family leads to crime as an inevitable alternative to stable networks (Arnold 1994, 180).

> [At seventeen] I was strung out on crystal meth. I tried to jump out of a car going sixty miles per hour on the freeway because I wanted a shot and my mom wasn't letting me get it. That's when I told her I was shooting up and I said that I wanted some help. Well, we messed up and put me in a state hospital and all they were doing was giving me pills and I couldn't even think. I spent three days there and left. Went home and that's when I went to work for the bank. And I started getting my little life together, had a car, was making good money, and [a friend] came and said, "Let's go," and I went, and I was gone again.

This woman acknowledges being tempted and influenced to use drugs by her peers:

> I know I can [stay away from drugs]. The only thing that makes me think that I wouldn't be able to is that I still got it in my head that it was fun. And even like, some days here, I'll be sitting here and I'll be depressed, and used to whenever I'd smoke marijuana it would make me laugh. So, I think about that a lot. But I know I can't. . . . I know for a fact for me to stay off drugs I have to stay away from people that do it.

Lifestyle

Living day to day with the strains of low-wage jobs, battering, drug or alcohol addiction, probation or parole requirements to meet, and children to care for created chaotic lives for the women. Many of their family members and friends were living similarly. Dissatisfying relationships, as when the husband or boyfriend would not work or drank excessively, also created stress. The following excerpts reveal more of the contexts of their lives.

Some of the women acknowledge the extent of their own dysfunctional behavior, especially regarding drug addiction.

> Most of my marriage [of six years] I've been high. If I'm not high on something, if I don't have some dope, I'll get some beer or some wine, whatever. . . . Drugs and alcohol have caused me problems all my life, and I've been in prison twice. . . . I'd leave [my husband] for three and four days at a time, on a high, and not even call, and then come home and expect everything to be okay. I have emotionally abused him. . . . And I'll be thirty-one, and I've got a little girl, and something's changing for me. I've done a lot of thinking. That little girl needs me. I've got a good man, and I've

got a chance of keeping that. If I screw up, I'm really stupid. The only way that I can screw it up is to use drugs and alcohol. And if that's all it takes for me to have a happy life is to stay clean, then I really need to get it together.

And,

I had a very fair probation officer who was very good to me. And he gave me chance after chance. What he said was he gave me enough rope to hang myself. But, he was very fair to me, and he asked me to go to drug treatment and I did. [But then] I left; really, I just didn't care. That's what it boiled down to. I liked the lifestyle at the time, and of course, I was so far gone on drugs that that was all I thought about.

This prisoner has cycled through new beginnings several times and was unsure of her ability to succeed through her own efforts.

It's real hard for me to make it on my own, real hard for me to make car payments, do a trailer, the lights and the phone, the gas, and the insurance, the food. It's real hard for all those things, and God forbid something goes wrong, like something tears up in the house, or the car, and then that's where I always start slipping backwards. And then I'm like, well, what's the use. And then I always end up letting the lights go out and then the car go bad and go down until I just don't have a car, and then I'm out on the streets, then I'm staying with a friend. Then I'm doing more drugs, you know. It's something that's happened about two or three times. This time it got really bad, real bad.

Some women are trying to pull their lives together in spite of past incarceration, drug use, single parenthood, or abusive relationships. For example,

If I would've had a car I could have made two years [of community college]. I know. But catching the bus, taking [my son] to the day care, catching the bus to school. From nursery to school then from school to work. Oh, my God. . . . That's when I started [to sell] drugs [again], to get me a car so my baby don't have to ride the bus in the rain, in the cold.

Another inmate is now more confident in her abilities and in what she will be able to do upon release:

Once I went to work and found out what I could do, it was no time 'til they made me a supervisor and I was proud of that position. Then I was really proud when they asked me to be the supervisor of supervisors. So then I started becoming more independent. Before I never thought I could do anything. Then I realized, yes I can.

Family life was unstable for most of the prisoners, including relationships with their children, partner, and parents.

> I finally got off drugs and me and my family got real close. We used to be real far. I couldn't talk to them. They didn't have no kind of communication from me because of the way I was. So, I couldn't ask them for nothing, they wouldn't do nothing for me. But now, they'll do anything in the world for me. My mother's been behind me 100 percent since I've been here. I went home and told her, "Mama, I think I'm going to have my sentence [probation] revoked. I'm going back to prison." Because the guy that I was having a relationship with, I kind of got angry with him [for shooting into my mother's house], and I got real drunk, and I was going to throw gas on him and set him on fire, and I knew then that I had to get help.

Realizing what she had lost through her drug addiction, this woman desperately wants to reestablish a relationship with her husband and daughter:

> There's people who have lost a lot of trust in me, and that's gonna take time to build that up, but my husband's willing to give me a chance. He has his doubts, but hopefully I really want to be able to stay clean and do the right thing. . . . All I want to do is love [my daughter] and show her that her mommy loves her very much. And that her mommy made mistakes and had to go to time-out for big people. I'll explain it to her when the time's right, someday. Mommy had a drinking problem. She'll understand it 'cause I'm her mother, and children have unconditional love for their parents. . . . We don't know each other well 'cause I went to prison for nine months when she was a baby, and then I've been gone for a year now. That's almost two years of her life [and she's three now].

Troubles with partners loom large for many of the inmates:

> I was in the wrong relationship with the wrong person. Their father was okay at first until he started on drugs. What he never understood was whatever he did and the drugs he did indirectly affected everybody around him. And he couldn't understand that. I've never done drugs, but there were a lot of things I had to put up with. My mother was, "When you're in a relationship you try to stay with them because of the children." That doesn't always work like that.

And,

> [My husband] had an alcohol problem and he would not work. I was getting really fed up with it. When I came to prison I felt like I had been rescued. A lot of people

don't understand it, but I felt like, God, I know that you rescued me from this relationship.

Pathways to Crime

There were 87 charges against the 40 women in the sample, ranging from shoplifting to first-degree murder. There were 17 violent crimes, 41 property crimes, 21 drug-related crimes, and 8 vehicular crimes. Seventy percent of the prisoners had charges that related to drugs in some way—outright involvement in a drug crime, being high or drunk at the time of the offense, or committing the crime in order to pay for drugs. For example,

> I had met my boyfriend who was a drug dealer. And at first it started out that he didn't want me to do anything, he didn't even want me to be in the room when he was selling something. Then it came to the point where he would leave the package and he showed me . . . how to cut that and to do this. And if he didn't have anything when he was on the block, then he would send someone to the house. And that's how I got started. But I was only involved in that maybe six, seven months. It wasn't long when I got caught and I learned my lesson quick. Thank goodness.

For 30 percent of the women this was a first arrest with prison; for 10 percent, a new offense but not their first; for another 10 percent, a probation violation only; for 23 percent, a probation violation with a new charge; for 3 percent, a parole violation only; for 20 percent, a parole violation with a new charge; and for 3 percent, a violation of both probation and parole.

Here is one inmate's story of violating her probation:

> The first judge ordered me to do three hundred hours of community service and he gave me eighteen months to do it in. But he said I had to go back to school to get my degree, 'cause I was a semester away from graduating. So he ordered me to go back to school. So I went to school and finished up, but then I still had eight months left to do my community service. And I missed seeing my probation officer one time and me and him didn't get along anyway, so he violated me. The judge said that my education wasn't the first and foremost. That the first thing I should of did was my community service, and then my education. But my education helped me get the jobs that I had, so I should've done that so I could have paid the restitution if it worked out. But he said that my community service should have come first.

The average length of sentence was 10 years, 11 months for thirty-eight women. The shortest sentence was 11 months; the longest was 47 years, 11 months. Two prisoners were serving life sentences with the possibility of parole. In North Carolina, for crimes committed after October 1, 1994, offenders are sentenced under the "new law," which mandates that they must serve a minimum of 85 percent of their sentence. Consequently, the Black Mountain inmates had been imprisoned under the old law (where an offender served 50 percent of her sentence—or less, once good time was factored in), the new law, or both. In this sample, 65 percent of the women were sentenced under the old law, 23 percent under the new law, and 13 percent under both.

At the time of my interviews, the average period already served was two years, five months. Thirteen women had been to prison two or more times (one woman had been imprisoned five times). Repeat offenders, especially those with three or more prison terms, are seen by staff members as "doing life on the installment plan." Recidivists tend to suffer from such chronic problems as alcohol and drug use, unstable relationships and abuse, and unemployment and poverty (Arnold 1990).

When asked to give the three most important reasons for committing their crimes, the inmates most often cited poor judgment (16 times), paying for drugs (11), being drunk or high (11), and economic pressure, desperation, and fear (8 times each). The next most commonly mentioned reasons were protecting self or family, greed, anger, and helping a friend or relative. Women of color most commonly mentioned poor judgment, economic pressure, fear, and paying for drugs; white women most often listed poor judgment, being drunk or high, paying for drugs, and desperation. Following are some of the inmates' explanations for committing their crimes:

> With my kids' father I was beat for everything. He gave me a curfew that I had to abide by. I had to be in at eight o'clock in the summertime and I had to be in at six o'clock in the wintertime. And I just got beat if I'd come outside or someone spoke to me. I went through that for so long I felt prison was the place for me. But I was wrong. I felt like that was the only way that I could get away. That was why my crime was committed.

For another inmate,

> What led to that? My stupidity. Nonjudgment. I didn't have no judgment of anything. I was abused all my life from infancy up, so I did not know how to make a proper choice. And I was forced into the situation. I allowed myself to be used in the situa-

tion. It was a common law robbery and I was being used to commit the common
law robbery. . . . 'Cause the guy that I killed was the one that had the gun, and then
we struggled over the gun, it went off and he was killed.

Mary Gilfus (1992) reminds us that often women turn to crime because
of coping and survival strategies. Women of color are dealing with the triple
oppressions of gender, class, and race (Arnold 1994). Drug dependency, escaping from abuse, and economic need are common factors that led the
women to the actions they took. Often, coping behaviors such as running
away, status offenses, and stealing began in adolescence as responses to desperate circumstances. Coping often meant behaviors at odds with taking care
of their children, especially if the acts resulted in separation due to a prison
sentence. Many of the women tried to maintain a sense that they were good
mothers, even if their daughters and sons were not living with them. Knowing
their children were safe and being cared for showed to them that they were
good and caring mothers.

Many of the inmates justified their crimes by pointing to their relational
responsibilities. This is clearly the case with economic need, when women
steal or write bad checks for money to pay the bills. Acquiring money illegally
to support a partner or care for a sick child was seen as being completely in
the range of their responsibilities and roles (Gilfus 1992). Kathleen Daly (1989,
789) points out that women cite economic need twice as often as men do in
giving their reasons for committing crimes. For those prisoners who were
addicted to drugs, their addiction was an alternative to lack of education and
employment—the drug scene provided a social network, and crime was their
way to get money (Arnold 1990).

In discussing how women ended up committing crimes, Daly (1994) used
five categories to map their pathways to felony court. I will use her classifica-
tions and briefly discuss two examples from each category. These are not
"neat" categories; for example, virtually all the women have been abused, and
there is a relationship between victimization and subsequent offending. I
place a woman in the category that most directly reflects her reasons for entry
into crime.

Street Women. Eighteen of the forty inmates followed this path to court.
They tend to come from environments as children and as adults that are
abusive and are marked by a high level of criminal activity by family, friends,

and partners. They are arrested many times, moving in and out of prison in what has become a way of life for many of them (Arnold 1994, 178). Drug and alcohol addiction is common, as is abandonment of their children. These prisoners face intense structural dislocation from the labor market, being undereducated, essentially unskilled women with poor work histories (Arnold 1994, 178).

This white and Native American woman, twenty-five years old, ran away as an adolescent and has been abused throughout her life. Her former boyfriend, also in prison now, was a drug dealer who abused her. She viewed herself as a good, loving mother, particularly because she had the parental rights of her daughter's father revoked after he battered her.

> There was a girl from my home town, she worked at the bank and she gave [bank checks] to me. So after I was on intensive [probation], I had been doing real good, but I was doing the check thing, but as far as my probation officer knew I was still doing good. But I was still out there. I was smoking a lot of weed. My mother and dad, they had my daughter. She was four when I got charged and five when I came to prison. There was just a lot of stuff going on. So, I got the checks and stuff, that was my means of getting my weed and supporting her, too. I'd be taking her stuff, buying her stuff. And then me and the girl got into an argument and she ended up turning state's evidence on me. But I had beat her up so I had new charges on me. I got an assault on a police officer, I got a simple assault, and four worthless checks and misdemeanor breaking and entering. She said I broke into her house.

Drug addiction rules this thirty-year-old white woman's life. She has prostituted herself, has been in and out of trouble since she was a juvenile, and also suffers from manic-depression, or bipolar disorder.

> I've used alcohol every day for the past fifteen years. I've had frequent blackouts. I say and do things I can't remember the next day. . . . I was a heroin addict for about three years. I used every day, otherwise I'd be sick. . . . I was a heavy, heavy addict; once I start smoking cocaine I can't stop. I could smoke a thousand dollars a day, I was bad. . . . I like anything that feels good and makes me not have to deal with anything.

Harmed and Harming Women. Six of the inmates have alcohol or other drug problems and trouble controlling their tempers. They may have coping or psychological difficulties. Depression is common. Many of the women had no problems as adolescents, but their adult relationships were unstable.

This white and Native American woman, aged forty-five, was abused as a child and in her adult relationships. However, alcohol was in charge of her life when she killed the policeman. She is serving a life sentence with the possibility of parole.

> I killed a police officer while drunk and driving, while in a blackout. In and out of blackouts, I don't really remember it all. [I was handcuffed and in the back of the police car] and a voice said to me, "You've got that gun on you, kill him because he's going to get you for that gun and you'll be in bigger trouble then." . . . It was a freak accident.

An alcoholic, angry and depressed, this woman is thirty-four, white, and the mother of two daughters. She was a teen mother, as her mother had been and as her daughter is as well. This was her first arrest, and she is serving twelve years.

> I was drunk and got into a fight with a girl in my own house. And because I beat her so badly and wouldn't let her leave they got me for kidnapping. . . . I didn't know what I was doing at the time that I was doing it. I didn't know it was kidnapping until they come and said we got you for kidnapping.

Battered Women. Although most of the prisoners in the sample had been physically assaulted, only three women committed their crimes in direct response. In the first case, the inmate had never been in any trouble, but she did have a childhood and adulthood of abuse. She, too, had been a teen mother. She is African American, thirty-eight years old, and serving eight years for involuntary manslaughter. The second case involves a white woman, aged thirty-four, who has two daughters. She had a turbulent childhood and lived in foster care for several years. Her marriage was also turbulent, involving drug and alcohol use and domestic violence. Her life sentence was reduced on appeal to twenty-five years. The first prisoner recalls:

> I couldn't believe the way [my husband] was beating on me and I just flipped. . . . My stepfather always kept a .38 beside him. I just went in and grabbed it, before he even knowed it. . . . Well, I sure didn't mean to take a life, but I meant to get him off of me. Shot him in the side and he died at the hospital three hours after I shot him. Man I been with seventeen years, two kids by him. Loved him to death. Yeah.

The second prisoner's memory is more clouded.

> I don't know, we were both drunk . . . there's so much I don't even remember about that night. . . . I came out of the master bedroom, my husband was sitting on the bed

with the gun . . . and he was talking about killing himself, and I don't know, I got the gun somehow. I don't know what happened.

Drug-Connected Women: The three members of this group use or sell drugs in connection with boyfriends or family members. Their drug use is recent and they usually have no prior records.

This woman, aged thirty, African American and Native American, has never been married and has three daughters. She never used drugs and had never been in trouble. Arrested for "maintaining a motor vehicle for a controlled substance" (she had a car her boyfriend had bought for her), she was given a sentence of ten years. It turned out her boyfriend had three other girlfriends he had bought things for; they were all arrested and incarcerated.

I was going with a boy that was selling drugs, so I was guilty by association. . . . My boyfriend was arrested a couple of weeks before I was. They went after everybody he was associated with. It was a major drug-ring bust. . . . I didn't really know he was out there like that. I was working twelve and a half hours [a day]. I knew he was doing something, but sometimes if you feel like you don't know you're better off. Stuff like that. It was a mess. I'm paying for it now.

This prisoner was serving a twenty-year sentence for trafficking cocaine. She is white, fifty-five, and has two adult children. A formerly battered woman, she says after a family member introduced her to the drug gang she was threatened and beaten over three years to make her act as a courier. She had no previous history of arrest or drug usage, and she claims she never profited from these illegal activities.

I was introduced to this group, and I ended up with threats because I had connections all over the county with all types of people, had worked with all types of people, and they believed that I would be ready and willing to take part and carry [drugs] and to do and all. And I wasn't ready and willing, but I had to. . . . They beat me several times. . . . Twice I ran away from them and both times I got almost killed by them, so I quit, I just did whatever they wanted me to do.

Other. Ten women had different pathways to court. The majority of this group broke the law out of economic need. As mentioned earlier, family obligations such as taking care of children or a husband who will not work force them into finding alternative sources of income. Bad checks, embezzlement, and forgery and uttering are common crimes for them. Several were teen mothers and single parents. Some of the inmates had no juvenile trouble, although others did; for some this was their first offense, but for others it was a return to prison. I placed two women in this "other" group because they did not fit elsewhere.

The first prisoner is white, thirty-four, and had no criminal history. She had been abused by her husband at the end of their marriage. She is serving ten years for forgery and uttering. The second woman is African American, thirty, and serving a four-year sentence for larceny. She, too, had never been in trouble before. After being battered, she separated from her husband, and she is raising her two children alone. The first inmate recalls:

> My husband drank real bad and for the last three years he would not work. I was the sole support of income. We had mortgage payments and car payments and the pressure really got to me. And to keep up with the bills is basically why I did what I did. I worked for a lawyer and when I got in a bind to pay the bills I would write an extra payroll check.

The other woman says,

> My oldest son [who was two] was sick . . . and I didn't have medical insurance, and I couldn't get Medicaid and that was the only way I saw then to get the money. . . . I knew that my son had to get medical attention. . . . I was scared because he wasn't being able to go to the bathroom, and I knew that he had to get to the urologist. And, then the economic [pressure], and then the desperation.

Women in prison tend to be in disempowered positions in the workplace, in their relationships, and in society at large. They may be drug addicted, and, even though many seek professional help, treatment programs do not seem to be effective. Their crimes were largely attempts to cope with the conditions of their lives. Although their survival strategies may not have been the best choices, given the limited options facing some of the women they seemed reasonable at the time. Other prisoners felt that there were no options. Desperation leads many women to commit crimes, primarily nonviolent ones; they must then face the consequences, including separation from their children and loss of freedom.

References

American Medical Association. (1992). *Diagnostic and treatment guidelines on domestic violence.* Washington: U.S. Department of Health and Human Services.

Arnold, R. (1990). Processes of victimization and criminalization of black women. *Social Justice* 17 (3): 153–66.

———. (1994). Black women in prison: The price of resistance. In M. Zinn and B. Dill, eds., *Women of color in U.S. society*, 171–84. Philadelphia: Temple University Press.

Belknap, J. (1996). *The invisible woman: Gender, crime, and justice.* Belmont, Calif.: Wadsworth Publishing.

Bureau of Justice Statistics. (1995, August). *Violence against women: Estimates from the redesigned survey.* Washington: U.S. Department of Justice.

Chesney-Lind, M. (1997). *The female offender: Girls, women, and crime.* Thousand Oaks, Calif.: Sage Publications.

Chesney-Lind, M., and N. Rodriguez. (1983). Women under lock and key: A view from the inside. *Prison Journal* 53: 47–65.

Daly, K. (1989). Gender and varieties of white-collar crime. *Criminology* 27 (4): 769–94.

———. (1994). *Gender, crime, and punishment.* New Haven: Yale University Press.

Dobash, R. E., and R. P. Dobash. (1992). *Women, violence, and social change.* London: Routledge.

Dobash, R. E., R. P. Dobash, and K. Cavanagh. (1985). The contact between battered women and social and medical agencies. In J. Pahl, ed., *Private violence and public policy*, 142–65. Boston: Routledge and Kegan Paul.

Fletcher, B., L. Shaver, and D. Moon, eds. (1993). *Women prisoners: A forgotten population.* Westport, Conn.: Praeger.

Gelles, R. J., and M. A. Straus. (1988). *Intimate violence.* New York: Simon and Schuster.

Gilfus, M. (1992). From victims to survivors to offenders: Women's routes of entry and immersion into street crime. *Women and Criminal Justice* 4 (1): 63–88.

Gondolf, E. W., and E. R. Fisher. (1988). *Battered women as survivors: An alternative to treating learned helplessness.* Lexington, Mass.: Lexington Books.

Koppel, M. (1987). *Lifetime likelihood of victimization.* Bureau of Justice Statistics technical report. Washington: U.S. Department of Justice.

NiCarthy, G. (1987). *The ones who got away: Women who left abusive partners.* Seattle: Seal Press.

Rice, M. (1990). Challenging orthodoxies in feminist theory: A black feminist critique. In L. Gelsthorpe and A. Morris, eds., *Feminist perspectives in criminology*, 57–69. Philadelphia: Open University Press.

Richie, B. (1996). *Compelled to crime: The gender entrapment of battered black women.* New York: Routledge.

Rouse, L. P. (1986). *You are not alone: A guide for battered women.* Holmes Beach, Fla.: Learning Publications.

Russell, D. (1975). *The politics of rape.* New York: Stein and Day.

———. (1984). *Sexual exploitation.* Beverly Hills, Calif.: Sage Publications.

Smith, M. (1997, June 30). When violence strikes home. *The Nation*, 23.

Stanko, E. (1990). *Everyday violence: How women and men experience sexual and physical danger*. London: Pandora.

Young, V. (1992, September). Fear of victimization and victimization rates among women: A paradox? *Justice Quarterly* 9 (3): 419–41.

C h a p t e r

5

Doing Time

I stayed in all this time and I've grown up a lot, I've grown up a lot. I needed that. I would take nothing for the time I've done, but I couldn't do it again. It's been a valuable experience and I've learned a lot, and hopefully I've helped somebody else along the way. But, it's broke me. They got their point across.

an inmate at Black Mountain

"**D**oing time" has many meanings for those in prison. To do "hard time" is to dwell on events in the outside world; to do "easy time" is to learn to become emotionally uninvolved in outside events. In the latter, the inmate's thoughts and energies are focused on her daily life and goings-on within prison, protecting her from things over which she has no control (Giallombardo 1966b). Part of hard time is "going through changes," involving mood swings, worry, and adjustment to being incarcerated (Mahan 1984).

Women and men serve their sentences differently. Men concentrate on "doing their own time," keeping others at bay and showing invulnerability. Women generally try to remain involved in the lives of their children and families (Lord 1995). Charles Turnbo (1993, 13) has found that, compared to men, women talk more to staff members, are more openly emotional, have more suicidal thoughts, and are more vocal about issues involving their family and children.

When considering the experiences covered in this chapter, inmates frequently spoke in relative terms—comparing Black Mountain to the North Carolina Correctional Institution for Women in Raleigh (referred to hereinafter as Raleigh). Every woman incarcerated in North Carolina enters the system there. She may stay as briefly as one night, or she may stay for years.

Inmates can be transferred to several different minimum security facilities during their incarceration, but the major point of comparison is the state's main prison. Housing over one thousand women, Raleigh is characterized by long lines, high noise levels, waits to see one's case manager, running out of food at meals, inadequate medical care, and the general problems of over-crowding. It is a self-contained "city" within the state's capital, and inmates never have to leave the prison grounds except for certain circumstances, such as giving birth at Wake County Hospital. It is also dangerous compared to Black Mountain.

> I hated that place. I felt that was the pits of hell for me. . . . The officers there, they don't have the means or the control of that place. It's so overcrowded that someone could get hurt there very easily. It's happened. I was on reception there and a girl got attacked with a straight razor, and by the time, the place is so large, they could get any help to that girl, she was cut all to pieces. And I remember laying on my bed crying, thinking, "Dear God, I can't live like this." It was hell.

Doing time at Black Mountain, therefore, is easier in many respects, and most women do not want to be sent back to Raleigh, where the only privilege is visiting. There are no opportunities for work or study release or community-volunteer passes, all ways to normalize life.

The average time already served when I interviewed the Black Mountain prisoners was two years, five months; the shortest stay was four months, and the longest was sixteen years. One woman gave this advice: "I got a saying, 'Do the time, don't let it do you.' You have to work with the system instead of working against it." "Time" has different meanings in the prison system. For example, every woman referred to "good time," which is time off for good behavior, for programming, or for working extra tasks; it is officially labeled good time, GAIN time, or merit time. "Doing my own time" refers to keeping to oneself, avoiding write-ups or conflict. "Straight time," or flat time, refers to a sentence without the benefit of good time or parole time. And, of course, the number indicating sentence length is another indicator of time, as is a parole date (Mahan 1984).

The Moral Career

Erving Goffman (1961) describes the life of inmates in total institutions, facilities that limit and control their movements, activities, surroundings, and ability for self-definition. Such institutions are characterized by rules and regulations, a strict barrier between those who are in power and those who are not, uniforms, their own lingo, and degradation of personal status. Catharine MacKinnon (1987, 170) observes, "To be a prisoner means to be defined as a member of a group for whom rules of what can be done to you, or what is seen as abuse of you, are reduced as part of the definition of your status." She goes on to say, "To be a woman is that kind of definition and has that kind of meaning." Social control of female prisoners, according to Meda Chesney-Lind and Jocelyn Pollock (1995, 166), compared to control of male inmates, parallels that of women in society—it includes all types of behavior and is more relationship based.

Thomas Arcaro (1984, 75–86) outlines seven stages in the moral career of the female inmate. A moral career is the progression of changes that occurs in sense of self and in relationship to others (Goffman 1961) as an inmate adjusts to the setting of a total institution. The process begins with a literal stripping of the self through strip searching, followed by accepting state-issued clothing and losing personal belongings. Impression management is threatened, since newcomers have few of the "props" needed to manipulate an individualized personality. Thus begins the process of status degradation, characterized not only by lack of distinct individuality but by loss of freedom and heightened external control (see also Moyer 1984).

The second stage involves distancing from the role of prisoner, wherein a new arrival will keep to herself and avoid identifying as an insider. This is a process of denial, which changes as contact with the outside is superseded by contact with life on the inside. In stage three, learning the ropes, the woman comes to understand the social structure of the prison, including hard lessons about trust, gossip, and how to monitor one's own behavior. Culture shock is common.

Learning how to do time marks the fourth stage. This involves figuring out how to cope with boredom, arbitrary enforcement of rules, lack of privacy, and unvarying schedules, as well as developing various coping strategies, such as establishing substitute family relations or involving oneself romantically with another inmate. This stage varies with the length of sentence, and can last from months to years.

Stage five, dealing with fear of denial around parole dates, essentially involves the experience of dashed hopes. An inmate longs for release, but she is denied time after time (and sees this happen to others as well). She comes to view the system as capricious, without fairness, and she needs to develop psychological defenses against this emotional roller coaster. Stage six, getting papers, takes place in this context. As a woman has her home plan accepted and gets a release date, mental strain can become unbearable. Fear that another inmate may undermine her impending release may verge on paranoia.

Finally, stage seven, getting out and shedding the inmate role, is necessarily a lengthy process. Upon release, the former prisoner has many adjustments to make, including rebuilding her sense of self and reestablishing social roles; she also, most likely, faces parole stipulations. Arcaro (1984, 86) observes, "This final stage in the moral career is marked by the ex-inmate becoming aware that she has been permanently affected by her life at [prison], and that she will continually have to deal with the social stigma of being an ex-con."

Powerlessness and Dependency

An environment as controlled as prison—in which women are told when to eat, get up, or go to bed, in which they are transported wherever they go, in which their contact with the outside is strictly regulated—fosters dependency and powerlessness (Clark 1995, Faith 1993). A "no touch" rule fractures any natural connection and spontaneity the women might feel and exhibit with each other that would provide nurturance and support under stressful conditions. Since adult roles and responsibilities are now limited (and in many cases eliminated), women not only have to accept authority but are given the message that they are not to be trusted with responsibility (Clark 1995, 312). The prison becomes the punitive parent, regulating the child through rules and sanctions (Clark 1995, 315). Keeping female prisoners in the status of dependent children makes them easier to control (Carlen 1983, Moyer 1984), and the women themselves feel infantilized. As one inmate told me, "This place here, they're not really hard on you. It's really, speaking for myself, it's feeling low self-esteem, feeling like you got a parent telling you what to do, and that's hard to accept, but you have to. . . . You start feeling like a kid." Another woman said:

> Honestly, [the officers] make me sick. They have an ego thing going. If you treat a person with respect, then you'll get respect. Sometimes there's one bad apple. But the majority of the ladies here, they just want to be treated like somebody. We know we are incarcerated. We're already tried and sentenced. No need to do it

over again. They tell you you should act like adults and then talk to you like you're two. I will never understand that, talking down to me.

Female prisoners receive a double message: to take responsibility for themselves, yet to not become too independent (Clark 1995). There is tight regulation over activities such as loaning personal items like toiletries, helping each other out with duties, and sharing possessions like clothing—normal activities that are prohibited within a prison (Fletcher et al. 1993). Such actions, now viewed as "trafficking" or "trading," are generally not even an issue in men's prisons (Belknap 1996), but in women's prisons they are met with write-ups, loss of privileges, or extra work duty. Many write-ups result from misunderstandings that are not negotiable, regardless of fault. One inmate shared this example with me:

> I went home on my home pass and I was told to have my daughter to have me back, and I don't even know what time, a certain time, right. But on the card that they give you the time is on there. She [the guard] told one time and on the card was another time. It messed me up, we went by what the card said. . . . And then another one was I gave my daughter twenty dollars to get her hair fixed, and my daughter wrote on a piece of paper the statement of why I gave her twenty dollars. But they said I was supposed to give her a money order, and I never gave money orders before. So I wasn't right then. They wrote me up for both of them, gave me forty hours' extra duty, twenty for each one, and, what else—took my home passes for a month.

Many women felt the rules and regulations were more strict at Black Mountain, a minimum security facility, than at Raleigh. The inmates wanted to avoid confrontations and not get sent back to the main prison, yet matters seemed out of their control.

> The rules will change from day to day, like one officer will say do it this way and another officer will say, "No, you can't do that," and write you up, and so-and-so said you could but that don't matter. You gonna take a write-up. We just go through a lot of mental anguish every day. We don't know what kind of mood the officer may be in or sergeant or even another inmate. You might just say something in joking and they might take it serious and it creates a problem there.

Another woman remarked,

> To me, this prison right here, it seems like a private prison 'cause it seems like they got their own rules. There's nothing here I see that says "DOC." Some of the rules

here you wouldn't believe. . . . It's just petty. I mean, you can't sit down, you can't comb a lady's hair outside; one person in the bathroom at a time [after 10 P.M.].

And more than one inmate told me that officers claimed they had to fulfill a write-up quota.

Well, their policy was that if they don't get an inmate, to write them up, there's so many times, they're not doing their job. That was told me by an officer. . . . She said, "Hell, it puts another extra paycheck in our pocket because we get a bonus." I'm like, "What?" "Yeah," she said, "We can get raises by as many write-ups we get."

What seems to be arbitrary control over actions is made worse by the lack of privacy in most prisons. There are no places to be alone, since prisoners must be accounted for at all times (Mahan 1984). Still, one of the benefits of the honor grade included, as one woman said, "doors on the bathroom stalls, shower curtains," and "when you're changing your clothes in your room you can shut your door."

Boredom is another consequence of control and loss of freedoms. According to Karlene Faith (1993, 167), boredom can be the "most miserable feature of the prison experience," given the regimentation of daily life and the herdlike atmosphere. Deprived of agency over their lives, many inmates gain weight, chain-smoke, sleep too much or not enough, become irritable over waits in line, and in general resent mail censorship, strip searches, and orders to "Move, *now*, ladies." Many prisoners I interviewed cited boredom as a prominent feature of daily life, although others felt they could be no busier than they already were with work, passes, and in some cases school.

For example, this inmate said, "It's boring, but that's about it. They don't have no kind of activity here. None whatsoever. Nothing but volleyball and badminton. It's nothing." Another woman remarked:

I have more freedom [than at Raleigh], and I don't even take advantage of the freedom that I do have. I go out every day to work. I don't do nothing on my job, I don't jeopardize my job in any kind of way. I work around some good people and I don't have nobody to try to bring me this or bring me that in. 'Cause I can go home and get the personal things that I need for myself or I can go out on CV passes to get it.

Adjustment

Being in prison is stressful and can create physical as well as psychological problems. Stress results from loss of freedom, loss of control of one's environment, loss of contact with family and friends, rupture of social roles, fear of losing bonds with one's children, and insults to self-esteem and self-concept (Fogel 1993, Giallombardo 1966a). Regina Arnold (1994, 182) reminds us that these women, structurally dislocated from the primary institutions of society, adopted strategies of survival that were criminalized, and now need to be resocialized within a criminal network and relocated structurally within the prison. Their ties to the prison world will increase as their ties to the conventional world decrease.

All inmates go through a similar adaptation, or prisonization, process, though not all of them will experience every aspect of it. For example, Rose Giallombardo (1966b) and David Ward and Gene Kassebaum (1964) argue in two early studies of homosexuality among female inmates that such behavior was the major mode of adaptation to the prison environment. Other investigators focus on pseudo-families (Mahan 1984, Propper 1982). Zelma Henriques (1996, 83–84) suggests that homosexuality among incarcerated mothers may be one means of dealing with the depression caused by separation from their children, whereas participating in a surrogate family allows for the continuation of mothering roles. Other researchers cite the importance of programming that includes support groups and information, education, drug rehabilitation, and job training (Sultan et al. 1984). Inmates themselves mention focusing on accepting the fact of incarceration, admitting responsibility for their crimes, and learning the difference between associates and friends.

James Larson and Joey Nelson (1984) and Doris MacKenzie et al. (1989) found that length of sentence and time already served had an impact on adaptation to prison. Persons who had served more time seemed better adjusted to prison life, a point with which the Black Mountain inmates agree. "You can tell a person who's been locked down two, three, four years because they more or less know what it's like. They've settled down, their wild streak is not there. They're getting serious with whatever it is that's going on." Another woman, in talking about who she can trust, says, "There's some ladies here you can trust. A lot of them is women that's been locked up for a while, that's kind of settled into it. In for two years or more, there's a big difference."

The types of adaptation that Larson and Nelson (1984) identify include isolation (withdrawing from outside bonds and constructing a life inside prison), solidarity (developing primary relationships with others in prison, especially through family or homosexual ties), and efficacy (transforming a sense of powerlessness to one of limited control through friendships). Although friendship and affiliation are major components of the female gender role, the finding that friendship and trust were important responses to powerlessness seems at odds with what I heard over and over again in the interviews regarding lack of trust. The prisoners at Black Mountain spoke of adaptation based on acceptance, isolation, state families, religious dedication, and resignation. Following are some comments about adjusting to prison life.

> I do know this, that when you do get put in prison you need to just set your mind to the fact that you are in prison, make the best of it, and to learn, immediately, that you have some people over you and that you have to do as they say. This makes it much easier. If you will just go along with the authority that's over you. Also to work as much as possible. This passes the time really nice. To make yourself tired out physically so that mentally you'll be all right.

And,

> Prison can be either good or bad. For some people, for most women it's bad because they don't accept the time they've got, and they always blame it on everybody else. Once you accept the crime and say, "I did it," whether you took it for someone else or whatever, you had to make that decision to do it. You have to live with your decision. Once you say, "OK, I did this, this and this, and this is what I got," and you start looking at it as time, and start living your life the best way DOC allows you, then you can't complain about it.

For some women, incarceration brought about a greater caution in interactions with others. For example, as this prisoner says,

> [I]t's hard in here, it's hard to live with women day in and day out. And sometimes I've found myself putting up shields and guards towards people. I don't want that to carry over with me. I was never like that. In some ways prison has affected me in a negative way because I'm not that trusting, free-spirited, free-hearted person I used to be. I'm very cautious. I feel like in prison, not speaking of on the streets, I feel like in here that you really have to watch what you say and do, and there's always an ulterior motive behind someone's actions.

For others, interaction was welcome within the spiritual context fostered by Bible study.

> Before I would go around preaching to someone, I want to make sure that I'm where I should be. I want God's light to shine through me. I don't want to cuss somebody out and then turn around and say but you should read this in the Bible or you should

read that in the Bible because that turns people off. That's not God's love coming through you. . . . But I love to sing, and I love to hear God's word, but I don't go around preaching to everybody. If we're having Bible study and they'd like to join us, I welcome them, they're more than welcome to come in and join us.

Relationships with Other Inmates

Once a woman is incarcerated, however long she takes to observe her fellow prisoners and the routine and rhythm of her new life, she will begin to interact with those around her, making her own impression and aligning with or avoiding other inmates. She learns to make herself scarce when certain guards are around, and she establishes relationships with other prisoners she feels comfortable with. Basically, she "learns the ropes."

When asked about free time, virtually all the women mentioned staying in their rooms. There they slept or read, where it was "safer and quieter." Half the inmates spent free time outside, sitting at the picnic tables, talking in small groups, and smoking. Less than a quarter of the women mentioned the day room as a place to spend time. Generally the television is on, and at the time of the study visiting took place there. The "smoke room" was cited by less than 20 percent of the women as a place to spend time. Since the time of my interviews, smoking has been banned inside prison buildings.

As Sue Mahan (1984, 359) says, "incarceration means forced interaction." There are people, perhaps sharing her room, with whom the new prisoner ordinarily would never associate. Some inmates are uncomfortable with those of another race, some despise prostitutes, some feel other women are not clean enough or look down on their personal habits (Giallombardo 1966a). As one inmate said, "I don't like it. I'm not used to this type of people. It's a new experience for me 'cause I've never had to be around people that lived on the streets, had to sell themselves for what they wanted." And another prisoner, although she was a drug addict, felt she was not like the other women. This belief helped her do her time.

What influenced me the most was knowing I had nothing in common with these people, and I don't want to say that I'm better than anybody else, 'cause I hate when people say that, it's just that I'm from, I have my values and morals instilled in me and a lot of people don't in here.

Given the limitations on prison activities, "prisoners establish their relationships through talk." Mahan (1984, 359) found that friends shared stories and gossip, whereas those who were not friends ignored each other. Perhaps the most frequent comment I heard about interaction with other inmates was that there are no friends in prison, only associates, so the term "friend" is always used loosely. There may be one or two people to talk to, but one never really trusts them. The element of distrust is *always* present.

> Well, I don't believe I would say [I] trust anybody in prison 'cause you don't really know 'em. Don't matter if you done ten years with them, you'll never know them because everybody will stick you in the back to get what they wanna get. You just don't know who will and who won't, so to just be on the safe side . . . you don't want to tell nobody nothing in here.

These two women echo her pessimism:

> The inmates, you have your certain little groups of friends. Those friends are supportive of you. As far as widespread support from the inmates, there is none. They'd rather tell on you and get you in trouble than they had to help you. I've found that out since I've been in here that women just will not help other women.

And,

> Trust is not something you have within these walls. . . . Women are evil. I want to believe people are basically good, but every time I believe it, I get knocked down. . . . As much as this is my world, this awful place, there's no trust, there's no dignity, there's no loyalty, there's no honor. I still believe there's good people in the world; this happens to be the place that draws the trash.

Indeed, Giallombardo (1966b, 100) found that inmates commonly held these views of women's nature: you can't trust another woman; every woman is a sneaking, lying bitch; and, with women, "you never really know."

Learning to distrust those around you in prison is based on experience. Gossip and the inaccurate retelling of stories create problems. Women can try to avoid gossip by keeping to themselves or displaying "false fronts" (Arcaro 1984). Says one prisoner:

> Here you don't have friends, you have associates. You really don't have anybody you could call a friend in prison, period. . . . You may say something and it goes and it may be turned three or four ways once it gets back. It's best to keep to yourself.

Or, as another woman remarked, "It doesn't pay to be honest. The one thing you learn from coming to prison is you learn how to lie, and if you didn't know when you got here, you better learn quick. You can't be honest, you just can't do it."

There seems to be no defense against an inmate who chooses to turn someone in with a lie, which sometimes lands a woman on a bus back to Raleigh. It is usually the accuser who is believed, not the person who must defend herself. One woman explained,

> See, what happened, I had a CV sponsor and a girl here who I know, she's gone now, well, she got really jealous of this lady's relationship, come back to the unit and told them that we were gay. And they stripped me of my CV passes to her. I can no longer go out with her. She cannot become a sponsor until the year I make parole. Because they believed it.

Here is another inmate's story:

> I got railroaded just because somebody wrote a statement on me and told a lie. It was a, I got charged with a 23 [a write-up for a sexual act], but what it was was that the girl said that I hemmed her up and exposed myself to her. Now anybody that knows me knows that that's not true. I mean, that's so out of my character. [But, I got sent back to Raleigh.]

The most trusted prisoners seem to be those from one's home town (the home girls, or "homeys") and those who have done long stretches of time together. As one woman said, "I have a girl that's here who's a real good friend of mine from home and I got another girl that she and I are pretty good friends. We've done this whole sentence together just about. But other than that, if they speak, I speak. I don't talk a lot." Homeys "talk about the old days" and are not as likely to twist stories:

> I don't communicate with half of the women here. I stay, if I'm not into a book, I start crocheting. It's very few of the women that I really talk to. Now, my homeys, from my hometown, I communicate with them. Other than that, I don't 'cause I come here to do my time and sometimes there's a mistake when you talk to other people, they stretch and take it elsewhere. . . . Women are trouble.

Racial prejudice and dealing with different personalities also have an impact on how the prisoners interact. On the surface, it looks like white women and women of color interact quite a bit. What they say, however, is something different (though no one admits to being prejudiced).

> A lot of people are prejudiced here, very prejudiced people. I've never met more

black people prejudiced in my life. I'm flexible, I figure to each his own. I can sit and I can hear the white people talking about the black people and hear the black people talk about the white people. But they all know for a fact I'm not [prejudiced].

One African American inmate felt she was in a no-win situation:

The blacks say I'm prejudiced and the whites say . . . I don't know. [Blacks] say I am, that I act better than anybody else, that I don't talk . . . they hold [my college education] against me sometimes 'cause I don't talk slang. I don't have any group. I can't sit down at the table and when they're talking about something I can't tell my war stories 'cause I don't have any war stories to tell.

"Different personalities" was mentioned numerous times as a challenge in coping with imprisonment. One woman summed up why she has no friends this way: "[Friends?] No. They can't help me. They in prison, too. What do I want to talk to them for, they can't help me."

Homosexuality among Female Inmates

Generally, people do not consider what prisoners "do with their sexual and emotional needs when they've been confined behind bars" (Burkhart 1976, 363). Although research indicates that one in four incarcerated women reports involvement in a same-sex relationship (Belknap 1996, 112; Harris 1988), this does not mean that they identify as lesbians (Faith 1993). Rather, as Mahan (1984) points out, female prisoners come out of a broader culture that is fiercely heterosexual in its orientation. Most of them have or have had relationships with men, and when they return to society they will likely resume them or begin new ones. Homosexual behavior for most prisoners, then, is an adaptation to their unisex environment. For others, who are lesbians, same-sex relationships are normal. And still others, finding themselves in an environment where they are not competing for male attention, find that they are truly attracted to women (Faith 1993). One inmate had this to say:

[A] lot of women have relationships, which is something you won't find in a men's institution. I mean, [the men] have sex, but they don't have relationships. But these women, it's more than sex to them. It's a relationship. You can get a woman who comes in off the street that ain't never been gay and is crazy about men, and she'll end up having a relationship. But it's just a substitution, I think, for lack of emotional and, you know. It's one way to try to have your needs met.

Many prisoners suspected the motives of those with same-sex involvements. For example,

> I think a lot of [the motive for gay relationships] is loneliness, despair, and in some cases I know for a fact that it's for financial purposes. I don't know what you'd call that, their friend or whatever, is willing to support them because they have no money coming in. I have seen women have relationships with women, leave this dorm hugging and kissing this woman and then go out to visitation and hug and kiss their husband, and I cannot comprehend that.

Such activity in women's prisons is not characterized by the exploitive, forced relations found in men's prisons, though individual experience may vary (Belknap 1996, Brownmiller 1975, Ward and Kassebaum 1964). Since homosexual behavior is against the rules and can result in disciplinary action, guards may be hypersensitive to asexual, friendly behavior and styles of dress or haircut, misinterpreting them as sexual (Propper 1978). Imogene Moyer (1984) feels this hypersensitivity prevents inmates from developing emotional ties to other inmates for fear of their being misconstrued, which results in increased isolation. As one woman described the situation at Black Mountain,

> [It's] definitely not [tolerated here], they do not like homosexuals. . . . If you get a 23, now, if you get caught in a sex act, you're gone [to Raleigh]. It's a rarity here. . . . They have relationships but it's like it's undercover. It takes a little while to tell who's going with who because, I guess because they're so scared they'll be found out. And they may never even have sex together, it may not even be a sexual relationship, just a companion relationship.

Researchers are interested in learning what influences same-sex behavior among female prisoners—are these women predisposed to homosexual behavior (the importation model), or are there prison variables that influence same-sex behavior (the deprivation model)? Robert Leger (1987), for example, finds that women who engaged in lesbian acts had earlier and longer criminal involvements, were likely to have had same-sex relations before entering prison, and were more aggressive compared to women who did not engage in same-sex behavior. Other investigators, such as Ward and Kassebaum (1964) and Giallombardo (1966a, 1966b), favor a deprivation model, wherein the loss of traditional female roles results in the substitution responses of homosexual relationships and pseudo-, or state, families (discussed in the next section).

The scholarship on homosexuality in women's prisons does not necessarily resonate with the inmates' own perceptions of their behaviors (Faith 1993). One influence is the shift in society at large concerning homosexuality. Although homophobia continues to be a major force, at the same time lesbians, gay men, and bisexuals are more visible in their everyday lives and are demanding their civil rights. These changes in the culture are not reflected in studies conducted thirty or twenty years ago, when lesbian role playing of butch and femme (based on heterosexual relationships) was the dominant model that homosexuals and heterosexuals both used to understand lesbian couples. This is no longer the predominant case, as changes in women's roles, combined with gay visibility, have expanded the conceptions of same-sex relationships. The detailed role playing described by Giallombardo (1966a, 1966b) as being characteristic of homosexuality in women's prisons has been replaced by a looser system and more flexible roles. Inmates report that few defining terms are used, mentioning only "boy" and "bulldagging" as common ones.

Faith (1993, 219) interviewed women in 1972 who had been involved in a study by Ward and Kassebaum in 1964. They responded with "hilarity" or "chagrin and anger" to how their behaviors had been characterized (as role playing, adaptation, etc.). They believed their feelings had been genuine and pointed out

> how in prison they had learned to overcome their fears of loving women, and how even though most of them (particularly those with children) would probably return to men when they returned to the "free world," they didn't want their "special friendships" with women to be denigrated.

Although homosexual behavior is present to some extent at this minimum security prison, at Raleigh it is both widespread and explicit. This does not mean all inmates approved of such behavior, or even that those who participated were without conflict.

In Raleigh it's not even hidden. They walk down the sidewalk holding hands. And the officers, they'll walk by you and some of them will say something and some of them won't. Most of them will say, "You all need to let go of each other," or "You all need to move back." Now if they catch you having sex, you know, some of them won't write you up, they'll tell you, "You need to stop that. You all need to get your clothes on." But some of them now, are just like, slap the handcuffs on you.

And,

> [T]hey've got the girls down there that got to do their bulldagging and stuff like that.
> I have no use for them. I could probably understand it if they were [lifers] and be in
> the big house for the rest of their life, but these girls that come in, they got a couple
> of months, maybe a year or so. I don't understand it. 'Cause it don't make no sense
> to me. That's just my opinion. . . . They don't tolerate the bulldaggering and all this
> other touchy-hugging-kissing sort of stuff like that, they don't tolerate it here. And
> the girls that's here know they'll be sent back to the main place, so. But, I think that
> it's just sickening.

The following comments from two prisoners (one lesbian, one heterosexual) demonstrate the spectrum of inmate attitudes. "If you're a homosexual you have no rights. They don't consider you, they don't respect that." And, "That is the awfulest mess in America. Here, there's some. That is really a sad situation. That's pitiful. . . . There's no way I'm going to go gay, that's just a little too deep."

State Families

Variously called pseudo-families, play families, make-believe families, and quasi-families, "state families" is the term the women in the study used to refer to the family-like units that inmates formed. The establishment of these groupings, complete with kin terms and the roles to go with them, is unique to women's prisons (MacKenzie et al. 1989) and is seen as a response to loneliness and the deprivations of prison life (Morris 1987). Thomas Foster (1975, 71; see also Burkhart 1976) describes such families as

> a structured peer group interaction that is characterized by role-taking among participants. . . . Strong in-group loyalties typify inmate family relationships and a functional division of responsibility and labour characteristically takes place among family members. Family members also are likely to lend each other mutual advice and assistance, look out for one another's interests, and participate in institutional activities together.

Although these units do not exist in male prisons, Alice Propper (1982) found that in coed juvenile facilities young men did become involved, participating as brothers and husbands, and sometimes as fathers and sons. According to Propper, state families and homosexual relationships are different modes of adaptation to prison life and should not be confused. In fact, in women's prisons the husband role is rare, and most homosexual relations take place in couple, as opposed to family, structures. William Holyoak (1972, 154) is, perhaps, one researcher who has contributed to this confusion, calling the homosexual activity of incarcerated girls "female homosexual family groups," taking the view that homosexual behavior is abnormal if it extends beyond a temporary mode of adaptation into a "fixation."

MacKenzie et al. (1989, 235) found that state families were much more common among newly arrived inmates than among women who had been imprisoned a long time. They speculate that state families are a coping mechanism for those adjusting to prison, providing a sense of security within a family-like unit. Once adjusted, however, inmates may no longer feel the need for these associations. Even though some researchers found no evidence of state families (Ward and Kassebaum 1964), the inmates at Black Mountain claim they are widespread in the North Carolina system. As mentioned, some of these studies were carried out twenty or even thirty years ago, which may account for some of this lack of agreement. On the other hand, Jean Harris (1988, 115), writing more recently about her time in prison in New York State, declares that she has witnessed a decline in state families; she links it to the decline of the nuclear family in society. From a different angle, James Fox (1984) points to the development of women's self-help programming, contact with outsiders such as volunteers, and increased visiting privileges as reasons for a drop in prison-family units in New York.

Although one prisoner said that "[e]verybody in Raleigh is somebody's family," and several women have been or are involved in state families, there was less of it in this minimum security facility. One inmate explained, "Once they get here they're put back out [through home passes]. It might be just for a weekend but they can reestablish those bonds to people they originally had them with. So, it's not needed as much." However, some women were involved in them even here.

> Yeah, and I said I never would. But I did. There was a lady, she went home the tenth, she was like the mother, an older lady, and she was like a surrogate mother to us. And then the girl that is here, ————, she's like a sister to me. . . . She doesn't draw any money, even, but I do, so what's mine is hers. I buy things for her, she smokes from my cigarettes, but I would do anything I could for her.

This inmate had an extensive family:

> I've got my state mom and my state dad, brothers, sisters. I even have children, I have a couple of children here. In fact, my dad got sent up here. She's "Don't tell nobody!" I said, "Are you ashamed to be my dad?" . . . It's just the masculine figure that you need.

Some prisoners are selective about the roles that they will take on. For example,

> I had one girl that kinda attached herself to me and used to call me mama, which was okay. If I would influence her in the right way then that's fine. But I've seen them daddies, they call each other daddy and brother, all the stuff like that. . . . I don't partake in that because we are women.

Most of those who claimed they were not involved in state families looked down on them. They had an understanding of why they were formed, but they still viewed them negatively.

> That's a crock. Insecurity. Insecurity that they don't have somebody that they can hover over or somebody that can protect them on the street that way. And in here they're willing to give it their all 'cause they got nobody else to give it to, so they give it to them.

Even though a state family might fill emotional needs, some prisoners still would not participate.

> I was called a granny [in Raleigh]. It makes me sick. "That's my grandpa, that's my daddy, that's my uncle, that's my brother." My God! . . . Just trying to have, I don't know, maybe they're needing that affection, just putting a title on somebody. . . . I needed some attention and love, too, but I would not go that route for no reason in the world. But some people maybe just couldn't take it, it was too overwhelming not to have anybody to hug on or kiss or whatever, and that have that heart-to-heart relationship, whatever.

And another inmate said,

> I see it like maybe the reason they do that is 'cause they don't know who they father is, maybe they don't have any sisters or brothers, maybe their mother's passed away, maybe they don't have any kids and want kids, want a mother, want a father, want a brother, want a sister. I don't want none of it. It's not real, for one thing.

Some women saw these relationships as being exploitive for financial gain, and others saw them as a way to keep people under control.

> I think it's something needed 'cause it's kept a lot of girls in line, out of trouble, because especially the parent figure will get on that child if that child's doing things against the rules or doin' things to hurt themselves or somethin'. That parent figure will discipline and it's kept things in control.

Katherine Van Wormer (1987, 265–69) views these as questionable benefits, coming to the conclusion that state families are dysfunctional. She sees them as encouraging emotional dependency by paralleling the passive roles of mother, daughter, and sister in the "free" family. As the most common relations in state families, they promote dependency rather than encouraging leadership. Furthermore, having such "relatives" constantly around means there is little psychological privacy, compounding the lack of physical privacy in prison. State family relations tend to be lasting during incarceration, and Van Wormer sees this as a source of emotional strain. Finally, the state-family pattern reinforces female oppression through the complacency that is fostered by inmates arranging themselves in these small groups. Women in prison do not organize and protest conditions like men do; state families, with their "childlike familial roles," are encouraged by prison authorities.

In an earlier work (1981), Van Wormer called state families "a natural response to an unnatural situation" (181) and considered this adaptation a way to "help insulate them from the pains of imprisonment" (183). The Black Mountain women held conflicting views of whether these families were positive, but they were in fair accord as to why the groupings were formed in the first place. Regardless of what they thought of them, the prisoners concurred that they filled a need—a need created from loss, isolation, and loneliness.

Relationships with the Guards

Getting along with one's jailers is based on more than personality factors. Officers are likely to be white, whereas inmates are disproportionately women of color. Guards and inmates both come from the working and lower-middle classes, yet there is a huge power difference between them. The criminal justice system is overwhelmingly controlled by men, so while the inmate population will be completely female, women's prisons will have guards of both sexes, and often a male superintendent (though not at Black Mountain). Most important, the job of the guards is to maintain order and security by enforcing rules and regulations. The negotiation of this enforcement determines, to a large extent, the relationship inmates have with guards (Fletcher et al. 1993).

When monitoring inmate behavior, guards have some leeway in how they secure compliance. Direct orders, threats of write-ups and actual write-ups, counseling (a verbal warning short of a write-up), polite requests, establishing rapport, providing services promptly or slowly, and using physical force mark the range of behaviors guards use (Zimmer 1987). At Black Mountain, access to pay phones (up to 10:30 P.M. on weeknights and 11 P.M. on weekends), the canteen, home passes, and CV passes are all privileges that can be taken away; extra duty can be assigned as a punishment. Lynn Zimmer maintains that female guards are more likely than male guards to have a social worker's orientation to the job and to attempt keeping up friendly relations as a way of securing voluntary compliance with rules. Some guards will adapt a mothering stance, listening to the inmates and offering advice (1987, 421).

Most prisoners reported getting along with a few guards and trying to avoid the others. Some were respected, and in general all were seen as just "doing their job." The social worker approach was validated in that guards occasionally asked inmates if something was wrong (often viewed as prying) if they seemed to be acting differently than usual. For example,

> I was going through some hard times. It was the anniversary of my sister's murder and her birthday—she got murdered right next to her birthday—so it was a very hard week for me. And I guess I was lashing out. I would not talk to anybody and if I did have anything to say it was not nice. I wanted to be left alone, I wanted to be left alone. She called me in and told me that she wanted to talk to me because she was concerned and wanted to know if there was anything that she could do for me. She really made me feel good because she told me she knew that I was a good person, that I come from a good family, and that she was just concerned that maybe other people were having an effect on me.

But some inmates felt the guards' inquiries were uncalled for and added pressure to their daily lives.

> A lot of them said the officers are bitches, that's what they call 'em, bitches, nosy bitches, 'cause you know, you don't act the same as you normally do, they say "What's wrong with you?" Some of them that's their job to do, to ask. And some of them you can sit in their face and they're like, "What's wrong?" And you know you

want to say something but you can't say nothing, and it's like, "Nothing, nothing." And they let you alone and stuff. But I don't find nothing wrong with it, it's their job.

And for this woman,

Last night we had a [volunteer] banquet, and they bowed their head in prayer, and I didn't bow my head, and ———— looked dead at me and then he came back and asked me why. And I said, "Well, you know that I'm Muslim, and I didn't think it would be appropriate for me to bow my head because if you all came to my house then you wouldn't get on my rug and pray." And he was like, "Well, I was just wondering. I thought you was being selfish." And I was like, "No sir, I was showing the most respect I could without harming myself."

Respect is a big issue for the prisoners, since their self-respect is under attack. They want to salvage some element of personal pride out of a situation of powerlessness. One element of control for the inmates is found in the bargain "If you respect me, I'll respect you." Of course, this is not really possible, given the rules and potential punishments of prison. If the women were truly to be respected, they could not be placed in such a setting to begin with.

There's a few here that I do respect, and will always respect, and I show them respect. The other ones I just kind of stay away from because the way I see it, respect is something that's mutual. If you want it, you give it. And I don't care if I'm an inmate or not, I'm still a human being. I'm a woman just like they are. Yeah, I may have committed a crime, but I'm paying for it. I've been paying for it almost a decade of my life. You don't have to talk to me like I'm a dog, 'cause I'm not. If I do something wrong, you write me up for it. Don't you stand there and you talk to me like I'm dirt on your shoe just because you get off on it.

As another prisoner saw it, "This is living hell, torture. . . . The guards are petty. It's okay for them to disrespect you but if you disrespect them then there's a write-up or it's taken to Ms. Brame a different way." Inmates commonly mentioned that they felt guards took out their domestic problems on them, that guards were on an ego trip, and that guards had negative attitudes and were hard to get along with. For example, one prisoner remarked, "And the officers, they come up with nasty attitudes. They having a problem at home, they come in and just take it out on the inmates and I think that's

wrong. I think they should get a grip on theyself before they come in here."
Another woman recalls:

> Anything I've asked them since I've been here has been negative, anything. Even the
> case manager. . . . She's like, "Oh, you need not worry about making your first
> parole, nobody never does." Well, excuse me, some of them do. I didn't say anything.
> [They could] give you a little hope, "No, no way. You're never leaving this dungeon."
> They're real sarcastic.

Some inmates felt the guards put their own needs first.

> [We were outside and the officer] was cold, she wanted us to come in. Okay, we'll
> come in. You can't say, "No, I'm not going." Okay. So, they don't want to be both-
> ered. Like they come to work and they watch TV, come to watch games, the ball
> games and stuff on TV. Sometimes they'll say, "I want to watch the game tonight,"
> especially ————. He'll come in and he'll actually turn from what you're watching
> and watch the ball game. And I mean, he didn't come to work to watch the ball
> game, he should come for a job. I realize that it is a privilege for us, but they come
> like this is their second home and they can do whatever they want to do here.

Except for a few who felt they did not get along with any guards, most
women liked and respected some of the officers. Given the naturally antago-
nistic power dynamic in the relationship, for most inmates to feel that there
were some good people trying to do their jobs at Black Mountain spoke well
of the institution. However, the dynamic is basically immutable. A prisoner
and her keeper are never going to be best friends: each will have bad days,
each will hold certain resentments, and the guards will always determine the
bottom line.

Enforcement of petty rules, a sense that officers were racially prejudiced,
and the fact that younger guards were telling older inmates what to do also
added to the tension of the environment. However, the number-one humiliation inmates experienced was the near-constant strip searching. Women are
always strip-searched after home passes, CV passes, and visitation at the
prison. They can also be strip-searched at other times. The policy is that there
needs to be at least three of these searches on each shift, so a minimum of
nine takes place every day.

Seen variously as a violation of self and as part of the guard's job, strip
searching can be used punitively. Teresa Albor (1995, 236) recounts one inmate's sense of defeat: "They wouldn't be able to admit it themselves, but

their search, of course, is for something else, and is efficient; their search is for our pride. And I think, with a sinking heart, again and again it must be, they find it and take it." Furthermore, for that great number of women who have been sexually abused, strip searches can be traumatic (Chesney-Lind 1997).

> My first night back I had been strip-searched twice that day and I was going again. And I'm the type of person, I'll talk to you. I'm like, "Well, this is only my third strip search today, so let's go ahead and do it." So I take my clothes off, and that's all I said. I didn't say it in an intimidating voice or derogatory way or anything, just saying that, making conversation. It's bad enough you have to stand there and take your clothes off in front of somebody. Might as well try to make it easier. And, 'cause that's something you really don't get used to. You just kind of block it out and do it. It gets routine, but still, it's still humiliating and embarrassing. And she's like, "We can strip search you as often as we like." I said, "No, I don't think you can," and quoted policy. Oh, she got an attitude then, and started talking junk to me. And then, I went and asked for my clothes and left. . . . And [later] she said, how did she put it, "I don't know who you are, and I don't care, but you don't need to be quoting policy to me about anything." I could have said something right then but I didn't. I said, no, just keep your mouth shut and go to bed. She said, "Why don't you just let me be the officer and you be who you are." And I said, "Okay, sure. Is that all?" . . . She done what she wanted to do, she degraded me.

Another prisoner recalls:

> So, I came in on third shift one night, and got strip-searched 'cause I was working second shift, that's a normal thing. . . . So I had got on these little underwear and my little bra I'd just gotten and she went back to control and called—one of the officers told me, and like I told you I get along with everyone—and she went in there and said, "I think we needed to start watching ———— because she's doing something at Taco Bell." And they're like, "———— what? Why do you think?" And she said, "The type of underwear and bra she had on. You don't wear those unless you're doing something." And I said, "Why would she want to put that kind of pressure on me? I mean, if anybody doesn't do anything in here, it's me. I'm just trying to get through it."

One of the inmates felt that strip searching was not about intercepting contraband. As she put it, "These women know how to do that. They could cough 'til doomsday and never find the money or anything else up there."

She thought a strip search should only take place if someone gave a tip or there was some evidence that an exchange had taken place. For many women strip searching was the worst aspect of prison, something they had to endure again and again. Several prisoners did not go out on CV passes or have visits because they would be strip-searched afterward, quite a sacrifice to make in order to avoid what they felt was a very degrading act.

Health Care

Women in prison tend to have serious health problems due to a combination of factors. They have a greater likelihood of coming from poverty, with limited access to preventive health care and with poor nutrition, they are likely to have little education about health, and they are likely to be drug addicted (Belknap 1996). There are also connections to the likelihood of being raped, domestic violence, and single parenthood—conditions common among female prisoners—and the high rate of depression and other mental illnesses among women in general (Fogel and Martin 1992, Lerner 1997).

Prison medical care is an arena of chronic contention, with voters and administrators trying to keep costs down and inmates suffering from lack of appropriate care, prompt response, and adequate staffing. Along with overcrowding, lawsuits concerning health and treatment matters top the litigation concerns of inmates, especially for women, whose medical care is often worse than men's (Pollock-Byrne 1990).

In general, nurses are available only for limited hours and access to doctors is restricted. Most women's prisons do not have a staff gynecologist, so services are arranged for as needed. Most prison systems have had to concentrate inmates with chronic medical needs, long-term illnesses, and pregnancies into one prison. Women at Black Mountain must wait to be transported to Raleigh for care unless they can arrange for services in the community. These delays can complicate their medical conditions (Chesney-Lind and Pollock 1995). Although the costs of staffing and equipment limit what prisons can do, it is also expensive to provide security when taking inmates out into the community for treatment (Lord 1995).

Nationwide, about 6 percent of female inmates enter prison pregnant, and about 90 percent of them give birth while incarcerated (Albor 1995). These prisoners are at a distinct disadvantage in control over their diets, access to prenatal care, exercise opportunities, appropriate work assignments, and having a stress-free environment. Some women desiring abortion may be denied their request; others may be pressured into having an abortion. Moreover, some prisons use inappropriate restraints for pregnant inmates, putting them further at risk (Barry 1989, Hufft et al. 1993, Ryan and Grassano 1993). Ellen Barry (1989) calls for a comprehensive, national body of standards to ensure that pregnant prisoners receive appropriate medical care.

Chesney-Lind and Pollock (1995, 165) argue that whether inmates should be able to keep their babies with them after birth is "a medical issue as well as a social and custodial issue." There are a handful of programs in which this is possible (such as those in New York and California), but generally inmate mothers and their newborns are separated within forty-eight hours, inflicting suffering on both mothers and children. The babies may have the good fortune to be placed with relatives; otherwise, they go into the foster care system. This forced separation, according to Terri Schupak (1986), disrupts the mother-child bond, and she advocates creating programs where children can remain with their mothers for their first few years of life.

Six women in this study had been pregnant while in Raleigh, and they had a range of experiences. One woman lost her baby at six months; her fallopian tube burst and she had to have a hysterectomy. Another prisoner recalls:

> They didn't believe I was in labor. My baby's head crowned before they would take me to the hospital. They kept telling me I was faking labor. . . . When you have a baby in prison, they take you at the last possible moment to the hospital. . . . You're allowed to stay there until the next day and it's normally less than twenty hours. And they take you back to the unit and whoever is supposed to come take the baby is supposed to get the baby twenty-four hours after the baby is born. . . . I was fortunate [my parents came]. Most of the girls aren't. Most of the babies go to social services, which is sad.

Except for the woman who lost her baby, these inmates were lucky enough to have family or friends claim their children. One of the women gave birth twice during two different prison terms, and each time her mother came and got the baby; another woman's mother came and collected her new grandson; and a cousin came and got another prisoner's son. In a daring move, one inmate gave birth to a little girl and arranged with a couple who had befriended her to pick the baby up. She listed the man as the father, thus avoiding having the social services department get her baby. She felt she was a mother "biologically only" and is very satisfied with her decision, since her daughter has a secure, happy home.

The women at Black Mountain felt overwhelmingly that the health care at the prison was adequate, and many mentioned that the nurse was excellent, doing the best she could under straitened circumstances. Six prisoners felt the medical care was not good, primarily because they found the doctor to be inadequate or did not receive attention when they needed it.

Depression was the most frequent among a range of medical problems. Twenty women (50 percent) suffered from depression; two others had bipolar diagnoses, one was diagnosed as psychotic, and two others suffered from anxiety or bad nerves. Ten of these inmates took the following medications: Prozac, Zoloft, Doxepin, Wellbutrin, Elavil, Mellaril, Risperdal, Benadryl, Depakote, and Paxil. Although I have no way of assessing if drugs are overprescribed in this prison, Shaw (1982) is concerned about the overmedication of female inmates, who are estimated to receive drugs at a rate two to ten times higher than that for male prisoners.

It is impossible to untangle the reasons for the high rates of depression and other mental illnesses among incarcerated women. Investigators have found that more than one-third—in one study, more than one-half—of women with severe mental illness suffered from physical abuse, and that depression is more likely among less educated and poorer women (Lerner 1997, 60). Separation from their families is a tremendous cause of depression among inmates, and those who are mothers suffer more from anxiety (Fogel and Martin 1992).

Other medical conditions the prisoners faced include back problems (mentioned by 19 women), headaches (16), respiratory difficulties, asthma, and bronchitis (9), menstrual problems (7), arthritis and bursitis (6), past or present cancer (5), and ulcers (2); several conditions were mentioned one time each, among them carpel tunnel syndrome, pinched nerves, and a yeast infection.

Prison as a Positive Experience

Doing time is difficult. It is about coping with loss of control and restriction of freedom. It is about establishing relationships in an atmosphere of distrust. It is about unmet needs and constant pressure. However, for many women, prison is an escape from a different set of losses, controls, and pres-

HARPER COLLEGE LIBRARY
PALATINE, ILLINOIS 60067

sures. Prison provides an opportunity to get off drugs and stay clean, to get away from abusive boyfriends or husbands, to acquire a GED or job training, and to have time to think.

> Coming to prison was the best thing that ever happened to me. It was the best thing. Because I was getting out of control. Alcohol. I was an alcoholic, still am. . . . When I first came in I had a real hard time because I was so angry. I was mad at the world. But after being locked up for a while I kind of settled up and realized what's going on. And it gives me another chance to work on myself. 'Cause I've been going strong ever since I was a teenager. Married, kids, and responsibilities when my husband got killed in a car wreck. . . . I don't think I would have [changed without prison]. I might even be dead.

References to death were common: "I don't even think it would have been possible [to change outside prison]. Something had to be done, either here, a treatment center, if not neither one of them, it just would have been death. Really." For a second inmate, "If I hadn't come to prison I'd be dead or serving more time due to more charges." And, again, "[A]t the rate that I was going [somebody would have killed me]." Another prisoner remarks:

> I don't know if I could have ever gotten clean enough [without prison]. But living the way I was living, with the drugs, and living with a drug dealer, I don't know if that would have ever happened for me. I think there's other means besides prison. For my case, I feel like I could have been punished within the community, taken out of my house, placed into a halfway house, placed under house arrest within the community. I feel like it's a shame that there is a lot of women in prison that could be punished within the community that have not committed violent crimes, first-time offenders.

And another woman admits, "I see myself a stronger-minded person to go out there. The more I'm, this is awful to say, the more I'm locked up, the more my mind, the better my mind. That's awful but it's true. The better my mind functions. The clearer I see things."

Mahan (1984) found that inmates felt they had learned whatever they had learned on their own. Clark (1995, 324) sees a woman's ability to regain control over her own life as involving several factors—"support from family and friends, positive experiences and relationships in her daily life, peer influence, inner resiliency, and (strangely enough) time." She believes that the individual must save herself, but that programs within a prison can facilitate change.

Nicole Rafter (1985) similarly views the prison as a shelter from abuse and a place where those in need can gain assistance. One of the Black Mountain women echoed this sentiment:

Prison is what you make of it. It can be a beginning point in your life or it can be the last moment you have left. You understand? But at the same time, prison can be a stepping-stone in your life for you to learn because it's hard to know that your family has turned on you and it's hard to know that you have no one to go to. But you always have yourself, when you have no one else. If you give yourself determination and hard will, you can make anything happen for you.

For some inmates who are serving very long sentences, these realizations come and go; years of introspection, taking every program available, and fading family contact all have the potential to create frustration. Longtime prisoners have been found to be self-reliant and well-adjusted, but bothered by boredom and lack of activities (Bonta and Gendreau 1990). They may be ready for release, but in the waiting for the days and years to pass to complete the sentence bitterness may set in. One woman remarks: "After my seventh year, there was no more growing process for me. I done everything. So now I'm just waiting. I'm waiting, that's it." An inmate who has served two years of an eight-year sentence says, "[P]rison helped me at first, it helped to clear my mind and get myself together. But like now I feel like I'm ready to go and I've paid my debt to society." And according to this prisoner, who has served eight years of a thirty-year sentence:

It's detrimental. It doesn't do any good anymore. It's making you bitter, angry, depressed, all sorts of things. . . . Five years, I think for anybody . . . because you're either going to be rehabilitated in five years or you're not. . . . You don't want to change. You like who you are.

Part of doing time involves contact with family and friends; another part, at this prison, involves work release and other programs. (They will be discussed in Chapters 6 and 7, respectively.) All of these relate to whether time is "easy" or "hard."

References

Albor, T. (1995, February 5). The women get the chains . . . *The Nation*, 234–37.
Arcaro, T. (1984, February). Self-identity of female prisoners: The moral career of the inmate. *Humanity and Society* 8: 73–89.

Arnold, R. (1994). Black women in prison: The price of resistance. In M. B. Zinn and
    B. T. Dill, eds., *Women of color in U.S. society*, 171–84. Philadelphia: Temple Uni-
    versity Press.

Barry, E. (1989, Spring). Pregnant prisoners. *Harvard Women's Law Journal* 12: 189–205.

Belknap, J. (1996). *The invisible woman: Gender, crime, and justice*. Belmont, Calif.:
    Wadsworth Publishing.

Bonta, J., and P. Gendreau. (1990). Reexamining the cruel and unusual punishment of
    prison life. *Law and Human Behavior* 14 (4): 347–72.

Brownmiller, S. (1975). *Against our will: Men, women, and rape*. New York: Bantam
    Books.

Burkhart, K. (1976). *Women in prison*. New York: Popular Library.

Carlen, P. (1983). *Women's imprisonment: A study in social control*. London: Routledge
    and Kegan Paul.

Chesney-Lind, M. (1997). *The female offender: Girls, women, and crime*. Thousand Oaks,
    Calif.: Sage Publications.

Chesney-Lind, M., and J. Pollock. (1995). Women's prisons: Equality with a vengeance.
    In A. Merlo and J. Pollock, eds., *Women, law, and social control*, 157–75. Boston:
    Allyn and Bacon.

Clark, J. (1995, September). The impact of the prison environment on mothers. *Prison
    Journal* 75 (3): 306–29.

Faith, K. (1993). *Unruly women: The politics of confinement and resistance*. Vancouver,
    Canada: Press Gang Publishers.

Fletcher, B., L. Shaver, and D. Moon, eds. (1993). *Women prisoners: A forgotten popula-
    tion*. Westport, Conn.: Praeger.

Fogel, C. (1993). Hard time: The stressful nature of incarceration for women. *Issues in
    Mental Health Nursing* 14: 367–77.

Fogel, C., and S. Martin. (1992, February). The mental health of incarcerated women.
    Western Journal of Nursing Research 14 (1): 30–40.

Foster, T. (1975). Make-believe families: A response of women and girls to the depriva-
    tions of imprisonment. *International Journal of Criminology and Penology* 3: 71–78.

Fox, J. (1984, March). Women's prison policy, prisoner activism, and the impact of the
    contemporary feminist movement: A case study. *Prison Journal* 64: 15–36.

Giallombardo, R. (1966a). Social roles in a prison for women. *Social Problems* 13 (3):
    268–87.

———. (1966b). *Society of women: A study of a women's prison*. New York: John Wiley
    and Sons.

Goffman, E. (1961). *Asylums: Essays on the social situation of mental patients and other
    inmates*. Garden City, N.Y.: Anchor Books.

Harris, J. (1988). *"They always call us ladies": Stories from prison*. New York: Charles
    Scribner's Sons.

Henriques, Z. (1996). Imprisoned mothers and their children: Separation-reunion syndrome. *Women and Criminal Justice* 8 (1): 77–95.

Holyoak, W. (1972, Summer). Playing out family conflicts in a female homosexual "family" group (chick-vot) among institutional juveniles: A case presentation. *Adolescence* 7: 153–68.

Hufft, A., L. Fawkes, and W. Lawson, Jr. (1993). Care of the pregnant offender. In American Correctional Association, *Female offenders: Meeting needs of a neglected population*, 54–59. Laurel, Md.: American Correctional Association.

Larson, J., and J. Nelson. (1984). Women, friendship, and adaptation to prison. *Journal of Criminal Justice* 12: 601–15.

Leger, R. (1987, December). Lesbianism among women prisoners. *Criminal Justice and Behavior* 14 (4): 448–67.

Lerner, S. (1997, July–August). Chemical Reaction. *Ms.*, 57–61.

Lord, E. (1995, June). A prison superintendent's perspective on women in prison. *Prison Journal* 75 (2): 257–69.

MacKenzie, D., J. Robinson, and C. Campbell. (1989, June). Long-term incarceration of female offenders: Prison adjustment and coping. *Criminal Justice and Behavior* 16 (2): 223–38.

MacKinnon, C. (1987). *Feminism unmodified: Discourses on life and law*. Cambridge: Harvard University Press.

Mahan, S. (1984). Imposition of despair—An ethnography of women in prison. *Justice Quarterly* 1: 357–84.

Morris, A. (1987). *Women, crime, and criminal justice*. New York: Basil Blackwell.

Moyer, I. (1984, March). Deceptions and realities of life in women's prisons. *Prison Journal* 64: 45–56.

Pollock-Byrne, J. (1990). *Women, prison, and crime*. Pacific Grove, Calif.: Brooks/Cole.

Propper, A. (1982, May). Make-believe families and homosexuality among imprisoned girls. *Criminology* 20 (1): 127–38.

———. (1978, Spring). Lesbianism in female and coed correctional institutions. *Journal of Homosexuality* 3 (3): 265–74.

Rafter, N. (1985). *Partial justice: Women in state prisons, 1800–1935*. Boston: Northeastern University Press.

Ryan, T., and J. Grassano. (1993). Pregnant offenders: Profile and special problems. In American Correctional Association, *Female offenders: Meeting needs of a neglected population*, 49–53. Laurel, Md.: American Correctional Association.

Schupak, T. (1986, Fall). Women and children first: An examination of the unique needs of women in prison. *Golden Gate University Law Review* 16: 455–74.

Shaw, N. (1982). Female patients and the medical profession in jails and prisons. In N. Rafter and E. Stanko, eds., *Judge, lawyer, victim, thief: Women, gender roles, and criminal justice*, 261–76. Boston: Northeastern University Press.

Sobel, S. (1982, Winter). Difficulties experienced by women in prison. *Psychology of Women Quarterly* 7 (2): 107–18.

Sultan, F., G. Long, S. Kiefer, D. Schrum, J. Selby, and L. Calhoun. (1984). The female offender's adjustment to prison life: A comparison of psychodidactic and traditional supportive approaches to treatment. *Journal of Offender Counseling, Services, and Rehabilitation* 9: 49–56.

Turnbo, C. (1993). Differences that make a difference: Managing a women's correctional institution. In American Correctional Association, *Female offenders: Meeting needs of a neglected population*, 12–16. Laurel, Md.: American Correctional Association.

Van Wormer, K. (1981). Social functions of prison families: The female solution. *Journal of Psychiatry and Law* 9: 181–91.

———. (1987, Winter). Female prison families: How are they dysfunctional? *International Journal of Comparative and Applied Criminal Justice* 11 (2): 263–71.

Ward, D., and G. Kassebaum. (1964). Homosexuality: A mode of adaptation in a prison for women. *Social Problems* 12 (2): 159–77.

Zimmer, L. (1987, December). How women reshape the prison guard role. *Gender and Society* 1 (4): 415–31.

C h a p t e r

Family and Friends

Mom had to go from pulling her own burdens to pulling the burden of raising my children, plus she has me as a burden again. So, it really increased hers trifold.

an inmate at Black Mountain

Social relationships are based on reciprocity, but women in prison find themselves extremely limited in this exchange. With no control over their time, limited access to resources, and lack of mobility, they find that dealings with family members and friends are circumscribed by prison rules and regulations. Keeping up social roles allows an individual to stay connected to society; these roles give definition and place in the social order. Without social roles, an individual is aimless; the lack of roles contributes to normlessness. When a woman enters prison, family, mother, and friendship roles are altered. She no longer can be a caretaker or provider, and the give-and-take of relationships becomes lopsided. Due to these changes, relatives who support inmates find that resources flow in one direction, often placing a strain on families' assets (Girshick 1996, Hairston 1996).

The importance of contact with family and friends cannot be overemphasized. It not only provides emotional support for the incarcerated woman but also allows some semblance of role maintenance, though redefined. Giving advice to children over the phone, writing letters to nieces and nephews, and getting visits from a boyfriend to talk about future plans are all ways in which women hope to maintain their roles. Numerous studies of male prisoners have shown that contact with family and friends lowers recidivism (see, for example, Holt and Miller 1972, Howser and MacDonald 1982, and LeClair 1978). Families are a valuable resource in rehabilitation, since strengthening family ties during incarceration creates an investment in others and extends networks into the community (Hairston 1988).

Contact with relatives and friends during imprisonment helps lower stress, enhances adjustment, and provides concrete aid such as money, clothing, and information. Feeling connected to others provides a sense of security during incarceration and helps inmates resume their social roles when they are released. Creasie Hairston (1988, 50) observes that "when primary relationships remain intact, a prisoner is more than a convict or a number"—she is still somebody's daughter or sister or mother.

Across the nation, the visiting rooms of men's prisons are crowded with mothers, wives, and children. The situation is different for women. Female relatives visit incarcerated women and men, whereas male relatives are scarce, especially in the visiting rooms of women's prisons (Girshick 1996). Female inmates get fewer visits from fewer persons than do men, and they are less likely to see their children. Families, partners, and friends show them less loyalty (Belknap 1996).

One of the major issues in visiting for women is that their prisons, since there are fewer of them, are more likely to be located farther from their families. Another major problem is that women in prison are less likely to have reliable partners who might care for their children during their incarceration. Men, on the other hand, tend to have their children living with their wives or girlfriends. This stabilizes the family unit and increases the likelihood of more visiting by the partners with the children.

Contact with Family and Friends

When the study began, visitation was six days a week, from 9:30 to 11:30 A.M. and from 2:30 to 4:30 P.M. It is now held only on weekends, reflecting nationwide cutbacks to reduce staff expense. Inmates can have one visit a week, and five inmates can have visitors at a time. Access to pay telephones is unlimited until evening curfew, but only local or collect calls, with a ten-minute time limit, are permitted. Officers review incoming mail for contraband. Community-volunteer passes and incentive-wage jobs are privileges that are granted when women work their way to Level 2 security status. Level 3 status grants the privileges of release for work or study and home passes. In the latter case, an inmate can be picked up by a family member and go home; if the distance is too great, they stay in Black Mountain. The passes are for 6 hours, 24 hours, 48 hours, and 72 hours (when a holiday is included). The following section covers phone calls, letters, and visits by family members and friends. I will discuss prisoners' contact with their children in a separate section.

Most of the forty women made telephone calls (83 percent of the total; by race, 93 percent of the white women, and 76 percent of the women of color). Among the major reasons for not making calls were having a block on their family's phone or not having one at all. Of those who did use the telephone, the white women made calls daily (27 percent), often (40 percent), or rarely (26 percent); the women of color made calls daily (20 percent), often (32 percent), or rarely (24 percent).

Seventy percent of the prisoners received mail. More of the white women did not get letters (40 percent) than was true of the women of color (24 percent). Of those who did receive letters, 33 percent of the white women got mail often, 13 percent once a week, and 13 percent occasionally. Women of color got letters daily (4 percent), often (20 percent), once a week (16 percent), twice a month (20 percent), once a month (8 percent), and occasionally (8 percent).

Visiting patterns showed a distinct difference by race. Forty-three percent of the inmates received no visits, but 60 percent (fifteen) of the women of color, compared to 13 percent (only two) of the white women, had no visitors. Of the ten women of color who did have visits, four took home passes, and the other six were visited (rarely) at the prison. Of the white women, one had home passes (7 percent), three had visits every week (20 percent), two had visits every month (13 percent), two had visits two to three times a month (13 percent) and five had rare visits (33 percent). Said one prisoner, whose mother visits only every two or three months:

> She would come every week, she would come whenever I asked her to come, but I don't. I rather she just wouldn't come at all. I just would. It stresses her. I've adjusted, after all these years, I'm adjusted. But she's not. She says it takes her days to get back normal. . . . That's why I call her as much as I do. To me, it feels the same. That way there's not that much attachment, doesn't stress her out so bad.

Another inmate had a different perspective on infrequent visiting:

> I wasn't even going to put anybody on [the visiting list] but my aunt 'cause she bothered me to come and see me, come and see me. I don't want visits because I

don't like the agony of the strip searching and [the saying good-bye]. Yes, it's tortur-
ous, nerve-wracking.

A third woman who had visits rarely felt that phone calls were enough. "That's plenty of support. As long as I know that they're fine and healthy, and that they're all right, then I'm all right."

Thirty percent of the prisoners at Black Mountain were married or had someone they considered their partner. One woman married her co-defendant, who was serving his own sentence. Another's boyfriend was in prison on a charge unrelated to hers. One inmate had married someone she met while in prison, and a few others had boyfriends they had met while incarcerated. These women were in touch with their partners, usually through calls, letters, and visits.

Overall, 55 percent of the women had money sent to them from family, partners, or friends. Family members were the most common sources of funds, followed by family and partner, family and friends, partner only, and friends only. The other 45 percent of the women relied on their own prison earnings. This second category comprised 52 percent of the women of color and 33 percent of the white women.

Sixty-eight percent of the forty women took CV passes. Twenty-eight percent did not take them—six women were not yet eligible, and another five were eligible but refused. (Information was not available on two of the prisoners.) Most of the women took CV passes once or twice a week, and a few did so three times a week. Others went out one to three times a month, and two went out rarely. Twenty-five percent of the inmates took home passes, whereas 75 percent did not. Of the latter group, twenty-five of the women were not yet eligible, and four were at Level 3 but did not take passes or had not taken them yet. One prisoner was not sure if she was eligible.

Most of the women were satisfied with their level of support; as one inmate said, "I feel a lot better knowing somebody out there cares about what happens to me." Many prisoners compared what support they did have to those who had less, and felt themselves very fortunate. One exclaimed, "I'd be a real basket case if it weren't for that [support]." Another remarked:

It's a big plus, I'm grateful. They have really stuck by me. Because my father has his
own business and he takes the time to come out and work around my passes and
stuff and make sure he's here to get me. It's just, some of the girls, I sit around and
look, and they don't really have anybody or those that do have don't really support

them. That makes your time hard, it really does. And I can really see that now since I'm in. If I didn't have my family beside me, God, I probably, I don't even know how to think about it.

And for this woman, who is in prison for the fourth time: "I really see that all I have is my family because they have stood by me from day one. They might not have sent it on time, but it was there. And they was there when I needed them."

Inmates with support are thankful for it; in some cases, their relationships with their mothers have improved.

I am very grateful for it. 'Cause I've met so many people that don't have any backing from their family or friends, so I'm very grateful for it. [My family was] there right from the beginning. . . . Me and my mom were always butting heads. She took it totally different from what I thought she would. I thought she was going to be all upset and fussing and stuff. She wasn't.

And,

I'm so glad I've got a family. Because me and my mom, we didn't get along when I was out there. Even before I started using drugs we didn't get along. But, we've gotten better. We've gotten closer now, since then. And I talk to her and I write her.

In some cases, the renewed relationship also entails setting limits:

They tell me not to worry about [feeling guilty], and I think about that since I'm trying to get my life together, that they would support me, but they also told me this would be the last time. If I ever come back to prison that they would not be there for me financially. They would support me emotionally, but as far as financially, no way. And my mother wrote me a letter, told me that if I got out and continued with drug use or any of the friends of mine, that my father would sell his business and they would sell their home and they would move out of state and take my child. A high price to pay if I use drugs. [They would be] protecting my daughter.

Women had no visits from family for a variety of reasons, such as illness at home, transportation problems, or the length of their sentence. For example, "My mother is disabled. She have arthritis in her legs real bad and she just had surgery on her right leg." And, "My mama don't drive and she always say she got to find a ride, or somebody to bring her." Another inmate said,

My mom is not a big writer [and she doesn't visit.] My mama don't like prisons. She hates prisons. She don't like seeing me in places like this. [When my father died two months ago] they let me go home for three days.

Those prisoners who have been incarcerated for many years usually see a change in contact patterns. One woman recalls:

When I first got locked up it was all the time. And, like, call me, call me, call me. And I would get letters. But after the first couple of years, it slacked off and probably a lot because of me. And now it's because of circumstances as far as the visiting. . . . But, I'm OK with it. I know they love me. When they do write, they make that clear and they all are ready for me to get out. So, I'm OK with it. It's an adjustment because even when I was an active drug addict for seven straight years, I was always close to my family. I never missed a holiday. I might've been high, but I was there. So, it was real hard to adjust [to] not being with them at times.

A sense of resignation was obvious with several inmates; as one said, "[I have very little support], I'm resigned. I don't really have any feelings about it. I do, I guess, it saddens. There's nothing I can do about it." Another woman echoed this sentiment:

I wish they would come and see me, but it seems like they just have their own world, their own family, and they don't owe me anything because I came here. And it's really not their problem that I'm here. It's mine. So. It would be nice if they could come but they've not offered to put their lives on hold for a day to come. I would for them but they haven't bothered for me.

The prisoners often have mixed feelings about inconsistent contact. They try to understand, but they also feel rejected.

They only do what they want to do. They don't have time to come up here, they don't have the money to send me. My mama's unemployed. . . . It hurts, it does hurt me. I wish my mom would be a little supportive, like drop me a line every now and then. She could at least come see me once a month or something. She don't. She did at first, but that dropped off.

And,

It doesn't really bother me. Sometimes I miss my kids and I miss my family. Most of the time I don't think about it. I try not to think about it. If somebody comes up here, they come up here. If they don't . . . I don't have but one person on the

visitation list. [This guy] is supposed to come tomorrow, but he might not come. It
don't really matter.

Many women wished they had more support but knew this put a strain
on their families. And, as this inmate put it, "Well, it's not enough, I want
more but I don't push it. I'm ashamed, really, being here, so I really don't
push it. I'll be home next month with my passes, I'll be able to spend more
time with them."

Contact with Children

The most severe punishment for a mother in prison is being separated
from her children (Baunach 1985, Clark 1995, Koban 1983, Lord 1995, Van
Wormer 1981). It strikes at her personal identity and her self-image as a woman
(Zalba 1964). Phyllis Baunach (1985, 1) points out:

> Whatever else they had, imprisoned mothers had one thing to hang
> onto before their incarceration: their children. Whether the relation-
> ship was healthy or otherwise for mother and child, when a woman
> goes to prison she takes with her the good memories of that relation-
> ship and cherishes the times spent in sharing joy and love with her
> children. Perhaps she truly loved and cared for her children in a
> positive healthy relationship; perhaps she reversed roles with her
> children and they primarily nurtured her; perhaps she paid little or
> no attention to her children at all. In any case, imprisonment engen-
> ders the feelings of loss and failure.

Being a mother is closely associated with self-esteem, and guilt at failing
to carry out the maternal role is widespread. Women fear they will lose their
children's love, and thus they lose confidence in their ability to mother (Baunach 1985, Koban 1983, Lord 1995). The "master status" of criminal now su-
persedes that of parent, calling the ability to be a good mother into question
(Faith 1993, Sobel 1982, Zalba 1964). However, as Allison Morris (1987) reminds us, sometimes a woman commits crimes precisely because she is trying
to carry out her responsibilities to provide for her children.

Continuing contact with their daughters and sons may be the most significant predictor of inmates' chances of reuniting their families upon release.

Unfortunately, many mothers in prison have little or no contact with their children (Bloom 1997, Henriques 1996). Because they are spread among different relatives or are in foster care, mothers have difficulty in seeing their children regularly. As mentioned earlier, women's prisons (because there are fewer of them) are often long distances from where families live. Arranging for transportation is a major hindrance and places a great strain on the family (Barry 1985, Sobel 1982).

The sons and daughters of male inmates, on the other hand, usually live with their mothers. Visiting is more frequent, and the family is more likely to be stable. Compared to female prisoners, male inmates are more likely to be located closer to their families, and they think their children are happier. However, as Linda Koban (1983, 181–82) points out, women in prison had closer relationships with their children before arrest. They were more likely to have had their sons and daughters living with them and more likely to have had custody; in addition, more female inmates plan to have their children live with them upon release (see also Barry 1985).

Incarceration challenges the parental role, threatening the parent-child bond. As Ann Adalist-Estrin (1986, 12) notes, "These disruptions in parent-child relationships undermine the mutual understanding of feelings, needs, and patterns in everyday family life. It becomes very difficult then for incarcerated parents to feel connected to their children and adequate as parents." Children are more affected by the incarceration of mothers than of fathers (Barry 1985, Belknap 1996), and they may be confused or angry that a parent has broken the law (Adalist-Estrin 1986). Children may wonder what they have done to cause their mothers to be taken away (Lord 1995). When a parent is incarcerated, the children are punished by the separation as well (Barry 1985), and both parties grapple with how to cope (Lord 1995).

The punitive environment of prison can undermine the sense of autonomy and responsibility a woman needs to mother her children (Clark 1995). Judith Clark (309) also points out, however, that even though prison is oppressive, belittling, and breaks the mother-child bond, inmates often feel that doing time gives them a chance to rebuild relationships with their children and that prison may have saved them from their destructive paths. For this to happen, however, there must be programs in prison that maintain or reestablish bonds with children.

Thirty-four of the forty inmates in the study were mothers, constituting 93 percent of the white women (fourteen prisoners) and 80 percent of the women of color (twenty prisoners). There were seventy-seven children alto-gether, twenty-nine with white mothers and forty-eight with mothers of color. Twenty-one of the mothers lived with their children before arrest (addition-ally, another three women had been living with their children but were on the run before arrest), whereas the sons and daughters of eleven lived else-where (one woman had two children with her and one elsewhere, so is counted once in each category); there was also one case of adult children living independently. Nine of the white mothers (64 percent) and twelve of the mothers of color (60 percent) lived with their children. If the women on the run are counted as living with their children, 67 percent of the white women and 70 percent of the women of color had been living with their children before arrest. Five of the white mothers and five of the mothers of color had their children living elsewhere.

Although examining the data shows that inmates of color are more disad-vantaged than their white counterparts (more broken homes, less educational achievement, lower socioeconomic status), these problems do not necessarily spill over into their relationships with parents and children. Laura Bresler and Diane Lewis (1983) maintain that there are significant differences by race in the inmates' relationships with their mothers, the role of the extended family in care of their children, whether contact was maintained with family mem-bers during incarceration, the extent of family assistance when released, and contact with children. In research on black female inmates and their chil-dren, Velma LaPoint et al. (1985) found strong interdependence of relation-ships among the mothers, their children, and their caretakers. The high degree of extended family involvement in child rearing existed during both normal times and crises.

Of the fourteen white women who had children, one was in daily phone contact with them, five spoke often (one or more times per week), four spoke occasionally (one or two times per month), and four never spoke on the phone. In two cases, family members who had their children had blocks on their phones. Of the twenty women of color with children, four spoke to them daily on the phone, six spoke often, another six spoke occasionally, one spoke rarely, and three never called their children. Mothers who called more often, especially daily, usually had their sons and daughters living locally. Long-distance calls were a significant financial burden on families.

Most inmates wrote to or received mail from their children. In some cases their children were too young to read or write, and in other cases the mothers wrote but their teenagers did not write back. Eleven of the white mothers wrote to or received mail from their children (79 percent), and sixteen of the mothers of color wrote or received mail (80 percent). There was no mail to or from children for three of the white and for four of the mothers of color.

Visits with daughters and sons are a much more complex consideration. Forty-seven percent of the inmate mothers did not see their children. A recent survey by the National Council on Crime and Delinquency found that 54 percent of children never visited their incarcerated mothers (Bloom and Steinhart 1993). There are the issues of traveling long distances, transportation, and whether there is someone to bring the children. Also, many mothers did not want their children to visit and be exposed to the embarrassment of the hostile prison environment (Faith 1993).

Five of the white women (36 percent) never had visits from their children. In two instances, the caregivers (the children's father and the paternal grandparents) would not bring them. Another inmate had not seen her two daughters, who lived with their paternal grandmother, in two years.

> My mama was having car problems, health problems, and then at the last of it, my ex-mother-in-law told my mom if she brought them to see me she wouldn't let her have them no more [on the weekends]. So my mom was kind of intimidated by her, so that creates a problem.

The parental rights of another prisoner had been terminated seven years earlier, when her children first went into foster care; there had been no contact with her two daughters since. In a final case, adult sons chose not to visit their mother.

Over half (55 percent) of the women of color did not see their sons and daughters. The reasons were varied. In a few cases, children lived out of state or were adults with their own busy lives. Transportation problems were mentioned four times. One of the caretakers would not bring a child, and in other cases the caretaking grandmothers were ill. One woman had severed contact with her children before prison and it had been four or five years since they had been in touch. Two inmates said they did not want their children to visit at the prison. For one, "I don't really like for them to come because it depresses me, so I'd just rather talk to them over the phone."

Of the white inmates, one had home passes and saw her children then. Three women's children visited every other week, one came two or three times a month, one prisoner met with her children (who lived out of state) once a year, and three inmates saw their children rarely. As one woman who visited with her children about every six months said,

> I really don't pressure that because it's so hard for them to come here and see me, and it's hard for me to watch them leave. But then again, it goes back to being teenagers. They've got more to do on the weekends than to come visit mom. I don't pressure or push that.

This prisoner recounts the family's visiting limitations:

> I can see my kids two hours a week. I have a daughter that's eight months old and [since being imprisoned] I've seen her less than twenty-four hours of her life. My other two kids I've seen less than forty-eight hours of their lives [since I've been imprisoned]. In Raleigh, I got to see my kids maybe once a month, sometimes just once every other month because the drive was so hard, and when the baby was first born, she got so sick when they would drive, they couldn't bring her up. And now that I'm here I get to see them more often. I get to see them at least every other week, if not every week. [But], I'm a complete stranger to my youngest.

Five mothers of color had home passes. Of those who were visited at the prison, one saw her children two or three times a month, one saw them once a month, and two saw their children rarely. One prisoner who had not seen her children since being imprisoned was getting ready for a visit.

> I can't wait [to see them tomorrow]. I had to get myself to the point where I could handle them coming and them leaving. I just got to the point where I don't cry every day. But now I think I can handle it, being here [at Black Mountain], it's more like a home setting [compared to Raleigh], that type of thing. I think I can handle it. And I'll be able to sit with them on my lap and stuff.

Upon release, most inmate mothers intended to live with their children. Of the white prisoners, 71 percent planned on living with all or some of their children, immediately or as soon as they were settled; 14 percent were not planning to live with their children; 7 percent were not sure; and 7 percent had independent adult children. Of the mothers of color, 65 percent intended to live with their children; 15 percent did not; and 20 percent had independent adult children. One woman who did not plan to live with her children felt that "[t]hey been with my mama so long it ain't right that I would come and take them, you know. It would really hurt her." However, she did plan to pay child support for the six children and help her mother out.

How Children Deal with Their Mother's Incarceration

As mentioned, imprisonment affects daughters and sons, who have their own emotions, losses, and coping problems to resolve. Stigmatization of their mothers may have an impact on the children's personal identity (LaPoint et al. 1985). None of the children of the Black Mountain prisoners were in the custody of foster parents. The commonly held view is that, given a choice, incarcerated mothers prefer that their own mothers care for their children during their imprisonment (Belknap 1996). However, according to Ann Adalist-Estrin, female inmates may be conflicted over having their children cared for by their own parents—the same parents they ran away from or were abused by (telephone communication, July 15, 1997). That the children do live with their maternal grandparents may reflect the prisoners' limited options more than what the women truly desire.

Almost one-fourth (21 percent) of the sons and daughters of the white mothers were split between family members, whereas over a fourth (30 percent) of the children of mothers of color were. For white families, there was no predominant arrangement. Children were living with the inmate's parents, former mother-in-law, their father, paternal grandmother, an aunt, or with friends. Four fathers had all or some of their children living with them. Legal custody also varied. Inmates had custody in only three cases; their parents might also have custody, as could the former or present mother-in-law, the children's father, an aunt, and friends.

Counting split arrangements, more than half of the women of color had sons and daughters living with their mother or with both their parents. Children also lived with paternal grandmothers, the inmate's grandparents, the inmate's brother, their father, aunts, inmate's sister, and a former husband. Three fathers had all or some of their children living with them. Three children were now adults. Inmates held full or shared custody in ten cases, with their parents or mothers, grandparents, and a brother being others who held custody of the children. Women of color had more of their children living with their own parents, and had a wider range of relatives caring for their children, than did the white mothers. They also retained custody more often.

Women who discussed their children's adjustment talked mostly about anger and emotional problems. One inmate, whose daughter was three years old, had this to say about their relationship:

Yes, I've parented her. My parents have really done the majority but she knows that

I'm her mother. She listens to me. We have a good relationship. I speak to her on the phone. She comes to see me. I write her letters. She'll get my letters and [my mother] will read them to her. She'll say, "Mom is my best friend." She had a real hard time dealing with it at first. She's very angry. She was angry at me. She would smack my picture and say that Mama was gone. She would cry. She would wake up in the middle of the night crying. She's doing better. I had lied to her and told her I was at work when I first came to prison. But she's old enough now. She's so intelligent. She's only three, but, God, she's smart. She wanted to know why I wouldn't come home from work when Mama and Papa was coming home from work. And I knew it was time that I come clean with her. So, I told her I was at a center because I had done something bad, that I was not a bad girl, but I'd done something that was bad and I was being punished. . . . And she just looked at me and said, "No, Mommy, you're not a bad girl." She's my life. I wish I had realized that three years ago.

This mother of a sixteen-year-old is quite worried about his acting out.

[He] is real rebellious. He's out of hand. He was in a home for children until about two weeks ago when he went back to [his father's people]. He's got a lot of anger and he has a right to have it. His father doesn't spend much time with him. . . . He's missing a dad and a mom.

And after serving sixteen years of a life sentence, one woman whose children were three, five, and eleven at her arrest had this to say:

Each child has to work through the anger and the bitterness of why and what caused their mom to be taken from them. Two went through it within themselves. One went through it verbally. That one was the tough one. . . . The inwardly one, I told him you are entitled to your feelings. I was supportive to them, letting them know it's OK to know what they're feeling. But it didn't make it all right, but it was something they had to work through. And I could understand why they had those feelings towards me. Because I allowed myself to get into that mess. And it was my fault that I was taken from them. And I took all the blame because I was the blame.

Acceptance is also fairly typical. One six-year-old told his mother on the phone, " 'Well, just don't do it no more, Mama, you don't go back to jail.' I said, 'OK, I'm not gonna leave you no more.' He said, 'OK, now.' " And another woman's fourteen-year-old son "is a lot of support for me. We've always been really close, we've always been there for each other. He accepts what I've done. He tells me not to do it again. But he accepts it and he forgives me for it. It means a lot."

In fact, several women felt they were especially close with their children, particularly their eldest, and that their relationships were characterized by openness. Two of the prisoners who had been teen mothers felt they were almost in a sibling relationship, since they and their children had "grown up together." Judith Clark (1995, 314) mentions that incarceration has an additional influence in that mothers may relate to their children's "powerlessness and frustration in the face of authority," creating a sibling-type bond. Another inmate mentioned that she felt her daughter was more like her sister, since her mother is raising her daughter while she is incarcerated.

Some children participate in the overnight retreats, sponsored by a church, held two to three times a year at a retreat center in the town of Black Mountain. These are special times, but not without their problems.

> The first [overnight retreat] I took my oldest son and he got really, really upset and he got sick. So the second time I took my seven-year-old. Well, [he] got really, really sick when it was over. He threw up everywhere, he was so sick. So the next time they had a retreat and had wanted me to go, and I told them no, I'm not going. They said, 'Good opportunity . . .' See, people don't understand. It's OK because we're adults and we can deal with it, but children can't. They don't offer the children anything when it's over here. I want to protect my children. I know you can't always but I don't want them to be put in a situation unnecessarily where they have to feel this way.

Youngsters have a difficult time coping with the brief reunion and then separation. One woman recalls:

> [My stepson] loves [me], too. He asks now when am I coming out so he can come and stay with me. We went on the family retreat and I made the biggest mistake I ever made in my life. I told him he was going to come and stay with me. I didn't tell him he was going to come and stay the night with me. And when it was over, that baby threw a fit. I've never seen [him] throw a tantrum until that day, and it tore me up. He had the preacher crying . . . me crying, he's something else.

Children also experience emotional problems in coping with their mother's imprisonment. One inmate says, "[My daughter] had a mental breakdown when I went to prison. A seven-year-old with a mental breakdown. She was seeing a psychiatrist two and three times a week when I first came here."

Another prisoner echoed this: "The kids are sensitive, especially when it comes to me and being here. It bothers them. They've had to, [one of them] had to go see a psychologist; [another one], they had referred him to [the mental health department]." Another woman observes:

My seven-year-old, he'll sit in my lap and I'll rock him and he'll cry and cry and cry. There's so much on them that I don't want them to come and visit that often. . . . With my children, I tell them it's time to go and they want to hang on. My six-year-old jumps on me and holds on to me. And it's just a lot for them 'cause then after they leave, they take my mother through a lot. And then she's like, the kids are stressed out and then go through things at school, and they act out and then it gets on her nerves.

Not all the children have trouble coping. One mother points out:

I just miss my kids so much that I just know I couldn't do it again, and I just pray that it's God's will that I won't have to come back because I wouldn't be able to stay away from my kids like that. It's ridiculous. I miss them to death. They're doing fine, it's the mama that can't. The kids are doing fine.

Overall, there were not consistent, striking differences by race on issues relating to children. The major contrasts were that more mothers of color did not place phone calls or receive visits from their daughters and sons and that children of color were more likely to be living with their grandparents. The first finding might reflect the lower socioeconomic status of people of color, seen in less disposable income, more ill health, and lack of transportation, all of which stood in the way of visiting. The second finding confirms the conclusions of many other studies that the family networks of women of color, African Americans in particular, are stronger than those of white women (Baunach 1985, Bresler and Lewis 1983, Hays and Mindel 1973, Vaux 1985). Mothers of color also had their sons and daughters split among more family members than did white mothers, which may simply indicate that they had slightly larger families (2.40 children, compared to 2.07).

The Experiences and Views of Family Members

Relatives play a major role in the lives of women in prison. They come out of existing relationships with them, they are in contact with them throughout incarceration, they have their children living with them, and they will continue relationships with them upon release. Thirty-five percent of the prisoners planned to be paroled to their mother, father, or both parents. Ten percent hoped to live with other relatives, and 8 percent intended to live with husbands (one of these women was to get married on release). If those family members are combined, over 50 percent of the inmates hoped to live with relatives. Thirteen percent of the women planned to live alone or alone with their children. Ten percent hoped to be paroled to a halfway house, and 8 percent intended to live with friends. Eighteen percent were not sure of their plans after release.

Prisoners are not alone in suffering from loss of contact with family and friends. Their daughters, sisters, partner, or friends also lose their presence and their role relationships (Fuller 1993). In a sense these persons are also serving the sentence of emotional loss, and they may suffer from societal stigma due to their association with a woman in prison (Fuller 1993, Girshick 1996).

I spoke with twelve relatives or friends who acted as surrogate family for ten of the forty inmates. Five of these family members were inmates' mothers (42 percent), and four of them had their grandchildren living with them. Another relative had an inmate's stepson living with her, but he had been in her care since infancy.

When asked what led to the crimes of their imprisoned relative, family members tended to mention drug addiction or associating with the wrong people. Some mothers also found some of the cause in the family environment. For example,

> One thing she was running around with the wrong people, people that were doing things that they shouldn't be doin', taking dope, running around, running wild. We spoiled her. She's the baby and she's spoiled. And we just practically had her way in anything. If she kept nagging on anything we'd give in. . . . It was our fault because we hadn't put our foot down and set the rules in the beginning. She just wouldn't listen when she got big enough and she thought she could do what she pleased. And she took off.

A second mother responded:

> Well, I think it's a lot of things, reason number one is the drug abuse. And I think second of all, I think that part of it has been . . . we were a dysfunctional family because my husband, I think we were dysfunctional in the fact that he was gone all the time, he was away from the home and then when he would come home . . . he

was a Santa Claus daddy. . . . And I think she learned at a very early age to be a real good manipulator and play one parent against the other. . . . She also had a father who would pay her out. He'd rescue her and all this, and him and I never agreed, like we just, we were never on the same team. . . . So, I think those are the major contributing factors.

One man whose wife (they married after her incarceration) killed her first husband said:

Well, my big thing is it was basically a lot of drinking, a lot of partying, a lot of drugs. Because [her first husband] had a couple of DUIs before, the whole family has an alcohol history and of drugs being used, and that's what it breaks down to. It's like I told [my wife], she's payin' for the lifestyle that she lived.

In the opinion of the former husband of a woman convicted of forgery and uttering

her job had a lot to do with it. 'Cause she worked for just a tyrant of a man. . . . And then our relationship went sour from alcohol and there were other things involved in our life, and just, I don't know, when she got in that downward spiral it just continued and everything pretty much self-destructed.

Family members and inmates also held some other views on what led to the women's crimes. For example, as mentioned earlier, one daughter did not believe that her mother trafficked in drugs because she was forced to, but instead felt she did this voluntarily for the money. In another instance, a mother thought her daughter was involved in drugs and committed larceny due to the influence of her friends and their drug needs, whereas the daughter maintained she needed the money to care for her children and that drugs had nothing to do with it.

The effect of a woman's incarceration varied among different family members. For relatives taking care of children the impact was enormous, altering their lifestyles and creating a burden. As Barbara Bloom and David Steinhart (1993, 30) explain,

They must deal with the trauma suffered by children whose mothers are arrested or imprisoned. They must define their relationship to the children as surrogate parents, and they must help the children cope with psychological and emotional problems. They must re-examine their relationship with the incarcerated mother and sometimes must reckon with personal disappointment or anger at the mother for her conduct and the resultant burden of care that has been thrust upon them. They must make time for visits with the incarcerated mother — visits which are often stressful for all involved. They must adjust their own households to accommodate children who are usually less than 10 years old. They must raise the financial resources to house, feed, clothe and care for young children, including some with special problems and needs.

For other family members the impact was not as life changing. As one said, "It's been a lot of hurt, you know, disappointment." A mother noted that scheduling visiting and home passes was a problem. "A lot of times I have to, like when I'm going to get her to bring her home or something like that, I have to maybe be out of work a day or trade shifts with somebody and double over. That makes it real hard."

Some mothers felt relief that their daughters were in prison. One said her daughter kept up more contact with the family as an inmate than when she was not in prison because "she says that when she's on the streets she doesn't want us to see her like that." She continues,

> There have been times I almost said to myself, well, no, there were times when she was really on the streets when I almost prayed that something would just happen to her because it was like, she's suffering out there, we're suffering, and I don't know where she is.

Other mothers held similar views:

> Even though I don't like for her to be there, it's the best thing for her. It's a relief she's in. At least I know where she's at, and she's got a bed to sleep in and she's got food and she can't get drugs. That's a relief on me in some way. 'Cause you never knew where they were. Or what they were into. And it just broke your heart.

And,

> My husband thinks it probably saved her life. And he says, if it keeps her alive and it helps get her on the straight and narrow then maybe, he said, she could have a good life, then it would have been worth it. Because I'd much rather see her in jail than a cemetery.

Half of the family members mentioned some aspect of unfair treatment of the women they were connected to. Two felt their relatives' sentences (each was serving ten years) were unduly long, especially for nonviolent crimes. They had served more time than "people caught for killing . . . and I'd think killing would be worse than stealing," as one mother said. A husband believed his wife had been "railroaded" and should have been indicted on a lesser murder charge. A sister-in-law felt her brother's wife got a "raw deal" solely because of her association with her brother; she "didn't deserve to be hit that hard," especially for someone with little trouble in her background. She also saw that her brother's wife did not understand the law—"I don't think she half knew what she was agreeing to and what she wasn't."

Prison rules and treatment were another area of concern. One sister-in-law felt the regulations were unevenly applied and that her brother's wife was not given privileges, such as home passes, she was entitled to. This inmate's mother-in-law especially wanted to take her daughter-in-law out on home passes to go to church and start meeting people there. She felt this was an important part of rehabilitation, and along with other family members was very frustrated at what she felt was an arbitrary application of rules. A mother, who at one time had worked in prisons as an educator, worried about how guards treated inmates. She pointed out:

> I don't think they really cared for me because I could see things that they were doing and the way they mistreated them, and yet they ought to treat them like human beings. And get respect from them. But then some of the officers, corrections officers and different ones, they treat them like dogs. And I think it could be one of your own in here, so you don't do that. At least treat them with respect and you'll get that back in return. I did, I had no problem. I was there for four years.

All of these relatives supported the prisoners by accepting collect phone calls, visiting, and sending money. One mother cut down on the number of phone calls and the money sent in to "be tough" and make her daughter realize she had to take more responsibility for her life. On the other hand, a second mother worried about her daughter's emotional state and told her to call every day. "Like I told her, whenever you want to call, whenever you want to talk, just call. I'll pay the bill some kind of way."

Friends of one prisoner, surrogate relatives, are trying to be encouraging and supportive in a way she never encountered in her own family. For almost two years they have accepted collect phone calls, visited, and sent money.

They would like to be a positive influence, to provide some guidance, and they hope she can realize the potential that they see in her.

Although they were all providing a good deal of support, in some cases the family members made it quite clear that their help was contingent on change in the inmate's behavior and attitudes. As one mother said, "I know in my heart that we have done everything for [our daughter]. And, I've also told her that if she goes back to prison, it won't be like it is now. She's totally on her own." She continued,

> And I said, and this is your last chance. It's not a second chance, it's your last chance. Because I will not live like this even if I have to take drastic means. Which she knows, I've told her that. And I intend to. I will sell my house and I will move to parts unknown, and I'll take [my granddaughter] with me. And I told her I will take her to court and take [her daughter] away from her. And instead of temporary custody I'll go for permanent custody. And, 'cause I'm not gonna have [my granddaughter] exposed to that kind of lifestyle. . . . And I'm not gonna jeopardize [my granddaughter's] future. Not even for my own child.

Another mother, who had custody of the youngest of her daughter's children, also set limits. Previously she and her husband had bought their daughter a mobile home and a car to help her get out of a lifestyle involving drugs and criminal activity. Instead, she ended up back in prison. Her mother says:

> Well, see, we had did that right before she went, tryin' to get her straightened out. And she, it just got worse. This time when she went in, we sold the car, we sold the home. So, she's gonna have to make it on her own this time. But, we're gonna be there. But we're gonna be tough. 'Cause we feel like this is gonna work better than setting her up and everything like we did before. We're gonna be there for her, if she chooses to go the right way then we'll be there for her. But if she decided to go back to drugs, we're gonna slip out of the picture.

Grandmothers taking care of children seemed to be in agreement—if their imprisoned daughters were not going to change, the children would stay with them. One woman's parents, as well as taking care of her two sons, were continuing to pay the rent on her apartment while she was in prison so she would have a home to return to. But as the mother said,

> I mean, we've bent over backwards. And we just can't do it anymore. Now it's up to her. She's either gonna do it and do right, or else we'll just take the kids. If that's

what it takes. 'Cause I'm not gonna put them in no foster home. I mean, I can't do that. But, she will not have visitation or nothing.

Building trust is an important aspect in some of these relationships. One supportive friend of an inmate said, "I'd like to see a person we can trust in the end." The prisoner had been very secretive over the years about her activities, and had even stolen from this man and his wife. Still, the couple befriended her and felt she would be "one of the few that would turn over." On the other hand, an inmate's daughter said that she and her mother have different interpretations of everything from her childhood to her adult life to the circumstances surrounding the crime. The only way to reconcile with her mother is to conclude that she sincerely believes her version of the truth, regardless of how far it is from the daughter's understanding of reality.

Two mothers were struggling with trusting their daughters because drug addiction had severely damaged their confidence. Said one,

I don't know how I would feel if she were out like tomorrow, how much I could trust her, to go to the store and come back. Because I don't know, she thinks she could, but there's still temptation. There are people out there just waiting to snatch her back to where she was.

The second mother voiced similar concern:

And I told her [trust is] something I wanted to have. Right now, no, I do not trust her. "I don't say this to hurt you, this is how I feel. No, I do not trust you. I want you to come home, part of me wants you to come home, and another part of me is scared." I said, "Because I can not and I will not go back to the way we lived." . . . 'Cause I told her. "The first time you don't come home, like you go to the store and you don't come back a week later like you have done, don't come back."

Most of the family members did not feel a need for others to support them in dealing with their incarcerated relative or friend. Some talked to select relatives ("[My husband] listens to me rant and rave . . ." And, "Well, my husband, we have a brother that we're very close to, him and his family. And then their children are grown and they know the situation. And they're very supportive of us.") or to friends ("There are a very few close friends that I talk or discuss everything about her with." And, "My boss at work knows."). One mother had a hard time accepting what had happened to her daughter:

Initially I was just devastated. I just felt like I couldn't think of anything worse other

> than if they'd told me she was dead. I had a real hard time with it emotionally. I
> ended up going to counseling. I had to be put on medication, it kinda helped me
> through that. . . . I think I have worked through a lot of it and I think I have, it's like
> a grieving process, and I think right now I'm just at the point where I've accepted
> what's happened, and I've just, I have worked through the anger.

Another mother had developed a support group with men and women in her town who had incarcerated children. Although the group had not met in quite some time, it had filled a need by ending isolation and giving strength to the parents by allowing them to talk and cry together. She also went to Alanon meetings, and through these various support meetings reaffirmed that she is a strong person with strong belief and faith.

Several women were sustained by their church membership, especially those who were mothering the inmates' children. One had her grandchildren christened in her church, and

> when they were small and I had to go to church for whatever, I just took them.
> There was always somebody there to help out with them. So now that they're
> getting older, I don't have to worry about when they go to church there.

This woman found particular support as an individual:

> My minister and his wife, they're wonderful. They are wonderful. 'Cause she calls
> me about every night to see how I am, so it's really been a lot of help just to think
> that somebody cares about me. They care if I go crazy or commit Hari Kari.

Another woman found divine aid.

> I just look to God for a lot of my help 'cause He [']comes my support 'cause He's
> always been there for me. . . . Things aren't too big or too little that He can't handle.
> If we put our trust in and depend on Him doing it.

Caregiving families got varying amounts of financial assistance for the inmates' children. One grandmother received AFDC of $236 a month for her two grandchildren; another received $180 a month in AFDC for one child. Medicaid and Social Security (paid due to their father's disability) helped another family caring for two of their daughter's children. One family did not seek social services support in raising an inmate's daughter.

Perhaps a bigger need involved the strains of child care, simply getting a break from the demands of having young children around when grandparents thought their parenting days were over. One exasperated grandmother reflected:

> You know, at this time you think when your kids are grown this is your time. And, I mean, this is like starting over again. And it's hard. I mean sometimes I feel like throwing up my hands and running the car off the road. It sometimes gets that bad. And I said if I didn't have a little bit of faith, I probably would. And a lot of people are giving me support. I mean, I couldn't handle it.

This woman was very active in meetings and community work, and her husband did his share of caring for the children. She felt a lot of men would not help as he did, but he had told her, "It's not your problem, it's *our* problem. We have to support each other." Still, she "needed a break" and looked forward to her daughter's upcoming release. She and her husband had sacrificed and changed their lifestyle to accommodate full-time parenting of young children. She tried to keep a sense of perspective and humor, though, as when remarking that "I've said if I had a child go to prison I'd rather for them to die. But I think I've had to retract that. Mamas have to eat a lot of words. And I think I ate those and digested them."

Another set of grandparents went through a period of adjustment but were able to incorporate the youngsters into their work lives, social life, and church activities. They have had them since their mother's first incarceration nearly seven years ago. Two other younger children live with cousins nearby, and the four siblings see each other on occasion. Said the grandmother,

> It just keeps me on the go! But it doesn't keep me from doing all the things I want to do because we do them together. We take vacations together and sometimes they take vacations away from us. So, it's all it is, just adjusting.

Other caretakers had different adjustments to make. For one,

> It's really put a big burden on me. I have a four-year-old child, which he was just over a year old, two at the most, when I took him. It's completely turned my life around. I had to quit my job to take care of the baby. Of course, now, I don't resent that one bit because I love the child, but you know what I'm sayin'! It put a lot of responsibility on me. . . . Between me and my other daughter, we take and share him. I've had some health problems lately so I let her tend to him most of the time.

Her daughter's other two teenage children live nearby with the former husband's family, but this grandmother does not let her grandson go to visit.

"That's sort of a bad influence . . . because they got some problems." She worries about the older children, but she has no control over the situation. Their father is also a drug user who has been in prison, and the children have been affected by this family instability. "These kids are disturbed by this real bad," she said.

One inmate's stepson had been brought up by his aunt in a stable and loving home. The prisoner had a long association with the family, even before marrying into it, and had behaved in something of a parenting role for many years. The two sisters-in-law were close friends, and the nine-year-old child was growing up in a supportive situation. Even though his father and step-mother were both in prison now, he was able to maintain close contact with his parents, thanks to his loving aunt and grandmother.

A man who married a woman in the study tried to reach out to her two daughters, now in the custody of the inmate's former mother-in-law. He gave the girls birthday parties and visited, but it was a very tense situation. The girls were negatively influenced against their mother, who had killed their father, as the former mother-in-law successfully controlled them and kept them away from the maternal side of the family.

Adjustment Issues

Family members expressed mixed views about how prisoners would re-sume their mothering roles once they were released. All of the inmate moth-ers want to reestablish a relationship with their children. One case will simply involve the freed prisoner moving back into her apartment, getting her sons, and starting over with a job. Her parents will help with child care (as they had before her incarceration), and they have offered to pay for counseling if their daughter felt she needed it.

In another instance, even though the inmate's two oldest children have been brought up by their grandparents, they are beginning to bond with their mother. Their grandmother said,

> I would encourage her because she says that she would like to have her children, and I believe she never really stopped loving them. Her addiction just affected her right then, [as] it did the children. But she never stopped loving them and caring about them. And I saw the relationship and their bonding when she came home the last two times. Then she said, too, "Mama, I know you and Daddy, you don't need this. You've been doing this so long, and you need to be just thinking about your-

selves." So, she knows that. And of course I told her, "Well, I'll do what I have to do, but I don't really want to be raising a teenager again."

Regaining custody of her two youngest is not as likely, since the third child knows his mother only slightly and the baby does not know her at all.

In two other cases, it will take much more time for the inmate to reassert her role as mother. A young boy who is "happy as a bird" living with his grandmother may remain there; she believes

> he won't want to stay with her or go with her. Just his reactions is gonna play a lot on it. I'm not gonna force him to have no dealings with her. . . . I don't think he ever will [want to go to her] because, where I could take him over to the place she lives and he says, "——— lives here" and he don't want to go over there. I think he suffers from bad experiences. He had some problems with that for a while [and] it took us a while to get him out of [them].

A second grandmother is hoping a bond can gradually be reestablished:

> I always call myself grandma to [my granddaughter], but she still calls me mommy a lot of the times. And I just, I'm hoping that when [my daughter] comes out that maybe by being here in the house that she can form a bond with this child. And maybe we can do it gradually like her spend more time with her. And like me push [my granddaughter] towards her mother when she comes to me. And that's what I want to do. And, because [my granddaughter] needs her mother, I mean, every child needs her mother.

Family members held a variety of concerns about parole. Getting a job, staying away from drugs, going back to school, and going to counseling with the children were all mentioned. Most of the concerns related to the inmate meeting the expectations of new behaviors. Many of the prisoners planned to parole to these family members' homes. As one mother said, "I think she kind of knows what I'll put up with and what I won't. And she'll go by my rules now."

Staying away from past associates is a big issue for family members. Friends of one inmate said,

> We would hope that if she was in our home that she would spend a lot of time with us in that sense so we could encourage her and stuff, and just to leave all her past friends, because all of them, to me at that point, were causing her trouble, you know what I'm sayin', the ones she did have, and start all over.

A woman said to her daughter-in-law:

> I know you'll have to when you see people, you'll have to speak with them, but as
> far as association with them in the same condition that they're in, I said, I just
> wouldn't approve of that. . . . And I certainly wouldn't approve of [her] gettin' out,
> partyin' and doin' all of that.

Drugs and drinking are out of the question for another woman, as her husband remarks:

> And I flat out told her before that when she does get out there's not going to be
> any drinking. I don't mind a wine cooler or something like that once in awhile, but
> there's not gonna be any going to bars and stuff like that. You don't do it, and I won't
> tolerate it.

One mother was optimistic that her daughter would be paroled to a halfway house. There, she would have support, and she could ease into taking full responsibility for herself and eventually her children. Furthermore,

> I think something good about a house like that is that wherein if she came back into
> my home I would have no idea if she had started back on drugs or not, but I understand that those who have been on it, they can spot it just like that.

Family members did feel that society has an obligation to assist women in prison, preparing them for release and providing opportunities on the outside. A sister-in-law wondered, "Is she going to be able to even build a life?" given restitution payments, finding affordable housing, securing transportation and a job, and basically getting back on her feet after prison. This inmate's mother-in-law felt that

> they need support groups for them to go to and be involved in, and you can't just
> throw them away. You got to show them love, and that's why I say usually about the
> only thing, when you think about it, is gettin' involved in church and church groups,
> and you just don't have that many outside people that are doing anything as far as
> them to go to to have a good, social, decent life.

Education and job training, as well as counseling, were cited as important programs for inmates to better prepare them for release. One mother felt that society does not care anything about prisoners and that the public does not even support the right to education within prison. In her view, lack of skills translated into lack of jobs and a life of homelessness, with crime as a means of support. As she saw it,

> I don't think money should go to building more prisons. I think money should go to programs, to rehabilitate them, to prevent them. Or places for them to go when they get out of prison. Because many times coming back into society, society won't accept them, but they need to have some place to go. Or they need programs of some sort to help them 'til they get a job.

Many relatives mentioned job training, a guaranteed job upon release, or both as enabling the self-support that they saw as key to the inmates' survival and staying out of a criminal life. Other suggested programs included ones to help prisoners understand why they had committed their crimes ("What went wrong") and ones to give them more direction to make up for their lack of guidance when growing up.

Several family members pointed to prison as a positive influence. Time to reflect and growing self-confidence were a few of the personal benefits noted. A man said of his former wife,

> [H]er self-respect and confidence seem to be very strong, a lot stronger than the last year or so we lived together. . . . I don't know necessarily if it's the system or just her herself that has changed it, but I can tell a very significant change in her in a lot of ways.

One mother thought prison was a safer environment than the streets, where "somebody could have killed" her daughter.

> I think she is tired of the life that she is living. Even though she's had our total support from day one, but I think the timing, she's tired of it, she's more mature now. She's had a chance in there to do thinking and soul searching and those kinds of things. I think this has helped her a lot.

Family Bonds

The family is the basic unit of society, and relationships within it embody the potential of support, comfort, and personal growth. Obviously, not everyone finds that, since an accident of birth places us in a particular family. In the overall study, there were some women who had been introduced to drugs or alcohol, beaten, or abandoned by their mothers. Overwhelmingly, however, abandonment involved fathers. The inmates mourned these lost relationships, missing the love and guidance that parents are supposed to provide.

In looking at prisoners' family ties, Bresler and Lewis (1983, 120) found that black women more frequently spoke positively about their mothers, particularly about relying on them for assistance, whereas white women made more comments about not getting along with their mothers. I found that as well. One black woman said, "I am my mama's daughter . . . and I am hers, so I have my kids with her."

One white woman had a very close relationship with her mother partly because they faced some similar experiences. The inmate was battered by her first husband, who isolated her except for seeing her mother, which brought them closer. When the mother was battered by her third husband, the daughter saw herself in the mother.

> I used to sit and it was like I was watching myself in her, and I remember when she used to tell me, "Why do you take it, why? How can you sit there and be that way? You're too strong-minded. Why do you let him do it?" And then I thought to myself, "Mama, look at you. Look at what you doing. What are you doing?" And finally she left him.

She continues,

> A lot of people tell us we're just alike 'cause we're not like mama and daughter, we're like friends, best friends. 'Cause neither one of us when she was married to my daddy and I was married to my first husband, we weren't allowed to have friends, so we had each other. We were allowed with each other but that's it. So, I can tell her anything, anything. And she's like me, she won't judge.

Many women had alienated their parents by their behavior or their own family's dysfunction, perhaps irrevocably severing the relationship. This was especially difficult to face, given their separation from their own children. Characteristically, one woman said of her mother, who had custody of her daughter even before incarceration,

> My mama wasn't really there for me when I first came to prison. I mean we had parted company so much that they didn't even want to hear my name. And now we're getting closer but it won't be like it was and it hurts. It hurts to know that. It hurts to know that I killed the love that they had for me.

Some women felt dependent on their mothers. Abandoned by her father and raised as an only child, one mentioned that she depended on her mother "for everything" and she did not realize she was capable of being independent. Another inmate said she was in a co-dependent relationship with her parent.

> I've always helped my mother, even when I was on my own. I still helped her, gave her money and stuff. My mother had it rough, she raised eight kids by herself. . . . I worked like twelve hours a day, seven days a week for six months to get my mother out of the projects, in order for her to move out. She's never been in the projects since.

One of the prisoners' mothers remarked wistfully,

> I think it's sort of an innate thing with us black people . . . we're just family people. And not to say that there aren't in other races. My family has always been very close. 'Cause my mother was very close to [my daughter] even though Mama's been dead since 1980, but she never saw her go to prison or any of these things. And I'm so glad she didn't because she loved her and she supported her and [my daughter] felt the same about Mama. And I've often said, "Oh, Mama, if you were alive she wouldn't have done this, she wouldn't . . ." Because children tend to go to grandmamas for support or whatever. She didn't have that grandmama to go to.

References

Adalist-Estrin, A. (1986). Parenting . . . from behind bars. *FRC Report* (1): 12–13.

Barry, E. (1985, March–April). Children of prisoners: Punishing the innocent. *Youth Law News*, 12–15, 18.

Baunach, P. (1985). *Mothers in prison*. New Brunswick, N.J.: Transaction Books.

Belknap, J. (1996). *The invisible woman: Gender, crime, and justice*. Belmont, Calif.: Wadsworth Publishing.

Bloom, B. (1997, July). Mothers in prison: Research, policies, and programs. *FCN Report*, 14, 1–2.

Bloom, B., and D. Steinhart. (1993). *Why punish the children? A reappraisal of the children of incarcerated mothers in America*. San Francisco: National Council on Crime and Delinquency.

Bresler, L., and D. Lewis. (1983, September). Black and white women prisoners: Differences in family ties and their programmatic implications. *Prison Journal* 62 (3): 116–23.

Clark, J. (1995, September). The impact of the prison environment on mothers. *Prison Journal* 75 (3): 306–29.

Faith, K. (1993). *Unruly women: The politics of confinement and resistance*. Vancouver, Canada: Press Gang Publishers.

Fuller, L. (1993, December). Visitors to women's prisons in California: An exploratory study. *Federal Probation* 57 (4): 41–47.

Girshick, L. (1996). *Soledad women: Wives of prisoners speak out*. Westport, Conn.: Praeger.

Hairston, C. (1988). Family ties during imprisonment: Do they influence future criminal activity? *Federal Probation* 52 (1): 48–52.

———. (1996, July 21). Unlocking the prison cycle for women. *Chicago Tribune*, section 6, p. 6.

Hays, W., and C. Mindel. (1973). Extended kinship relations in black and white families. *Journal of Marriage and the Family* 35: 51–57.

Henriques, Z. (1996). Imprisoned mothers and their children: Separation-reunion syndrome. *Women and Criminal Justice* 8 (1): 77–95.

Holt, N., and D. Miller. (1972). *Explorations in inmate-family relationships*. Research Report no. 46. Sacramento: California Department of Corrections.

Howser, J., and D. MacDonald. (1982, August). Maintaining family ties. *Corrections Today*, 96–98.

Koban, L. (1983). Parents in prison: A comparative analysis of the effects of incarceration on the families of men and women. *Research in Law, Deviance, and Social Control* 5: 171–83.

LaPoint, V., M. Pickett, and B. Harris. (1985). Enforced family separation: A descriptive analysis of some experiences of children of black imprisoned mothers. In M. Spencer, G. Brookins, and W. Allen, eds., *Beginnings: The social and affective development of black children*, 239–55. Hillsdale, N.J.: Lawrence Erlbaum Association Publishers.

LeClair, D. (1978). Home furlough program effects on rates of recidivism. *Criminal Justice and Behavior* 5 (30): 249–59.

Lord, E. (1995, June). A prison superintendent's perspective on women in prison. *Prison Journal* 75 (2): 257–69.

Morris, A. (1987). *Women, crime, and criminal justice*. New York: Basil Blackwell.

Sobel, S. (1982, Winter). Difficulties experienced by women in prison. *Psychology of Women Quarterly* 7 (2): 107–18.

Van Wormer, K. (1981). Social functions of prison families: The female solution. *Journal of Psychiatry and Law* 9: 181–91.

Vaux, A. (1985). Variations in social support associated with gender, ethnicity, and age. *Journal of Social Issues* 41: 89–110.

Zalba, S. (1964). *Women prisoners and their families*. Sacramento: California Department of Social Welfare and Department of Corrections.

Addressing Chronic Needs
through Programming

It's nothing but learned behavior that has to become unlearned in order for you to become anybody, and before you even leave this place and go back out and become a law-abiding citizen. I will always say that prison does not rehabilitate a person. It is only here to set you on the right track. It's up to you as to whether you want to be rehabilitated and whether you are repentive and sorry for your actions and what brought you here. That is the number-one factor in anyone's life, whether they be in prison or out of prison. You can be in prison within yourself. And so when we came we were in prison within ourselves plus the physical body was in prison, so it was a double prison there for us.

After sixteen years of incarceration, this inmate has seen women come and go, perhaps again and again, and has gained this wisdom concerning people and personal change from her own experience. What might help change one person may be meaningless to another. Regardless, the vast majority of women in prison have much in common. They have chronic needs (abuse histories, drug addiction, low educational levels) that beg to be addressed, and their personal willingness and ability to change at this particular point in their lives has bearing on that potential transformation.

The programs available to prisoners are the other key variable. In general, programming "does little to overcome marginalization from the workforce and leaves many who have a history of drug abuse, or who are parents, untouched by relevant programming" (Morash et al. 1994, 197). Programs vary widely by state and by whether they are intended for men or women. As Nicole Rafter (1987, 28) points out, "Even in prison, women are second-class citizens." Gender stereotypes shape the nature of programming for female inmates. In general, they have fewer privileges, less opportunity for work release, inferior medical care, and less access to educational and vocational programs. Because there are fewer prisons for women, inmates of different security levels may be housed together, meaning that restrictions will be at a level higher than needed for most inmates. Fewer in number than men, incarcerated women are given much less attention in every state's correctional budget and can participate in fewer activities and programs, whether recreational or educational. Women are housed farther from their families, making visiting more of a hardship and less frequent (Morash et al. 1994, Rafter 1987).

Historically, women have been penalized by gender assumptions, especially in the types of job training they receive. These tend to be such low-paid, dead-end, traditionally female occupations as cosmetology, clerical services, food preparation, and factory work like sewing or assembly. Their unique needs were also ignored, and it was not until the dramatic increase in the number of incarcerated women, pressure from outside organizations, and the push of women's rights advocates that treatment of female inmates was finally examined (Belknap 1996, Fox 1984, Morash et al. 1994, Moyer 1984). Among the indicators of the special needs of incarcerated women are that most of them are the primary caretakers of young children, they have high rates of drug addiction and of sexual and physical victimization, and they are burdened with poor work histories (Morash et al. 1994).

Although there is debate over whether "equality in treatment" is the appropriate response to the lack of attention given female prisoners, policy and program changes have begun. Even so, however, states are grappling with "tough on crime" stances and budget crises while they try to determine how to treat male *and* female inmates. As Rafter (1993) points out, equitable treatment does not mean identical treatment but attention to the special needs of both women and men. James Fox (1984, 34) notes that programs first introduced at Bedford Hills in New York State had a backlog of prisoner requests, demonstrating strong interest among inmates in self-improvement and change.

All of these considerations are important variables in planning and assessing programming; it is crucial, however, to understand the context in which the programming takes place. The goal of simultaneously rehabilitating and punishing creates a paradox. Punishment is easy to establish with incarceration—loss of freedom by itself is a punishment. But can there be rehabilitation within a context of loss, control, humiliation, and distrust?

The challenges to the distorted thinking of injured and abused human beings will not succeed unless safety and trust are established. Can that environment be fostered within prison walls? A culture that defines inmates as "other" is a rejecting culture, not a supportive one—inmates are "the lowest of the low." Incarcerated persons develop flat affect or lack of emotion because prison is not a safe environment in which to have or show feelings. Can programming break through that defense mechanism? Is it even fair to attempt to do so? If isolation is a protection against the humiliation of prison, should programs seek to reverse it?

If women are to be released back into society functioning at a healthier level, ways must be found to address their chronic needs and the trauma in their lives, and to give them new tools to deal with issues involving emotions, economic self-sufficiency, parenting, and self-esteem. A co-therapist for the Women at Risk program, a community-based alternative to incarceration, sees prison as "a place to build your rage." Other program providers referred to the emotional atmosphere of groups, which had to be addressed before providing program content could even be attempted. Certainly the counseling-type programs found creating "safe space" their biggest challenge. Yet, without safety, no growth or change is possible.

Overview of Participation at Black Mountain

The Black Mountain Correctional Center for Women has an array of programs prisoners can involve themselves in, on- and off-site, some led by contract employees and others by volunteers. According to Sue Mahan (1984, 375), programs can help inmates protect themselves from the hostility of prison life. Individual counseling or twelve-step programs can help guard against the dehumanizing aspects of incarceration; for other women, Bible study and religious services provide defenses against their low status. In fact, church members constituted the majority of the volunteer pool, establishing ties to the outside and helping with re-entry into society after prison.

Programs that had the most participation among the 40 inmates (counting women who took part in more than one program in a category) included substance abuse (39 women), leisure activities (34), individual or group counseling (30), religious programming (21), and educational or job training (16). Three inmates had participated in overnight retreats with their children. Some of the prisoners in the study had recently arrived at Black Mountain and were not yet taking part in any activities; the work schedules of others prevented them from attending groups. Sign-up sheets for different pursuits often had acquired long lists of names before an inmate could add her own because she was at work or involved in some other activity when the sheets were posted.

The women saw substance abuse programs as being very helpful. Narcotics Anonymous (NA) and Alcoholics Anonymous (AA), DART (Drug and Alcohol Rehabilitation Treatment) Aftercare, and the off-site, twelve-week, intensive substance abuse treatment group were mentioned many times as useful and influential. These were followed by Women at Risk group therapy, church or Bible study, and retreats as programs that women gained from. Many inmates also participated in community service efforts, such as the adopt-a-highway program, the women's club at the prison, and helping with patients at the Black Mountain Center. Other occasional projects included working with Habitat for Humanity, feeding the homeless, and washing vehicles. Think Smart, which brings inmates into schools to talk about prison life, is well received by young people. When two women who had participated in the study spoke to students from the high school in nearby Asheville, one member of the audience said, "They changed a lot of my opinions. They made me realize how much I want to be my own person, not just a number." The Black Mountain program director commented, "These women are concerned . . . they don't want the kids to go down the same road they've gone down" (Blake 1997, B2).

There were few negative comments about programs. However, some prisoners felt none of them were helpful. One remarked, "If they don't like you, they send you to all these classes to build your self-esteem, you get back over here and they strip you of it." Another had a different approach to personal change: "I usually deal with things on my own. I just always done that." Many inmates felt NA and AA should not be mandatory or complained that other inmates broke the rule of confidentiality; many women also did not find the self-help groups to be a positive experience.

As for other programs that might be offered, prisoners mentioned most often wanting more counseling, either individual or group, particularly to deal with domestic violence. Twelve-step programs other than NA and AA were also suggested. The women mentioned efforts to strengthen mother-child ties, such as MATCH (Mothers and Their Children) and Mother Read (both at Raleigh); one of them commented,

I know that North Carolina needs more programs for mothers. They do not have enough. More like, they started the MATCH program in Raleigh, but, only a certain amount of inmates can sign up for that. The majority of women in prison are mothers. That is really, I think, very important. To keep that relationship, to keep that bond. More than a two-hour visit. You can't get up and play with them or you can barely hold them on your lap without being told "Don't do that." That's something that I think needs to be changed.

Prisoners wanted more educational classes (art, health, or topics of interest), exercise programs, Bible study opportunities and religious services, outings, and crafts. For example, one woman thought exercise would be an excellent way to release energy:

It should be mandatory that if they do not have a nurse's written statement that they are not physically able to walk that we should have to walk at least two miles a day, morning and afternoon. . . . I'll tell you those women that lay down and sleep, they would not run these halls and yell and scream and curse and the other, and they'd respect the officers a lot more because of it, they'd be tired out and mentally they would feel better.

Frustration over gaining weight was frequent and a reason for supporting more exercise options:

They need some kind of exercise thing here, a class, something. I'm gaining so much weight. I'm on a diet now, but I have gained so much weight, I'm talking on the extreme. I weighed 120 pounds, that's my normal weight. I weigh 175 pounds [now]. This is since last September and I don't eat no more than I ate then. It's just that I'm not getting to move around and stuff. . . . I've had anorexia before and I already perceive myself as bigger than what I am anyway, and this just bothers me.

In addition, two women mentioned that officers could use a program to improve their communications skills and moral values.

More than half (twenty-four) of the prisoners felt that they needed more schooling in order to get a job upon release. Nine women felt fully qualified for employment; eight hoped to gain help in self-presentation, interview, and other job-seeking skills. Some inmates felt more experience and technical training would help them in the job market; encouragement and more responsibility were also mentioned.

More inmates (eight) declared that they would take "whatever job they could get" than indicated any specific category of employment. Factory work was mentioned by six prisoners, followed by office work (four). A few were planning to go to school, and three women hoped to become nurses. Other fields of interest included cosmetologist, store manager, forklift driver, substance abuse counselor, cook, waitress, photographer, bartender, dietitian, working with developmentally disabled people, and opening a business; one woman would be receiving supplemental security income upon release due to disability.

Education and Job Training

Fewer than 20 percent of all North Carolina inmates convicted of felonies are able to read at the twelfth-grade level. About half score at the sixth-grade level. Upon incarceration, 75 percent of prisoners do not have a high school diploma, and approximately 70 percent do not have one upon release (Carolina Justice Policy Center 1997).

Women tend to participate more than men in adult basic education programs in prison (Morash et al. 1994). Rita Simon and Jean Landis (1991) suggest that female inmates' utilization of educational opportunities mirrors their greater participation in education outside prison. In their survey of forty state women's prisons, all had educational programs, including college-level courses.

Eighteen of the forty women (45 percent) already had a general equivalency diploma or had graduated from high school before they entered prison. Twelve inmates had completed their work for the GED while incarcerated, and ten did not have their GED (although four of them were working toward it while at Black Mountain). Other options for education included classes at Asheville-Buncombe Technical Community College (A-B Tech); occasional classes at the Mountain Area Health Education Center (MAHEC); the Alpha Beauty School; classes for nursing assistant certification; and Shaw University. There were two slots for inmate study release and eight slots for inmates in vocational rehabilitation.

Vocational and technical training add to inmates' knowledge base and provide them with applicable skills and experience for release. What is needed are programs that will lead to economic self-sufficiency, not simply any job. This need becomes plain when one remembers that the crimes of female prisoners are primarily about getting money (Moyer 1984). However, the women themselves usually choose stereotypically female jobs within the already narrowed range of options provided. Nontraditional programs are not as popular, but they are the ones that lead to jobs that pay higher wages and offer benefits (Chesney-Lind and Pollock 1995).

As Sister Winifred (1996, 168) tells us,

> Without adequate programming, these women return to society older but still without skills and education. . . . Those reaching middle-age—allegedly a time of increased creativity and productivity for women—are unable to meet their innate potentials. They function at a minimal level, and their prospects for meaningful contributions to society are hampered or nonexistent. Failure to address their specific needs creates an even greater societal problem when these women are released from the correctional system.

Basic reading and writing skills are essential to an inmate's job prospects and chances for self-support. But, as Sister Winifred notes (1996), vocational and technical programs must also be in place to provide marketable skills.

In her survey of all state prisons for women, Sister Winifred found that North Carolina (as well as Hawaii, Nebraska, West Virginia, and Wyoming) did not have technical or vocational training programs for female inmates. However, although there are no such opportunities on the prison grounds, inmates at Black Mountain do participate in the vocational rehabilitation (VR) program of the Division of Vocational Rehabilitation Services, part of the North Carolina Department of Human Resources. Vocational rehabilitation works with persons with disabilities or impediments to employment (e.g., those with mental health or substance abuse problems). The main goal of VR is to get people back to work, and the program provides evaluation and various forms of support, such as work adjustment training at Handiskills (a community workshop), paying for uniforms, shoes, and other clothes, or subsidizing rent for a few months at Steadfast House (a local halfway house for women with substance abuse histories).

According to the VR unit manager, inmates request VR assessment, which demonstrates their motivation to better themselves. Upon release from prison, persons who stay in the area might remain at their job. Replacing transportation provided by the prison during incarceration (but paid for by the inmates) is usually a problem for the parolees, however.

The vocational rehabilitation program may refer an inmate client to Handiskills, a community workshop that aims to teach adults with disabilities to be productive members of the workforce. Up to six prisoners at a time work at Handiskills, along with community members who have various physical and mental disabilities. According to a job placement specialist, the inmates often feel uneasy around handicapped persons, but with time they get more comfortable. Often the women come in with an attitude problem ("the world owes them"), but working on attitude is part of the program.

Typically there is a period of four to six weeks of client evaluation involving paperwork, testing, and taking on different jobs in the workshop. Inmates, who are not paid at that point, focus on attendance, attitudes, job training, and setting goals. Once they begin work, they are paid according to their productivity. Inmates can be clients at Handiskills for one week to one year. Once they are on work release through Black Mountain, they can begin searching for a job in the community.

Some businesses do not want prisoners who have committed crimes like murder, assault, or arson. However, many employers in the community are receptive, having found that the women are productive and have good attendance. The Handiskills job coach sometimes goes along on a job interview. The organization is trying to help prisoners find long-term jobs that provide opportunity and good pay, taking the view that someone who has committed a crime has not lost the right to better herself.

Vocational rehabilitation pays for various training courses, such as those involving office and computer skills, certification as a nursing assistant, forklift driving, cosmetology, and earning the GED. These courses are provided at different locations, among them Handiskills, A-B Tech, the Carver Community Center, and the Alpha Beauty School. Meetings of AA and NA are held at Handiskills for clients twice a week. For the most part, the jobs the women were training for reinforced "either the traditional role of wife and mother or the sex segregation of the labor market" (Simon and Landis 1991).

According to the job placement specialist at Handiskills, the prisoners come there as broken people. They need to overcome years of depression, oppression, and insecurity, a tall order in an average stay of three to nine months. However, the organization tries to instill in the women the ability to stand on their own two feet and to build a new life rather than return to their earlier environment.

Handiskills has a very high success rate in placing women in jobs. An inmate is discharged from VR after a successful sixty-day follow-up period. While at Handiskills, prisoners are not paying room and board, transportation costs, or any court-ordered fees. However, once they are on work release, with a job in the community, there are deductions from their paychecks (listed in order, until funds are exhausted): $70 per week for room and board, $3 per week for transportation, $30 per week for the inmate's account at Black Mountain, and child support and restitution payments; any balance is deposited in an account in Raleigh for their use upon release. (These deductions have all increased since the time of the study: weekly room and board is $87.50, transportation is $1.50 per day, and $35 is deposited in the accounts at Black Mountain.)

Nineteen of the women were working at incentive-wage jobs within the prison; the jobs paid 40¢, 70¢, or $1 a day. Assignments included kitchen work, cleaning the living unit, or working in the canteen or clothes closet. Most prisoners arriving at Black Mountain started out in the kitchen, with a grueling schedule.

> In Raleigh we had to work, we worked five 8s [8-hour days] and on the weekend we had to pull 14 [hours] and had one day off. Here we're working six 8s, but if they need you they can call you in to come early and you don't get diddly-squat. If you work 14, 20 hours in that dining room, you still only get $1. And you only get six days' GAIN time. But if you have anything over 168 hours, it has to be [at least 8 hours] to get one merit day. So, you're working yourself to death to get one merit day.

Several women felt the low pay was very unfair.

> They ought to stop [forty cents to a dollar a day] 'cause people who don't have people to send them money in it's hard for them to live off five to six dollars a week. Because you have to buy your own, everything that you get you have to buy, your deodorant, shampoo, powders, you name it, you have to buy it. And if you don't have the money you just bum off of somebody else or you just do without.

And this inmate's comment represents those of many women who felt trapped by a complete lack of resources:

> I'm burned out and I mean that. The only reason right now that I continue to work is because that six dollars a week is better than nothing. That's the only reason why I hold in. Otherwise, I would lie and I would say something medically was wrong. That's the only reason. 'Cause I am burned out.

There were twenty-six slots for work release. A prisoner might be eligible but might have to be put on a waiting list, meanwhile remaining in her unit job or at Handiskills. Six of the women in the study were in VR, and one was in an off-site substance abuse program. Fourteen others were working in the community. Of these fourteen, ten had jobs that were related to food service. Five worked in fast-food jobs, one was a restaurant cook, two worked in food service stores, one worked in food service at a retirement community, and one was a waitress. Two other inmates worked in offices, and one was a certified nursing assistant. Only one woman held a nontraditional job, as a forklift driver. The overrepresentation of "female" jobs is evident, and the pattern is consistent with work release for female inmates across the country (Morash et al. 1994).

Becoming eligible for outside work, finding a good job, and keeping it were not simple. Prisoners complained about waiting lists, too few program slots, unfair bosses, sexual harassment, low pay, transportation for job hunting, and the ever present possibility of "messing up" while in the community. Mahan (1984) refers to the pressures of not breaking petty rules while on the job. Making phone calls, seeing a friend, talking to others, and keeping pocket change were all grounds for being disciplined. "Prisoners on work or school release found themselves in constant jeopardy of breaking one rule or another" (Mahan 1984, 365). One inmate told of an action, deemed an escape, that had landed her back in Raleigh.

> I was working at Burger King and I was having problems with my mom getting money, and I had some of the money in a bank. And so I told them I had to go to the bank, but they didn't let me do that, they said it had to come through the trust fund. So I left and went to the bank and I got the money, wired it to my mom, and when I got back, they was at my job. So, then I caught the bus to downtown Asheville. I panicked. And then I stayed down there about two or three hours, and I turned myself in the next day.

A second woman, who had no family support and really needed a job, was frustrated:

> For it to be honor grade, I can't tell. I don't understand. Where's the honor? The only privilege I see now is, yeah, I've got a CV pass and I can get work release. But yet I earn work release but you tell me I might have to sit another two to three months because I'm on a waiting list. So what was the use of me trying to get work release? You're not going to give it to me until you get a space. I don't agree. That's wrong. If I earn that privilege I should be able to go out on work release, not have to sit until you are ready.

Another aid the women have in job training is a series of workshops brought to the prison by A-B Tech. These start with a six-session program, "Getting a Good Job: Tips, Tools, and Techniques." Women wrote a résumé and talked about attitude, interviewing, attendance, and so forth. The program leader remarked that inmates would come in with individual problems that affected group dynamics. Flexibility and checking in at the start of a session helped the women be "present" for the classes and helped create a good learning environment. Events at the prison brought on instability among the women, making them at times flat, sluggish, or depressed. Some prisoners displayed emotionalism and a certain cynicism over who would hire them given their records. Even so, when the women worked on a concrete project like a résumé they seemed empowered and optimistic.

Substance Abuse Treatment

In 1996, 63 percent of offenders admitted to prison in North Carolina were identified as needing treatment for substance abuse (Carolina Justice Policy Center 1997). Women have been found to have tested positive for drugs at the time of their arrest at a higher rate than men and to have used major drugs more often than men before incarceration (Bagley and Merlo 1995). Kate Bagley and Alida Merlo (1995, 135) report that in 1991 women made up 28 percent of all clients in drug and alcohol treatment programs in the United States. Looking at drug use alone, women represented 34 percent of the clients in treatment; looking at alcohol abuse alone, they constituted 23 percent of the total.

Substance abuse treatment for women must address many needs, yet Prendergast and his colleagues (1995) found that most programs did not include services related to physical and sexual abuse, physical and mental health problems, limited educational and vocational skills, and (for nonprison programs) care for children. Compared to men, women substance abusers have higher levels of emotional problems, more psychosomatic symptoms, and lower self-esteem (Prendergast et al. 1995). Fletcher et al. (1993, 44) report that the most important aspect of institutional programming is to build an inmate's sense of self through uncovering her individual strength. In their study of female prisoners in Oklahoma, they found that those who received treatment for alcohol abuse had lower self-esteem levels than substance abusers who did not receive treatment.

For women, DART is the main treatment program in Raleigh, followed up at Black Mountain with DART Aftercare, NA and AA, and off-site treatment at Blue Ridge Center Substance Abuse Services. Given that 70 percent of the crimes committed by women in the study were related to drugs, substance abuse treatment is certainly needed. Ninety-two percent of the prisoners have used alcohol and 80 percent have used other drugs. Fifty percent of the inmates did not plan to have any substance abuse treatment once released, 45 percent did (fifteen in twelve-step programs, two in outpatient programs, and one in both), and 5 percent were not sure. A higher percentage of white women than women of color plan to continue in some sort of drug abuse treatment (60 percent, compared to 36 percent).

The substance abuse treatment program at the Blue Ridge Center has five slots for inmates in their outpatient, twelve-week program; five to seven other women from the community are also involved. The week's activities are varied. Education about such issues as HIV, cravings, women's health topics, and stress management is mixed with activities like meditating and going to a gym. Group therapy is held once weekly, and inmates attend two twelve-step meetings each week (held at the prison). Behavior modification technique is used two days a week, and keeping a daily journal is required. One inmate said about the program:

> I loved going. I hated the thought of going, but once I went after the first week, I wish I could go every day. They did nice things, we didn't just go to a classroom and sit. It was like we sat in a circle and had therapy and we all ate together, went out to outside meetings where the public was, went to a halfway house on Fridays and ate with them. It was fun.

According to one of the co-therapists, the women come in with lopsided beliefs maladaptive for healthy living. Substance abuse is but one of the multitude of interrelated problems facing the prisoners. The inmates are very similar to the community clients. They share having lost their children to other family members or social services due to the inability to care for them. They share DUI arrests, living on the streets, domestic violence, and emotional abuse. Perhaps the only difference is that the therapists are aware of certain limitations on inmates, under which they cannot make phone calls or mail out letters and packages.

Getting and staying clean and sober is an enormous personal challenge. One co-therapist said that repeat offenders often come in finally ready to make a change. They are tired of prison and tired of separation from their children. They begin to realize they have to behave differently for things to change. Still, adjusting to a job paying the minimum wage, compared to the income from drug dealing, is hard to accept. It is hoped that through the program they learn how to keep their needs and wants in perspective. More than one woman has told the therapists that "prison saved my life." For most prisoners, completing the program is their first or second accomplishment ever. At a graduation ceremony they receive a certificate and a necklace, valued by the inmates. One woman had attended an earlier version of this program and found it a life-changing experience.

> [I]t's a truthful program, and if I want to live it, I've got to work it. And I'm gonna work it. And I'm gonna get all this out of me. Half of it's gone, really. The part with feeling like I was the black sheep of the family, and I was left out a lot. My grandmother would set the table, she would forget to set me a glass of milk and a plate and stuff. "I know I set you one there, ————." But there wasn't one there. But she didn't do it on purpose. So all that kind of came up.

DART Aftercare is held once a week and focuses on maintaining a commitment to sobriety. The group leader at the time of the study was a woman with a background as a correctional officer, a probation officer, and in recovery. She knows that using and abusing alcohol and drugs is at the heart of the crimes the prisoners commit. Aftercare tries to get at the problems they will face upon release. Anger management is a big issue in the group. Since drinking and drugging had been ways to handle anger, recognizing the emotion and practicing new methods of dealing with it are crucial in adapting to the outside, which will be no "bed of roses," either.

The leader acknowledged that attendance was inconsistent and that how a particular session went depended on the mix of persons there. The goals are to plant the seeds of change, to encourage the women, and to treat them with respect. However, there is no formal support system for inmates once they are released. Having been treated as children within the prison, they are set free and expected to behave as adults.

Prisoners spoke very highly of DART Aftercare. Unlike AA and NA, this group did not seem gossipy, and honesty and openness were fairly typical. Judith Clark (1995, 316) reminds us that in prison there is little opportunity for women to talk frankly about their drug problems without feeling exposed. In NA and AA, very few prisoners interviewed felt that confidentiality was respected, though some did not care who knew about their personal business. As one woman pointed out, "A lot of people won't even go to an NA meeting 'cause they know somebody in that NA meeting is going to get out of that chair when it's time to go and come out that door and go, 'You know what she said?' " Inmates also felt that others were insincere. Clark (1995, 320) also found this during her incarceration at Bedford Hills in New York: "Others talk openly and fervently about themselves in their groups. Yet they shed those understandings as soon as they leave the meetings, reverting . . . to old habits and behaviors back on their living units."

Meetings of AA and NA are led by community volunteers. These programs were mandatory for many women, which was resented because those inmates who did not take the twelve-step structure seriously disrupted the meetings. Sometimes the gatherings simply degenerated into telling "war stories," talking about gay behavior in prison, or gossiping. One of the volunteers who helps direct AA sessions agreed that they were not "regular" meetings. The circumstances were altered, and

> many times they're in there to vent, not necessarily to share experience, strength, and hope, but just to vent. And I try real hard to give them that place to do that because sometimes I think that that's the only place that they might feel safe enough to do that. I understand that it turns into a griping session and everybody jumps on the bandwagon. . . . It's a kind of a balancing act as to how far we can let that go without it being destructive and allow some of it to be constructive.

"The prison shouldn't make people go to meetings to get their CV passes," said one inmate; "It's a 'self' thing, [you] can't make someone go." Another observed,

> The NA and AA, the fact that they make some girls go, the ones that they make that don't want to go are hindering the ones who wanna go from getting out of it. . . . It's a very good program for those who want help, but don't mix them with the ones that don't want help.

Some women felt no need for AA. "I just sit there. I don't know what they're talking about. I've never had any of the experiences that they've had." But another inmate commented, "I go to NA, I go tonight. I get a lot out of it even though I don't use drugs, but it still keeps my sanity."

One prisoner attended AA at Handiskills, which she preferred: "They talk more, the people there. I get more out of it than I do here." Some women favored an outside twelve-step program, but they had little opportunity to attend.

> Well, we get to go out to church, shopping, stuff like that. To me what I would really want for myself is to be able to go out to outside meetings, to AA meetings, NA meetings. For them to let a sponsor take us. Because it's so hard for me to share things with the ladies here. There is a lot of things I need to share and don't usually. That's something I would like.

Counseling

More than four in ten incarcerated women nationwide report that they had been abused at least once before beginning their current sentence. Of these, 34 percent reported physical abuse, and another 34 percent reported being sexually abused. Thirty-two percent said the abuse had occurred before their eighteenth birthday, and 24 percent said they had been abused since turning eighteen (Bureau of Justice Statistics 1994, 5). The chronic needs of women in prison arising from abuse, family dysfunction, use of alcohol and other drugs, lack of education, and low socioeconomic status require a response. We cannot put inmates back out on the streets without attempting to heal some of these wounds.

A few of the women felt as this one did—"Nobody can help you, you got to help yourself before somebody can help you with it." However, they still saw a role for counseling. Some were concerned with confidentiality. For example, asked if she would go to an abuse group, this prisoner said, "It's not that I don't need it, 'cause I do need it, but I wouldn't do it due to that fact it's with all the inmates." Yet, a second prisoner held a different view about counseling.

> Do they not realize, let me tell you, if they would stop pressuring you so much with all these treatments, these programs, it would probably be a less, probably fewer people returning back and forth to prison, because if you keep pushing every person to keep reliving their past, they're going to relive their past. Once you go through a successful program, you dig up the past, you burn it, you throw it away. Leave it alone, don't keep digging in it. They don't understand that.

Almost all of the Black Mountain inmates had been battered as adults—85 percent had been physically abused, 83 percent had been emotionally abused, and 43 percent had been raped. While in Raleigh, a few women had been in abuse groups and found that helpful. There is no abuse counseling per se at Black Mountain. Forty-five percent of the prisoners said they would like abuse counseling, 50 percent said they would not, and 5 percent were not sure. One woman, after eight years, had been through many therapy-type groups and was looking for "some advanced counseling or therapy session." Others wanted counseling about abuse in a small-group setting ("because it's easier to express yourself when other people have been there and learn how they feel"), and still others felt they would only go if the counseling were one-on-one.

Given the widespread history of domestic violence among the women, the lack of targeted services to deal with battering is a gaping hole in programming. As one inmate said, "Each and every one of [us] somewhere down the line has been abused. We need to pull together and gain something from it. So I would definitely be in favor of [an abuse group]."

Perhaps the goals of the Family Violence Program at the Bedford Hills Correctional Facility in New York State could be adopted at Black Mountain. According to a handout about the program (dated March 5, 1990), these include creating a safe, supportive environment for women to begin to identify and address the experiences of victimization in their lives, developing an understanding of the impact of that victimization, and coming to understand the implications for change in their lives. Individual and group work are used to empower and support each woman. Learning effective skills for handling conflict is the beginning in creating options for a safer, more effective life, where free choices can be made. Many women at Bedford Hills have found prison to be the first safe place in their lives, a haven from which they can begin to address the violence and abuse directed against them.

Although there were no specific programs at Black Mountain on domestic violence, there were counseling options for the inmates. Eleven of the women had seen a psychologist, psychiatrist, or both. There was some satisfaction with this one-on-one work, though several women mentioned not trusting the psychologist, who allegedly "talks to the officers about confidential information." One prisoner had this to say:

> I had talked to the psychologist here . . . and [a friend I trust] was in the office in there in programs cleaning one day and walked in on the psychologist giving a full report to [the program director] and [her assistant], and I will never divulge one word to that woman. And I think that's illegal. That's doctor-patient confidentiality.
> . . . I didn't hear it with my own ears but the person who told me about it I do trust.

Another prisoner claimed that the psychologist had told her that the program director had asked for a report on her counseling session. Whether or not these breaches of trust were taking place, the belief that they were undermined an important service the inmates needed.

Women at Risk, sponsored by Western Carolinians for Criminal Justice, is a local program aimed at diverting women bound for prison into community-based supervision. It has three parts: court advocacy, to achieve the diversion of the client to the program instead of prison; case management, to assist the women with employment, follow-through on opportunities, advocacy with social services, and substance abuse recovery; and a weekly group therapy session. Two closed group therapy programs were held for eight weeks at Black Mountain around the time of the study interviews. Ten of the prisoners had participated and were very favorably impressed. Said one:

> I really and truly believe that [Women at Risk is] going to be really helpful to the women. I was in their first group and it was a learning experience, and it was more, really and truly, what it ended up to be more of, was them helping us to make it through what we're dealing with. Where I think they came in to get us prepared to go back out. What they're helping us is to make us make it through. They're doing great at it. . . . Women at Risk, they pretty much pinned it down. A lot of us are so angry over [officers degrading us], almost everybody that was in the group had anger over different points of view and different things, but it almost always came down to that you were so mad at one point that you couldn't handle [it]. Once they got to the part where they actually seen where we were at, they started teaching us to deal with the anger, how to deal with people, how to take time to spend with yourself. They taught you how to live within yourself, to survive and not necessarily to think that you had to depend on all these other women in here. . . . They gave us a place to go and talk.

The co-therapists determined that inmates were trapped in parent-child relationships with the guards, who represented the critical parents. Inmates found the guards to be more personally involved with them than at Raleigh, resulting in more emotional control and more petty day-to-day interference. These relations triggered memories of childhood abuse and created an emotionally abusive atmosphere. This issue became a focus of the group; as guards establish a parenting role, they also are enforcing regulations that keep inmates separated. No-touch rules and those against lending common items like laundry detergent break natural give-and-take bonds that people have with each other. This disconnection fed into the rage that the women felt but constantly had to suppress.

The groups evolved into therapy concerned with handling the emotional strains of incarceration. The direct and honest approach of the co-therapists helped create an atmosphere of safety, but whether much more than that was accomplished was questionable. The needs are so great that islands of safety may be the most that individual programs can offer.

Another such effort, "Getting Free, Growing Whole," was an eight-week, closed, self-help group intended to guide the women in reclaiming the self, emotionally, spiritually, and psychologically. It was directed by a local therapist in private practice. As was true of other groups, the context of prison made it difficult to get in touch with feelings in a safe environment. Confidentiality is suspect, conflict between individuals is frequent, and the guards' lack of respect undermines the inmates' sense of autonomy and self-esteem.

Although the therapist for this group hoped to establish a safe place, it became evident that most of the prisoners had never had that experience, either as children or as adults. She used a wide variety of methods to assist the women in personal change—journal writing, art therapy, music, story telling, guided imagery, and meditation. However, although some participants became happily involved in these therapies, the very methods themselves did not feel safe to others. Meditation, for example, requires an ability to connect with a sense of peace within the self, which is virtually impossible in the presence of deep trauma experiences. Women who survive through suppression and isolation find expressing their real selves very threatening.

According to this therapist, the prison was operating like a dysfunctional family. Lack of safety, respect, and trust created the need for such maladaptive behaviors as hypervigilance, chain-smoking, stifling feelings through eating, and excessive sleeping. The group attempted to reclaim some sense of self and to instill a belief that no person can be robbed of her dignity by someone else. However, the wounding of these women began long before they entered prison, and unless help with reentering society after release is provided their wounds will be inflamed again and again.

Health Care

Women who enter prison have good chances of being in poor health. Drug-related lifestyles mean increased likelihood of problems associated with

IV needles, high-risk sexual activity, and poor nutrition (Nadel 1996), and low socioeconomic status and inadequate access to health care are significant underlying factors (Epp 1996). As noted by Jennie Lancaster, head of North Carolina's Female Command (the state's five women's prisons), there is more mental illness and AIDS and less formal education among female inmates than in the general population. Add high rates of substance abuse, and you have women who have not taken very good care of themselves (Lawsuit 1997, B6). As Jan Epp (1996, 96) points out, women sent to prison have not earlier "actively pursued their physical well-being by exercising, eating properly and getting physical exams and consultations on a regular basis. Many smoke and abuse drugs and alcohol."

Health care needs at Black Mountain were addressed by a nurse on duty five days a week, six hours a day; a doctor in attendance one day a week and on call other times; a psychologist present two days a week; and a psychiatrist who visited once a month. A volunteer chaplain also sees inmates who need assistance or need to talk.

The nurse treats what maladies she can and makes referrals. So, in addition to treating medical ailments, she also hears of various psychosocial problems. The inmates' myriad physical complaints are related to the stresses of prison life, to relationships with guards, other inmates, and family, and to separation from loved ones and loss of control. Anxiety about release to the old neighborhood is heightened by lack of preparation and support. Money is another big concern, as a minimum wage job is not adequate for support.

Providing health care in prison is a complicated process involving guards' and inmates' attitudes and prison rules, in addition to medical complaints. According to the nurse, much more is involved than treating illness. Some inmates, for example, are manipulative and try to use illness to get out of work or other responsibilities; others make constant complaints that are not serious, attempting to get attention. Given that health care was free at the time of the study (prisoners now pay three dollars to see the nurse and five dollars to be taken to the emergency room), some inmates demanded services that they may not have absolutely needed. The move to have prisoners pay for their health care is occurring nationwide in hopes of cutting down on frivolous requests; however, there is some concern that it may also cut down on necessary medical visits (Clayton 1997). For guards, responses vary between shifts in how medical needs are handled. Some override the nurse's order for an inmate's bed rest if they believe she is malingering, thus undermining the nurse's authority. The prison nurse is also limited by the requirement to prescribe only from a set list of drugs and by regulations governing who may be referred, to whom, and when.

As mentioned earlier, depression and related disorders are common, and ten to fifteen women are taking medication at any given time. Questions have been raised because women are more likely to be treated with drugs than are men (Morash et al. 1994). Female inmates themselves, moreover, are wary of the control aspect of medication. When receiving such treatment they feel groggy and out of control, and other people respond to them less. A further cause for concern lies in prescribing drugs for women who abused these same drugs before incarceration and who may use the system to gain access to them again. Some inmates reported that prescription drugs were the only ones available for abuse at the prison.

Overall, inmates were satisfied with health care at Black Mountain. However, in June 1997 Prisoner Legal Services filed a class action suit on behalf of nineteen inmates about conditions at NCCIW in Raleigh. The complaints concerned lack of timely treatment, inadequate emergency services, poor care for inmates with chronic diseases, and failure to follow the recommendations of outside specialists (Lawsuit 1997). Women who had spent time in Raleigh had mentioned poor medical conditions as one reason they felt Black Mountain was a better facility.

Religious Programming

Many prisoners found comfort and guidance in their faith, some having strengthened their beliefs since incarceration and others having held those beliefs before. Staying in their rooms reading their Bibles was mentioned often as what women did in their spare time. For others, religion was not much of a factor in their daily lives. There were several Bible study programs, and in addition to Sunday worship church groups provided five other services or programs. Going to church on a CV pass was a common event, both because that was what prisoners wanted to do and because most volunteers came from churches and wanted to bring inmates to their services.

Different churches were highly involved in activity programming, rotating the monthly birthday parties and sponsoring the overnight retreats. One church supported a weekly game night, and another donated books to the prison library. Prison Fellowship also holds programs at Black Mountain.

One volunteer chaplain, who served from 1986 to 1991, in addition to

leading worship, established Steadfast House, a halfway house for female parolees with substance abuse histories, and is now involved in planning overnight family retreats. These are coordinated by the outreach ministry of St.
James Episcopal Church, and give six to eight prisoners and their children an
opportunity to bond and have fun together. The retreats are held two or three
times a year at In-the-Oaks Episcopal Conference Center in Black Mountain,
where participants go hiking and swimming and make memory books and
take photographs. In the chaplain's opinion,

> It's been very beneficial to the mothers and to the children to have the children be
> able to bond with their mothers. I remember there was one mother who said that,
> we asked her if she had slept well that night, and she said that she didn't sleep at all,
> and she said, "I just wanted to stay awake and see my child sleeping because I had
> missed him so long." So, you get that bonding, they sleep in the same room. It's
> private, it's a lovely place. They have all kinds of activities going on. We plan for
> them, we plan every minute, but we do have quiet time.

The volunteer chaplain at the time of the study coordinated varied religious programs, services, and seminars. Earlier in her chaplaincy she had
taken inmates to social services, court, or appointments, but today these tasks
are handled by CV sponsors. In her work at the prison she has found that
many inmates were brought up with a strictly religious "Thou shalt not" attitude; they know their Scriptures, but often only the hellfire-and-brimstone
version. Her approach to spirituality was to offer the inmates more-balanced
options: church services, family retreats, and retreats concerned with self-
esteem and substance abuse. She applied for and received grants for these
activities, and with the development of the volunteer program there is today
a broader range of ways to encourage wholeness among the inmates.

The volunteer chaplain believes that change comes about through spiritual influence. The most powerful force for change lies in the religious community and in religious convictions. Therefore, there will always be chaplains
and religious activities in prison.

Programming for Mothers and Children

Given the high number of incarcerated women with children, there is a
surprisingly low number of correctional institutions nationwide to accommodate their needs. Most facilities do not have special visiting rooms, let alone

toys and games for mothers and children to play with. Visitation time also varies, with a few prisons allowing daily visiting, and a few others permitting contact only once or twice a month. In a survey of forty states with women's prisons, nineteen had home furloughs, with varying regulations (Simon and Landis 1991). Only three states, New York, Minnesota, and California, allow children under two years of age to live with their mothers in prison from birth (Henriques 1996, 86).

The chronic desire of inmate mothers to remain in contact with their children is not theirs alone. The children also want to stay in touch with them. The journal *Pediatrics* reports that nearly one in fifty children in the United States has a parent in jail or prison (cited in Spindler 1995), disrupting family bonds. The family is where we acquire our values, learn respect for authority, and develop our self-esteem. The evidence shows that many incarcerated individuals grew up with an absent parent, thus closing the circle (Mustin 1995).

Except for the family retreats mentioned above, home passes, and regular prison visiting, there is no ongoing programming at Black Mountain to maintain the mother-child bond. Women whose children do not visit regularly at the prison or who do not have home passes are given priority at the overnight retreats, which St. James Episcopal Church hopes to expand to four per year. Although the family retreats are a wonderful opportunity for mothers and their children, the program is limited in how many families can be accommodated. Clearly, more such efforts are needed. Said one inmate, "I think they should do more things like treating us with more time with our kids because it's going to affect them [for] a long while and they're the next generation." Women were interested in having the Mother Read program and MATCH, both presently at Raleigh, at Black Mountain as well.

Community Volunteer (CV) Passes

More than a hundred volunteers are involved with the Black Mountain facility; a majority of them are CV sponsors, taking prisoners off-site. Most women (68 percent) accepted CV passes, as mentioned earlier. Five eligible women (13 percent) did not take passes: they felt it would be too hard to get in touch with a sponsor, that they might not find a compatible sponsor, that there was nothing they were interested in doing with a sponsor, or, in some cases (knowing most sponsors were from churches) that they did not want to go to church or talk about religion. One inmate said,

> The only thing I'd really like to do on a CV pass is go fishing, and other than that I don't care about going out there with those people. . . . 'Cause those little old ladies who come in here, bless their heart, they're doing good for all these girls.

Another remarked that most of the CV sponsors

> come out to take you to church or take you shopping or take you to their house or take you to feed the ducks or something like that. And I respect them, I give them the utmost respect, I would never disrespect them in no kind of way, but I don't have an interest in that. Going shopping is not going to benefit me. Church, yeah, it would benefit. But I have a personal relationship with God, I could go in my room, shut the door and pray.

The prisoners cherished their time away from the unit while on a CV pass as a change of pace: taking care of an errand, buying goods outside the prison canteen, seeing a movie at a theater, and in some cases establishing a long-lasting relationship with a sponsor. The process was not without stress, since paperwork could be mishandled and the pass not scheduled properly, or a money request might not go through. The sponsor and inmate have to fill out an activity sheet detailing where they are going and at what time, complete with phone numbers and addresses. The schedule is to be followed, and if there is a change the sponsor must call the unit. Any money the inmate spends has to be accounted for with a receipt. And upon return to the prison there is always the humiliating strip search.

Release Preparation

It can be argued that all of the programs mentioned in this chapter, from work release to counseling to home passes, are preparation for reentering the community. Program providers all cite equipping the inmate with the skills and confidence needed to survive without returning to crime as one of their goals. However, much depends on the inmate's own support system, since the criminal justice system does not provide follow-up and help upon release. Women often leave prison without the ability to address the problems that led to their involvement in illegal activities and are thus often worse off than before (Hairston 1996).

There are no regularly scheduled targeted programs for reentry at Black Mountain. Inmates sentenced under North Carolina's so-called old law receive "good time," which immediately cuts their sentences in half. Virtually all prisoners receive GAIN time, a certain number of days off their term, depending on custody level. However, inmates sentenced under the state's "new law" can receive GAIN time only up to a point, since they have to serve a minimum of 85 percent of their sentences. At Black Mountain, where women are held at Level 3 minimum custody, prisoners receive six days GAIN time off their sentence each month. Merit days—acquired by working overtime on a unit job, undertaking projects like raking leaves and shoveling snow, and so forth—are another way to get time off. Every eight hours of merit duty add up to one day of GAIN time. Of course, time could also be lost due to infractions.

When inmates come up for parole depends on the length of their sentence, whether they were sentenced under the old law or the new law, and the various calculations of time off for good behavior or merit days. No one formula for parole hearings is applied equally to prisoners. The women submit a home plan to the parole commission, stating where they intend to live and whether they have a job (or how they mean to find one). A parole officer investigates the living site for its suitability. (For example, if the inmate will be on intensive probation or under electronic surveillance, the officer needs to determine if the living situation is conducive to the monitoring.) The commission sets the particular conditions of parole (e.g., whether there will be drug screening or treatment), but other stipulations are universal, such as paying supervision fees and reporting to the parole officer. Under the new law, parole is referred to as "post-release supervision," and some inmates can be released without any supervision at all. Moreover, women can be set free the first time they come up for parole or kept in prison until their term is up.

Many prisoners prefer to "max out." By serving their full sentence, they do not have to report to a parole officer. Parole is a state of "suspended freedom," in which inmates are subject to all the pitfalls that continued regulation implies (Faith 1993). Parole officers are supposed to provide guidance and punish wrongdoing simultaneously. As part of the criminal justice system, they are socialized by the views of prosecutors and judges about punishment, as well as by the sex role stereotypes of the larger culture (Erez 1992). This combination is not positive for female parolees. For example, "Women will be required more often to improve domestic relations, whereas men will be required more often to improve their employment situation or other aspects of their breadwinner role" (111).

As one of the few supervised halfway houses in the Black Mountain area, Steadfast House can be part of the home plan. Opened in 1989, it is a project of the jail ministry of the Asheville-Buncombe Community Christian Ministry (ABCCM). It houses five women, most with substance abuse histories, and the house director (in this case, someone also in recovery). If the woman is a vocational rehabilitation client, VR will pay her rent for three months. In any case, the rent is very low ($100 for the first month, $140 for the second, and $200 thereafter), easing the women into bill paying and other responsibilities and helping them to save money for a place of their own. Women stay for from three months to a year, and the goal is for them to save at least $1,000 in the first three months to help them toward independent living. They do not pay utility bills, but they are responsible for their own food and for cable television. Residents usually apply for food stamps in their first days there; for medical and dental needs, they often go to the ABCCM medical clinic.

House rules forbid drinking and other drug use, sex, and violence, and require attending at least three twelve-step meetings a week and respecting other people and their property. Any additional parole stipulations must be followed. The women's children can visit at any time, and they have the run of the house. Visiting men are restricted to the foyer and the living room downstairs. After one month there, women start to use their weekend passes and can stay with their families or husbands or boyfriends; permission of their parole officer is required if they are leaving the county. With all weekend passes, the residents need to inform the house director of where they will be staying and how they can be reached in case of emergency. Women cannot stay out overnight at other times.

The five beds at Steadfast House do not begin to meet the need for a supervised, supportive environment for released female prisoners. In fact, bearing in mind that women pose less risk to the community, are far less likely to engage in criminal activity after release, and, even when they do, commit less serious crimes than men (Bureau of Evaluation 1986), it appears that an increased investment in community programs for them would be a wise policy move. Furthermore, as Clark (1995, 327) points out, women in prison are not isolated individuals but "continue to relate to and affect their families, communities, and society." What happens to them during incarceration affects their children, and hence all of us. In Chapter 8 I will look at community involvement with the women at the prison and at how these relationships affect both inmates and volunteers.

References

Bagley, K., and A. Merlo. (1995). Controlling women's bodies. In A. Merlo and J. Pollock, eds., *Women, law, and social control,* 135–53. Boston: Allyn and Bacon.

Belknap, J. (1996). *The invisible woman: Gender, crime, and justice.* Belmont, Calif.: Wadsworth Publishing.

Blake, B. (1997, May 26). A look at life from behind bars. *Asheville Citizen-Times,* B1–2.

Bureau of Evaluation. (1986, May). *Women in prison: How much community risk?* Madison: Wisconsin Department of Health and Social Services.

Bureau of Justice Statistics. (1994, March). *Women in prison.* Washington: U.S. Department of Justice.

Carolina Justice Policy Center. (1997, April). *Legislative Update.* Raleigh: Carolina Justice Policy Center.

Chesney-Lind, M., and J. Pollock. (1995). Women's prisons: Equality with a vengeance. In A. Merlo and J. Pollock, eds., *Women, law, and social control,* 155–75. Boston: Allyn and Bacon.

Clark, J. (1995, September). The impact of the prison environment on mothers. *Prison Journal* 75 (3): 306–29.

Clayton, S. (1997, May). Fee-for-service programs: Is it time? *On the Line* 20 (3): 1, 3.

Epp, J. (1996, October). Exploring health care needs of adult female offenders. *Corrections Today,* 96–97, 105, 121.

Erez, E. (1992, March). Dangerous men, evil women: Gender and parole decision-making. *Justice Quarterly* 9 (1): 105–26.

Faith, K. (1993). *Unruly women: The politics of confinement and resistance.* Vancouver, Canada: Press Gang Publishers.

Fletcher, B., L. Shaver, and D. Moon, eds. (1993). *Women prisoners: A forgotten population.* Westport, Conn.: Praeger.

Fox, J. (1984, March). Women's prison policy, prisoner activism, and the impact of the contemporary feminist movement: A case study. *Prison Journal* 64: 15–36.

Hairston, C. (1996, July 21). Unlocking the prison cycle for women. *Chicago Tribune,* section 6, p. 6.

Henriques, Z. (1996). Imprisoned mothers and their children: Separation-reunion syndrome. *Women and Criminal Justice* 8 (1): 77–95.

Lawsuit challenges women's prison care. (1997, June 29). *Asheville Citizen-Times,* B6.

Mahan, S. (1984). Imposition of despair—An ethnography of women in prison. *Justice Quarterly* 1: 357–84.

Morash, M., R. Haarr, and L. Rucker. (1994, April). A comparison of programming for women and men in U.S. prisons in the 1980s. *Crime and Delinquency* 40 (2): 197–221.

Moyer, I. (1984, March). Deceptions and realities of life in women's prisons. *Prison Journal* 64: 45–56.

Mustin, J. (1995, June). Parenting programs for prisoners. *Family and Corrections Network Report* 5: 1–2.

Nadel, B. (1996, October). BOP accommodates special needs offenders. *Corrections Today*, 76–78.

Prendergast, M., J. Wellisch, and G. Falkin. (1995, June). Assessment of and services for substance-abusing women offenders in community and correctional settings. *Prison Journal* 75 (2): 240–56.

Rafter, N. (1987, Spring). Even in prison, women are second-class citizens. *Human Rights* 14: 28–31, 51.

———. (1993). Equity or Difference? In American Correctional Association, *Female offenders: Meeting needs of a neglected population*, 7–11. College Park, Md.: American Correctional Association.

Resnick, J. (1982, November). "Women's prisons" and "men's prisons": Should prisoners be classified by sex? *Policy Studies Review* 2 (2): 246–52.

Simon R., and J. Landis. (1991). *The crimes women commit, the punishments they receive.* Lexington, Mass.: Lexington Books.

Spindler, S. (1995, June). The need for parent/child programs. *Family and Corrections Network Report* 5: 3.

Winifred, Sister M. (1996, August). Vocational and technical training programs for women in prison. *Corrections Today*, 168–70.

Community Involvement and Societal Change

When you get this woman out of prison, who sometimes doesn't have a high school education, her reading skills, her writing skills, her social skills, aren't quite what other people's might be. She doesn't have a good job history, she doesn't have a good support system. All she knows is that when things got tough she used or drank, or had some other compulsive behavior. She was addicted to men, or any of those kinds of things. This isn't just one issue. One little lady from the church is not going to do it. . . . We need programs that are going to help them get that education and have a job. We need day cares that are gonna take care of these kids. We need attorneys that are gonna help these women get their children back, get the child support. All of those things. Those are things that are gonna take time and money.

These words do not come from some ultra-liberal social theorist. They come from the publicly expressed view of a CV sponsor at Black Mountain that rehabilitation should be part of the correctional program. Despite policy makers' get-tough stance, studies consistently show the public to believe that rehabilitating offenders is a social goal equal to or greater in importance than general deterrence, punishment, or protection of society (Applegate et al. 1997).

The mission of the North Carolina Department of Correction is "to promote public safety by the administration of a fair and humane system which provides reasonable opportunities for adjudicated offenders to develop progressively responsible behavior" (North Carolina Department of Correction 1992, 2). One way to achieve this aim lies in the volunteer program found at every prison throughout the state. At Black Mountain, volunteers attend a two-hour orientation meeting, followed by six hours of contact with an inmate on-site or off-site supervised by an active volunteer, before they can assume their responsibilities. Men and women can be volunteers, but only women can be off-site sponsors.

According to the state's volunteer handbook, there are seven reasons why "civic-minded citizens may wish to offer their services as volunteers in a correctional facility" (North Carolina Department of Correction 1992, 8–9). These include economics (helping inmates become fully functioning members of society again), public safety, personal satisfaction, personal growth, a chance to expand interpersonal relationships, training and experience, and public awareness. I interviewed sixteen community volunteers for this study, whose involvement ranged from ten months to ten years, the latter antedating the prison's opening in 1986. Three persons had been volunteering for ten years, one for nine years, six for six or seven years, three for one to two years, and three for just under one year.

Recruitment

Most volunteers are brought in through churches; others are recruited through personal contacts and through contacts the inmates make. Fifteen of the sixteen volunteers came from churches; one was involved in the original legislative funding for the prison and in the discussions about the site through her position as executive director of Western Carolinians for Criminal Justice (WCCJ). A few started with the jail program at Asheville-Buncombe Community Christian Ministry (ABCCM); others were drawn in through the monthly birthday parties sponsored by area churches; some were conducting religious services and Bible study.

Several of the volunteers felt a "calling" to work with women in prison.

I'm an ordained deacon in the church and I felt that I was really led into this ministry because, for one thing, I had hospice work and I was ordained for that, but something just led me into this place. And I remember very clearly, I was sitting in my armchair and I said to my husband, "You know, I think I'm going to go over to the prison." I didn't even know where the prison was. So I went over and I asked to speak to the superintendent, and the guard there said, "Do you have an appointment?" And I said, "No, but I'll wait." I did not know the superintendent, it was before Renae Brame . . . and so I spoke to her and I asked her if I could help in any way. Well, I did help for about a year and I taught Sunday school. I had another little helper who helped me sing and all of that, but I said to one of the persons, they need a chaplain here.

And so I went to [the superintendent] and told her about it. I said, "I wouldn't be qualified to be chaplain," and she said, "Oh, yes you would." So, I said, "OK, I'll try it." And that's what I did, and I did it for five years.

Another woman, who has been a sponsor for six years, remembered:

I felt some years ago, probably fifteen or more years ago, kind of a calling. . . . I really felt called to do it. I felt also that I probably was not up to it. I felt like I would be manipulated, taken advantage of. I didn't think I would be strong enough. So I fought these feelings of wanting to do it, and there were several workshops in Asheville that were maybe forty hours long for volunteers, and I didn't do them. And I thought about it a lot . . . and kept putting it off and putting it off. And then ————, who has volunteered her whole life in prisons, said that our churchwomen at Warren Wilson Church were doing the September birthday party out at Black Mountain and would I help. So I did go out and felt quite at home.

For other women, volunteering at the prison seemed to be an "accident." One who helps lead AA meetings and is also a CV sponsor said,

A friend at church asked me to help her become a volunteer. I was just going to be her transportation. She's never been there, not to this day. And here I am. So, it was quite by accident. . . . When I went to the orientation, I told her, "Well, I'll just go through the orientation, get established, then when you can we'll start going together." Filling out the paperwork, it had several options [for] what you could participate in. I'm almost eleven years sober. . . . So [AA] was on that form and I thought, "Well, I can't do anything else but I can do that."

Most church volunteers are recruited through presentations by active volunteers or announcements published in the church's newsletter about the need for people to drive inmates to worship services, to participate in the monthly birthday parties, to help with a dinner or event, or to become CV sponsors. Some volunteers meet inmates who are attending their church and become interested that way. Other churches have a prison ministry program.

The original reason I got started in this is that the prison is basically in my backyard. So when the prison first came, [and] I read the articles in the paper that the prison was coming, I was interested in it because I didn't know if this was maximum security or minimum security. What if they escape and come to my house? So I had an interest right there and with what was going on. And then through my church, [they] put a plug in through United Methodist Women. We have an emphasis on women in prison and their children. And so because of that, and because of having the prison practically in my backyard, and just an inner desire to help, to see if I could make a difference for some women, I got involved in it.

This woman saw

a notice in our [church] bulletin that . . . there were some Catholic women at the prison who needed a ride to mass on Sunday and there were no volunteers from the parish . . .[;] that seemed like a terrible situation to me. Somebody whose life needs to be turned around and they couldn't go to mass and that was what they wanted to do, I thought that was really awful.

Another observed,

Then there were people in our church that were doing prison ministries in Black Mountain. They introduced me to the volunteer program. I took the orientation and basically they helped train me into what to expect and what to do and what not to do by being with me. We went to town, did things together. . . . And from there I have honestly felt that God has chosen me to work with women in prison.

The executive director of WCCJ had a different motivation for involvement:

[W]e've been interested in the prison since before it was a prison, with mixed feelings because of our mission for prison alternatives. It's not in keeping with the thrust of the organization to support expanding prison units, particularly for folks who would be at this prison. [They] could be equally served by prison alternatives at no risk to the community and less expense to the taxpayer. So on the one hand, we found ourselves supporting [the prison]; it was an awkward situation in that we were supporting a unit we thought might not even need to be. On the other hand, because of the work that I've done since being in Asheville with imprisoned women, I knew firsthand the burdens that family members were having because of their trips to Raleigh and back.

The executive director of WCCJ was also asked by the governor's office to suggest names of community members to sit on the Resource Council, which she has been continuously involved in. Several other volunteers who participated in the study were or are members. The Resource Council "is to provide assistance in stimulating positive citizen and community involvement and volunteerism at the prison facility" (North Carolina Department of Correction 1992, 17). Alternating in bimonthly meetings with the Core Volunteer Committee, the Resource Council works on expanding the volunteer program, recruiting new participants, and supporting the prison staff; it also raises funds for projects. The superintendent is free to engage this nongovernmental organization in an exchange of ideas for bettering the lot of inmates.

The major activity of the Resource Council for several years was to lead in raising money for the new chapel and activity building, under construction during the interviews (in 1996) and now in use. Council members raised fifteen thousand dollars by involving prominent local citizens, building upon and increasing positive relations between those inside and those outside the prison. This structure has added needed space for activities. The administrative offices have moved from the residential building, and a dining room, new kitchen, and library have made a significant difference in programming and living space.

The Core Volunteer Committee, also meeting bimonthly, plans activities and resolves problems that involve volunteers. Its members recruit volunteers, plan two training sessions a year, and organize birthday parties, get tickets for cultural events, arrange for participation in area festivals, and so on.

A problem with volunteers is that there never seem to be enough sponsors to take the prisoners out on CV passes; some have several sponsors and others cannot seem to connect with even one. Although there are over 120 volunteers, only about 50 take inmates off-site. Making the connection between CV sponsors and prisoners is not easy, in part because the inmate is responsible for contacting the volunteer and many feel uncomfortable calling and asking to go out. This may be due to being shy, to concern about compatibility, to seeing that the volunteers are mostly older, retired women and being concerned about the age difference, or to knowing that volunteers mostly want to take inmates to church, where not all inmates want to go. Said one volunteer in her mid-forties, "I don't think there are many women my age. A lot of the volunteers are older. They are senior citizens and they have more time than we do. With working women it's really hard to find the time to do that with their work and their children." Another volunteer observed,

> There's such a wide difference in age and experience between the women who organize and participate in the volunteer program and the women that are behind bars. [We need] to try to broaden the community volunteer pool to include younger women who might have more in common with women who are there.

Concerning the over-representation of church members among volunteers, one of them said, "I don't know how you would change that. And the prison system doesn't know either." Another points out,

> Across the state the church volunteers at prisons are the overriding volunteer group, and maybe that's nationally, but certainly that's true in North Carolina, and in some prison units that's pretty much all that there is in terms of outsiders coming in. They're there for religious reasons . . . but [here] there's also some interest in other social, educational, and individual benefits and matching inmates with sponsors.

Perhaps one reason for this overriding involvement of church members is that they can draw on a built-in support group of others involved in the work, sometimes even an organized prison ministry. Inmates' participation in worship services, and perhaps potluck meals afterward, creates a sense of safety and community. Still, not everyone can work with women who have suffered traumatic experiences. "[At first I thought] I could get all these women from my church to be sponsors. Not. All people, women or men, aren't geared up for that. Some people can't, it actually hurts them inside. They just can't face it. There's a part of them that just can't." Another volunteer puts it this way:

> My concern is that it's a very specialized work, and I do not feel that just anybody can do it. It takes a special kind of person. It's a very special ministry, very special needs there, that are very hard for very many people to understand. There's a tremendous amount of fear. One thing that I have been struck with, I think that we would be absolutely aghast if we knew how many people we passed by on the street, in the malls, in town, in a grocery store, who've been in there. I don't think we realize. And if we realized we'd probably walk around paranoid, going crazy all the time for those who tend to be afraid of those kind of people.

The Volunteer Program

Prisoners and their sponsors can get involved in a host of ongoing programs, seasonal events, and individualized activities. In addition to monthly birthday parties, Bible study, and worship services, there are holiday events like the Christmas party, the Billy Graham Chorale, and the Angel Tree. There are also many cultural events—plays (produced by Warren Wilson College and by the Asheville Community Theatre), Arts Alive, the Swannanoa Chamber Music Festival, the Swannanoa Gathering, and museum exhibits at Pack Place in Asheville among them. On CV passes, inmates and sponsors can also shop, hike, or walk, go out to eat or to the movies, spend time at the sponsor's house, go to church, and do various errands to take care of business. They can also go to special outside groups or meetings, such as with their children's school counselors. Still other particular arrangements can be made.

The volunteer chaplain at the time of the study had aggressively sought out grant money to fund overnight retreats for the inmates. One grant was for adult children of alcoholics, which allowed them to engage in personality typing and examine family roles. Another local grant funded overnight retreats for inmates and their children.

Volunteers would like to see other programs at the prison, including more physical activities. One observed, "I think maybe there's not enough physical things for them to do. . . . They sit. That's all I see them doing when they have any free time, or whatever. They sit and smoke." Another commented, "I hope that they will be able to get a reading program because even though some of them don't necessarily say they're illiterate, their skills are lower than what they could be." Several volunteers felt that instituting an aftercare program should take priority.

> The support of other people is vital within the unit but after they get out of there they're bombarded with so much in such a short space of time. They have a list several pages long of "You need to do, you must do, you will do" things from parole, they have the parole office to deal with, they have community service people to deal with, they have employers to deal with, they have rules [at Steadfast House] or wherever, all those things. Plus deal with the issues that got them up there to begin with. So sometimes it's just overwhelming. As much as I tell everybody we need the volunteers, we need support for the unit, we need the support to be connected before they leave, that it's already in place before they walk out the door.

Another volunteer echoed this concern.

> [T]he thing that bothers me is that they have basically no real follow-up program, and that's where it's sadly [lacking], we're sadly in need of that. When they get out of here, they tend to, I'm not saying all do, they tend to get back in the same patterns. And if we had someone who could keep after these people and keep in touch with them, and bring them to church or maybe not to church, or just keep up with them,

keep in contact with them to say, "Well, are you doing OK, do you have a job, are you going hungry, how are your kids doing?" This kind of thing.

Matching volunteers with inmates and communication between them were mentioned as rough spots in the program. For example, staff members will post a sign-up sheet for an activity, and many more inmates will want to take part than there will be volunteers available to take them out. Having raised expectations that will not be met, such incidents create dissatisfaction among inmates. Another issue

is the problem of matching people who would like to sponsor a girl with a girl. [After the orientation] we have a follow-up with those new volunteers to which we invite an equal number of girls who hopefully need a sponsor or who haven't been out very often. But often the girls who come are the outgoing ones who have already made contact with sponsors and who are already going out. . . . So, somewhere along the way there needs to be some means of determining which girls who are eligible to go out haven't gone out because they're too shy to make contacts or [for whatever reason].

One sponsor recalled a follow-up session:

From the basis of that one meeting I wouldn't have felt real comfortable calling, saying I want to sponsor ———— because I don't want to impose myself on anybody who doesn't want me because those women are in such a powerless position. I think that's something I feel sort of sensitive about. It's like the bull-in-the-china-shop kind of thing. Just my presence is sort of overbearing in a way because they have no power and I do. That's no basis for friendship unless you sort of forget about it. . . . When you talk to [some of the prisoners] you can just feel that you are being sort of sucked up to, even when there's no reason for it at all. It's sort of awkward, but they're in a needy position.

Staying in touch with the inmate a volunteer sponsors is also a challenge.

[Getting in contact] just seems awful to me. She has to call on the pay phone and I can't really call her. I have to make the appointment, I have to set up the leave for her, and if there's something that I think would be a good idea, I can call and set it up, but I can't call her and say, "Do you want to do this, does this sound like fun, or are you off work that day?" I can just set the appointment and then if she can't do it then she would call me. But that's just awkward I think.

A variation on this was also mentioned. "It's very hard to communicate with the women in this program because I can't call them at all, and they can call me, but they're not always very responsible about doing that."

Another problem is that when an inmate requests a "special," a withdrawal of money to go shopping or to go out with a sponsor to dinner, the request sometimes has not been processed. The inmate learns of this as she is ready to walk out the door with her CV pass. One sponsor who experienced this frustration adds, "We get the feeling there are some staff people who, they try and feel some sense of compassion. There are others that are very rough."

Most volunteers have high praise for the staff at the prison and their dealings with them. For example, one couple who volunteered with a monthly religious service felt

> [the staff and administration] are just super. We are super impressed with [the program director] and Renae Brame and [the volunteer chaplain] in terms of their approach to the work that they're doing and their willingness to stick their necks out a little bit and bring volunteers in to do all this stuff that they can't do single-handedly.

Another compliment involved the superintendent:

> I think Ms. Brame does a wonderful job. I will say this. I have never met an inmate who ever said she didn't listen. That's the one thing that they always say. They don't always like the decision, but they always say that she listens. I think that's a very honorable situation.

One volunteer felt she received support from the prison's staff, "except for some [guards] who act like it's a real imposition for them to have to deal with you." Another questioned whether the guards did, in fact, respect the volunteers: "There is not a good staff-volunteer relationship. Volunteers come in and there's been times when I have stood at that window for five minutes when waiting for a staff person to acknowledge that I'm there. And it's a volunteer coming in and giving their time." Another recalled a miscommunication:

> [An inmate] had been in our seminar. She didn't have her CV pass [yet]. She cried a great deal at the seminar and I said, "I'll come see you." And I made an appointment to see her. And when I went the officer did not tell me that my name wasn't down there. I wished he would have told me right away; I would have left. So he called [the inmate] down and we sat and talked. The whole time he was [glaring at us], it was unnerving. Am I sitting too close to her? What am I doing wrong? So finally, I looked

at him and I said, "Sir, do you want me to leave?" He said, "Yes." So he sent [the inmate] upstairs and called me into the control room. He said, "I don't know how long you've been around here, but you can't come in and talk to people." I said, "Well, I didn't. I had an appointment." And he said, "Well, it's not there." I said, "Well, why didn't you tell me?"

Most of the volunteers felt the support of their family, other volunteers, and their church, along with appreciation from the inmates and the prison staff, kept them going. Said one, "My key support is my family. If I didn't have them there's no way I could do what I've been doing or have gotten accomplished what I have gotten accomplished." Another remarked, "We're relatively often told by either women that we work with or the administrative staff at the [homeless] shelter, 'You're doing wonderful things. People really appreciate it, thank you,' [and] 'I need you, keep on coming' [that] kind of stuff."

Some felt more ongoing training would be helpful, although only one volunteer was really adamant about it. She pointed out that the Core Volunteer Committee was started with the goal of taking over the volunteer training,

to get more in-depth training, the same that [the prison ministry of ABCCM] had done. And I said, "Well, at least, if we can't do as much in-depth as they did, we could at least have four good programs a year." . . . I was concerned that so many of these women did not have the slightest idea of what an arrest is, of what an arraignment is, what a woman goes through, what happens to her children, the whole system.

The rules of the volunteer program have evolved over the years. For example, in a statewide change, the minimum age for volunteering was raised in 1997 from eighteen to twenty-one. Sponsors at Black Mountain now can only take out one inmate at a time (except for certain educational programming), down from the original two. This change in the rules came after the discovery that two inmates were going to assault a sponsor, steal her car and money, and try to escape. (A third prisoner heard about the plan and reported it to Superintendent Brame.) The two women involved were sent back to Raleigh, but all the inmates suffered as a result. Said one sponsor,

The girls are complaining because they're the ones who are suffering. Well, we're suffering from it, too. But you turn the picture around and look at it. They're making a statement. Number one, we're going to protect our volunteers. I appreciate that, and so therefore, I cannot fight it, though it's disappointing because we had [gotten] to take two apiece when we got to church or an educational thing. The other thing is it's a statement to the women, "Don't do that."

Interacting with Inmates

Taking women away from the prison opens the sponsor up to a myriad of feelings. She may feel some discomfort (What will we talk about?), fear (Will I be taken advantage of?), a sense of adventure, a sense of satisfaction in helping someone, or uncertainty at the possibility of a close friendship and the involvement that entails. Sharing time in activities, over meals, at church, or shopping gives the inmate and sponsor a one-to-one experience.

Many of the volunteers mentioned the possibility of manipulation, and some stated point-blank to the prisoners what their limits were.

> I've made it very, very clear to women in the beginning that these are the rules. We have rules for passes. . . . I don't walk on water, and I speed continuously. So, I'm not perfect. But in that I will never, never lie for you or about you—that means don't do anything and expect me to support you in that if it's a lie. Don't try to get me to take things in for you or carry messages for you or whatever it is. Tell a lie and go somewhere else. . . . I've always told each and every one, the very first pass. These are the rules, as long as you don't ask me to break them, we'll get along great.

This sponsor also addressed the issue with inmates:

> I realize that some of them are in there and they will con you, and just really take advantage if you'll allow it. . . . I just in a nice way try to set them straight and let them know their limits. I realize there has to be rules and they have to know that too.

Several sponsors indicated that prisoners had tried to use them. One wanted to mail a package to her family and in another case wanted to pick up her paycheck at work. The sponsor knew to say no to both requests; finally, the inmate "stopped trying to manipulate me or pull the wool over my eyes." Another volunteer said,

> [There was one woman], she called and she wanted me to go down and buy enough yarn for an afghan and she didn't say, "I will pay you back." . . . I support her all the way, but now she's beginning to make some demands. . . . So that's when I had to

> learn to draw the line. . . . She'd write me and say, "I need shampoo," little stuff like
> that. But then the gifts became, the requests became, bigger and bigger.

Although some are cautious, this volunteer maintained her own perspective: "Of course we're aware of the fact that there are people who will manipulate. But there are people everywhere who manipulate, so I don't know if it's any more prevalent among the sixty-eight [prisoners] out there than it is elsewhere."

Sometimes what seems like a violation of the rules is not, and it may be hard for the sponsor to tell.

> They're told they're not allowed to meet friends or their family. The first time's a
> coincidence, the second time we're to report it. [One time an inmate and I] came
> out of the restaurant and she started talking to these people, and I was sorta turning
> to get her away. And [the inmate] realized I didn't recognize this guard because she
> wasn't in uniform. So that was just my stupidity. And the first woman I ever took out
> was a young, beautiful woman . . . [;] we were in Wal-Mart and this guy kept following
> us around. I got scared. I didn't realize she's just gorgeous. I've never had a problem.

Another volunteer mentioned a few times when she violated rules by not keeping the inmate she sponsored in sight. Once, after they had settled down in a restaurant with their food, a prisoner realized she had left her sweater in a store; the sponsor let her retrieve it. Another time the sponsor had to drop something off at a school, and she left the inmate in her car with the car keys and her purse. Even though these are certainly rule violations that created escape possibilities (both situations have been used in volunteer-training sessions to illustrate what not to do!), the sponsor trusted the inmate in each case, a trust that was not betrayed. One volunteer said of the need to stick close by the inmates, "I feel very silly trailing them around because you sign a statement saying you won't let them out of your sight. . . . And you feel very conspicuous when you do that. But I think they realize that that is a part of our responsibility."

By extension, possible manipulation could also mean possible physical violence. In fact, some of the inmates have been convicted of assault or murder. They have earned the privilege of being at a minimum security facility by following rules, behaving without aggression, and participating in programming. Still, the fact of not knowing people who have been convicted of crimes extremely well leaves room for doubt. Some sponsors do not take inmates to their homes, feeling that minimizes their risks. Another relies on her faith in God to deal with her fear.

> Let me tell you how I approach it, a lot of people are afraid to take these ladies out. . . . I have decided that my approach to it is not fear, it's if I can walk and talk to God close enough, I don't have to fear. Because nothing will happen to me unless it's with any plan in which to glorify God's name somehow, someway through it all. . . . If my life is taken or one of my children's lives, and I am helping them to walk and talk with God, I have nothing to fear because when Jesus comes I'll be able to go home to heaven with him.

This sponsor trusts in the judgment of the prison staff. "I figure if they're going out with me on a CV pass they've been checked over and they haven't done anything wrong, no little infraction in the last month, or they wouldn't be going out on a CV pass. I feel like they keep a real close rein on them, so that protects me."

Sponsors are often very generous, though the acts seem small to them. One woman drove the prisoner she'd sponsored home upon release because she was concerned for her safety.

> [H]er son didn't have a car and her other family members weren't real reliable. . . . She was thinking that she was probably going to take the bus to ———— and wait at the bus depot for a relative to get her . . . and I thought for a woman in prison for up to a year, and have that restricted environment, and to just let her out on a bus, let her go to ———— to a bus station, I mean, I wouldn't do that myself, let alone someone who's been shut up for a year. So I told her, "When you find out when you can go home, if it's OK, I'll take you home." 'Cause it was just to ————, it wasn't a big deal for me. And I had grown to really like this girl. . . . So I got a call from one of the ladies there at the unit, one of the officers . . . and she said [the inmate] was being released the next day and I could come get her. And I said, "I'll be there at nine in the morning." And I picked her up at nine in the morning and she was waiting. . . . I took her to ————, dropped her off at this apartment her son had. So that, talking about what it does for me, that was very, very rewarding for me to be able to take her home. I knew she got there safe and sound.

Although not all sponsors have the means to treat inmates to meals, this woman said, "When I take them out I pay for their meal because I cannot buy them anything else, nothing, but I can buy them something to eat. So that's what I do."

As mentioned earlier, most sponsors come out of churches, and they have differing views as to what role they should take outside a literal worship service. Said one, "We have prayer at the house, and a lot of times they'll come by, they say, 'I wish that I could feel more, not this burden, this load, but I feel so depressed.' And maybe we'll have a prayer for them. My husband happens to be a minister. He's retired. So we counsel with them in certain ways at home." Another sponsor, acknowledging that some volunteers promote accepting God, said, "Because of their guilt they [the volunteers] bring on altar call after altar call. This is just not a fair way of dealing with their emotions. And yet, I don't want to speak against those that are really pushy about it. My feeling is that that's not my style."

A former volunteer chaplain felt that the content of the religious message made a huge difference.

> I get tired of hearing people coming as volunteers, particularly in a religious situation, where they are always saying, "God's gonna get you for that," and all this kind of stuff. I want them to hear, here's something good and constructive in the Gospel rather than the bad, the punishing, because this is what they've always heard.

This lay minister, too, believed that services provided by volunteers can have a powerful positive message.

> We are a patriarchal society. We are a white, male society. So what we are taught is white, male stuff. [T]he message that keeps getting left out is the message that you are a precious daughter. You are worthy of love, you are worth more than what has happened to you, and you need to be healed. I want you whole.

Impact on Inmates

Volunteers believed their work had an overwhelmingly positive effect on prisoners. They felt it helped relieve tension, created bonds of friendship, allowed for a sense of normalcy, and restored faith in humankind. Said one, "I think if you just treat them like they're a person when you go out, I think that gives them a real boost, just treating them like a friend." Part of this friendship, found another sponsor, was that inmates asked "me questions that they wouldn't ask somebody up there" at the prison. And again, the ambiguous role of religion was noted:

> I think the impact of the volunteers 90 percent of the time is very good. I think most of them are there to share friendship and whatever in that area. There are some

volunteers who will preach, try to save souls, try to act like a warden. Their impact is not good. But they're in the minority.

Leaving the unit, even for a few hours, gives the inmate a break from her surroundings and the regimentation of prison life. Birthday parties with games, fresh fruits and vegetables, and cakes are a change of pace. One volunteer thinks "it helps to relieve the tension and maybe depression. And I'm sure getting out goes a long way in relieving tension, and reassuring them of the compassion and love of other people." Said another, "I'm sure it's got to be a lift for them . . . to be able to go to town and feel normal, go and be normal."

Most volunteers want to be a positive role model for the inmates. One remarked,

I really feel that the volunteers' responsibility is to be role models and that's partly what they tell us when we go through the orientation. You're a role model. [When they come to my house] and see a stable family in action, it's probably a tremendous influence on them.

Another sponsor reinforced this notion:

Hopefully we're enriching these women somehow with just being someone who cares. I know when I take the girls out, lots of times I take them out just shopping. They have clothing exchange or they want to buy just some lipstick or something. They're very grateful, and they'll ask me, too, why do I do this, and maybe they've never had anybody do anything kind to them. So, I'm hoping that by my doing this to [help] them out, to just [be] kind to them, that I'll plant a seed. And they'll go out and do that when they get out of prison and pass it on to somebody else. I think it's really important. People look to other people all the time.

One woman felt the volunteer program had little impact on the inmate she sponsors; "she is a very assertive, strong person. . . . I don't think she needs to be changed in any way [and] I don't think she'd ever say, 'I'm a different person because of [my sponsor].' "

But for most of the prisoners, the volunteer program provides many opportunities for growth and change and for access to outside resources. Probably its biggest impact is to let prisoners know that they have not been abandoned by the world. This lay minister noted of the women coming to his services, "The stories we have heard of how they walk with God, even in their addiction, even in their prostitution, it's mind-boggling. What they don't have any faith in is humankind. They have a deep faith in God, and no faith in humankind." And remarking on this deep need for human contact, another longtime sponsor recalled, "[I heard an inmate say volunteers] restored their faith in humankind and [gave] them hope."

Impact on Volunteers

The most common effect of knowing and interacting with the inmates was developing a better understanding of their lives and what they experienced in prison. "It affects me," said one experienced volunteer.

> I've driven home many a night saying, "Thank you, Lord," because they often tell you—you don't ask—but they often tell you why they're here. I had one woman tell me the very first [pass] why she was there. And the horror of their life has been so terrible, their parents have been so inept. It sickens me to realize how in-depth. . . . You wonder what you and I would have done if we had been in that situation. . . . And I know that doesn't say that we shouldn't have them incarcerated, but it also makes me realize that they weren't given much to start.

Another observed,

> I think I have a better understanding, I suppose, of what the inside of a prison system is like, of what it might feel like to be one of the women in that situation, a better empathy. I guess if anybody had asked me before I'd gone there what the women were like, I would have said they were just like anybody else, but now I know that really is true. They're not a breed apart. Even though you know that before, you really understand it after you know them and talk to them and so forth. They are people.

This sponsor has come to believe that

> women have a real disadvantage in prison. Their sentences are usually longer than men's. I think they're probably looked down on more. Most of them in prison have very low self-esteem or have some kind of abuse in their background. Another thing I've found with the ladies I've taken out is that usually one of their parents have died [or is absent], and I think that makes a difference, when they were younger. Sometime in their life they're either without a mother or a father. And I think that's a real void that affects their lives.

A volunteer whose past experience and job brings her into contact with inmates found that she gains "more understanding of what staff deals with and maybe the additional things a community might do to make it a better place for the women."

Some sponsors felt a "high," an excitement at being involved with the inmates. For example, "I'm kinda a people person so it thrills me. I go away with a charge, like, this is great. And probably I go away with a little bit of guilt thinking I wish that I could be more regular at it. I wish I could be here more, doing it more." Another remarked, "[It's] probably the most fulfilling, satisfying feelings that anybody could experience." "I usually come home 'up,'" said a third, "really up after taking them out because I know they really appreciate it."

Other reactions were gratitude, frustration, and a sense of personal growth. "So I guess it has made me much more aware of the fact that the justice system doesn't always seem to act justly. And I've also realized that there but for the grace of God go I or a niece." Another volunteer was frustrated at the results of a race- and class-based system, where nonwhite and poor women "are in prison for what you or I [white and middle-class women] could get away with. It's not fair." And some volunteers mentioned how they had grown personally, learning skills or picking up information from prisoners they had sponsored ("One woman rode motorcycles; I learned a lot about motorcycles from her"). On a deeper level,

> Shortly after I started going there I got involved with a lady and became her sponsor and took her to the incest survivor group, which I had never openly admitted to being raped. . . . And in that, again I thought I was doing this for her, and as it turned out, it was for me [as well] and my growth emotionally and also spiritually.

A couple who conducted religious services as lay ministers had this to say:

> We have just met some amazing ladies in prison. They're very needy and there are some that belong there, but there are just some really strong people there that we have learned an awful lot from in terms of their ability to survive, and their faith, and their ability to teach, to talk about their experiences in such a way as to bring tremendous understanding. . . . Their testimonies are so powerful, and we almost always go away having received far more than we brought. . . . And these are the same people that so much of society discounts as not being important.

Volunteers' Views on Societal Change

There were quite a number of suggestions for helping women in prison and viewpoints about societal change on the part of the volunteers. These ranged from prevention to educating the public to more prison-based programs to aftercare to finding alternatives to incarceration. Several women spoke of the need to examine why crimes are committed in the first place.

> There's reasons why they're doing these crimes. And if we were addressing some of those things then maybe [it could change]. I don't know that just locking them up and taking away frills is going to change a heart. I don't know that . . . would happen. To me, if it was me, it would make me more angry.

Noting the impact of early dysfunction, this volunteer observed:

> A lot of what I have been able to see with the women is the things that happen in their lives early on. Many come from addictive family backgrounds. It isn't just the incarcerated woman who has addiction problems, but that this was a family problem. They come from abusive homes, physically, spiritually, emotionally, sexually.

This volunteer also pointed to the powerful role of abuse:

> If society can come to understanding the evil of abuse, but they don't want to because they want to continue abusing. . . . I think society does have a big problem. And the big problem is that they're willing to accept being abused and to abuse, and not recognize the evil of abuse nor stop abuse themselves, doing it themselves or stopping other people from abusing.

Prevention makes the most sense to another sponsor:

> I think one way is just in the rearing of our kids. Really the only way to stop problems is at a young age at the very beginning. And it seems like our society is putting the fix after it's already been done. We need more support systems or educational opportunities for our children before they get in any trouble.

Other volunteers saw a need for stronger societal support of women while they were incarcerated. For example, mother-child bonds must be strengthened:

> I think society as a whole needs more awareness of the problems faced by the women in prison. And I think one thing that we don't do here [at Black Mountain]

that could be done is to see that children of incarcerated women who do not have transportation for visitation, that could be provided. When this prison was opened it was my understanding [that women] from Gastonia [in North Carolina's western Piedmont] west, more or less, would be incarcerated here. But as the prison cap went into effect, then wherever there was a vacant bed and whoever was the next on the list went there. So, it seems to me they're from more scattered areas across the state.

Having more sponsors to bring inmates into the community was viewed as an excellent way to break down stereotypes of female prisoners. For example,

By the fact of having [inmates] come to our church once in a while, [the congregation is] finding out that they're people like you and I. I think the world doesn't know that. Except I think more people are seeing that with drugs—more families, unfortunately, who thought they'd never deal with this are dealing with it. So, some of that is changing.

And, similarly, another sponsor who brings women to church felt their presence provided "a greater opportunity to be aware of the women who are there." "People don't realize," another volunteer said, "they haven't the vaguest [idea] of what goes on there. They just think they're all behind bars, that one of them will stab you or something if you take her out. But people haven't been educated."

There's "no quick term solution here," as one volunteer put it. "It's not only one person or one thing, it's the whole society." For the public to want to undertake the kinds of programs this volunteer is implicitly talking about, and the prevention work that so many know is needed, there has to be a change of heart. We need to stop seeing the prisoner as "other." "If it's somebody else and the people seem so distant from you," one sponsor observed, "it's the old thing if you can dehumanize people you don't have to take them seriously." These "others" are people with access to different resources than the mainstream middle class. "From the color of your skin, the class that you grew up in, to your family background, to your educational level, to how you feel about yourself, their resources are just vastly less than ours are," according to one volunteer. "So it truly is," she continued, "it's only by grace that we're not in the same situation, because a lot of it we had no choice in, and they have no choice in."

References

Applegate, B., F. Cullen, and B. Fisher. (1997, September). Public support for correctional treatment: The continuing appeal of the rehabilitative ideal. *Prison Journal* 77 (3): 237–58.

North Carolina Department of Correction. (1992, April). *Volunteers make a difference: Volunteer handbook.* Raleigh: North Carolina Department of Correction.

C h a p t e r

9

No Safe Haven:
Policy Recommendations
and Concluding Remarks

As someone deeply involved in jail and prison work for more than fifteen years, the executive director of Western Carolinians for Criminal Justice (WCCJ) felt "really offended by their challenges."

> I think society ought to work to keep as few women [in prison] as possible. I think that's the best thing that we could do to help women in prison. And that's always really pulled at me in terms of being a part of the Department of Correction, that by bringing [the program] Women at Risk to the prison are we making it too easy for the prisons to keep taking care of these women when so many of them could be better helped in the community. But I really do think that the best thing we can do is to figure out ways the women don't have to go in and do their time.

Women in prison have sizable obstacles to overcome. First, they are stigmatized as *women* in a patriarchal society. Then, they are disproportionately women *of color*, predominantly *poor* women, and overwhelmingly *abused and battered* women. They have violated norms of behavior, become *criminals*, and they have been separated from society as *incarcerated women* (adapted from Richie 1996, 160). These intersecting status positions hold not just the key to understanding women in prison but also the key to change—overcoming inequality and ceasing to see people as "others." It is easier to stigmatize despised groups as "evil or unworthy" than it is to work for social transformation (Sidel 1996, 168). These stigmas are powerful forces in the Black Mountain women's lives, and they must be met with equally powerful forces for change.

Natalie Sokoloff and Barbara Price (1995, 12) point out that a major overhaul of the criminal justice system is unlikely in the near future. However, it is very useful to acknowledge that this system reflects the sexism, racism, and class biases of the larger society. White, upper-class men make laws for the benefit of white, upper-class men, and these laws are primarily enforced by men. Those who are arrested and convicted tend to come from the lower social classes, made up disproportionately of members of minority groups. In fact, social class is the single most significant variable in the criminal justice system's treatment of women. The higher the social class, the more favorable the treatment at every stage of the system. Etta Morgan-Sharpe (1992) found race and gender to disadvantage people of color and women significantly in state after state in the criminal justice process.

The prison environment itself is an inherent drawback to any prison reform program. As Phyllis Baunach (1985, 126–27) states, "Philosophically, prison administrators want to generate a sense of independence and responsibility among inmates. However, this philosophy is antithetical to prison operations, which of necessity focus on security. In reality, prisons foster dependence." An environment in which most aspects of inmates' lives are controlled is not going to be conducive to personal growth and development. As Elaine Lord (1995, 262) sees it, "Prison does not allow women to experiment with their own decision-making but rather reduces them to an immature state in which most decisions of consequence are made for them." On another point, Donald Cressey (1965) tells us that prison administrators try to balance conflicting program demands from outside groups against incompatible internal ideologies and goals. Administrative survival often wins out, which rarely results in the best programs and services.

Still, several women in this study spoke of how incarceration was helping them. They referred to certain positive aspects of prison, primarily having time to think about their priorities, breaking away from the fast life, getting drug abuse and physical abuse counseling, and gaining their GED, job experience, training, or all three. Seen in a context of life experiences that have involved economic marginalization, abuse, addiction, and few resources to deal with their problems, prison *against this backdrop* does become a resource. Patricia Van Voorhis and her colleagues (1997) found that male inmates who felt they benefited most from incarceration were those who had no employment before arrest, had limited opportunities, and were nonwhite. Being part of the underclass of America makes life outside prison less attractive (Wilson 1987). Incarceration, however, should not and can not be society's answer to poverty, systemic unemployment, and poor educational systems (Tonry 1995).

Policy Recommendations

Keeping in mind the broader context of social inequalities and the contentious prison environment, the following recommendations cover three areas: prevention, programs inside prison, and alternatives to incarceration. Each recommendation is made with an eye toward addressing women's chronic needs, seeking solutions that are based on the root causes of their offenses, and comes out of a feminist critique.

Prevention

Meda Chesney-Lind (1995, 114) notes that every dollar spent on incarcerating women could be better spent on services preventing them from becoming so desperate as to commit crimes. As noted, the major issues in this area are economic marginalization, sexism, drug addiction, abuse, and racism.

• According to the U.S. Census Bureau, 15.1 percent of all persons in the United States lived below the poverty line ($11,522 for a family of three, and $14,763 for a family of four) in 1993 (cited in Sidel 1996, 69). One of our biggest problems in this regard is the minimum wage. Millions would be lifted out of poverty if the minimum wage were raised to a livable wage. A full-time minimum wage worker making $5.15 per hour still has earnings below the poverty line for herself and two dependents. At the time of the study, the minimum wage was $4.25 an hour, yielding an income of only $8,160 per year. For single women with children, these incomes are a disaster. And women and children in 1993 made up 77.4 percent of all Americans living in poverty (Sidel 1996).

Women on Aid to Families with Dependent Children (AFDC) are also living in poverty, although with the advantage of at least having health insurance for their children and themselves. A national health insurance program would assist millions now living on welfare, as well as the working poor, to improve the quality of their lives and their ability to work and to learn at school.

For many repeat offenders, economic marginalization is a major factor in breaking the law. These women are disproportionately nonwhite, have inconsistent labor force participation, are undereducated and unskilled, and are structurally dislocated from the labor market. Research on female repeat offenders has found that women with some type of economic means are less likely to commit property crimes (Jones and Sims 1997, 337). And, a study of recidivism in North Carolina, which followed inmates released between July 1, 1992, and June 30, 1993, found that "unstable employment was a significant predictor of rearrest for drug offenses among females but not for males" (Jones and Sims 1997, 346).

• We must address gender bias in schools, including sexual harassment of girls, how teachers treat girls, and the gender bias of books and materials used in the classroom. Girls, including teenage mothers, must be encouraged to stay in school to get the training they need for jobs to ensure their self-sufficiency (Merlo 1995). Girls with low self-esteem do not grow into women with healthy self-esteem. Young girls struggle to maintain their sense of self within a hostile environment that bombards them with messages designed to convince them that they are sex objects (Greenberg-Lake Analysis Group 1990). Schools can play a major role in combating this propaganda by encouraging girls' intellectual development and academic achievement, fostering social skills, and aiding in positive group interaction.

• We must continue working toward gender equality in all social institutions, including criminal justice and the media, pass the Equal Rights Amendment (ERA), and continue to challenge attitudes of female inferiority. Sexism is ingrained in social institutions, laws, popular culture, and in our notions of femininity and masculinity. A sexist double standard of how females and males are to behave is reflected in our double standard of punishment. Women are not to be violent, even in self-defense, and they are punished more harshly than men. During incarceration, they have less access to libraries, exercise, programming, education, and rehabilitation than do men, and women serve longer sentences, since they are not released early due to chronic overcrowding as men often are (Chesler 1994).

Edwin Schur (1983, 240) tells us that "the 'normalizing' of femaleness must itself be a major feminist goal. Activists must therefore directly concern themselves with trying to undermine the reproduction of sexism as it occurs in routine male-female interaction." He goes on to say that the "prevailing patterns of deviance-defining can be changed. Those patterns which—at a given time and place—prevail do so primarily because of the social power that upholds them. . . . Since it is imposed, it can be deposed" (1983, 241).

• We must insist that juvenile female offenders be given educational and job-training programs that will enable them to achieve economic self-sufficiency. Life skills and parenting programs, drug treatment, and abuse counseling need to be offered to young female offenders to equip them to lead productive lives upon release (Bergsmann 1989, Immarigeon 1997). We need to stop incarcerating girls for status offenses, especially as they involve sexual behavior, and find other means of dealing with their nonconforming actions (Naffine 1989). If these girls come to our attention at this point in their lives, we need to do all we can to reduce the likelihood of seeing them as adult offenders. Rather than penalizing and stigmatizing them, we should help them in their resistance to their oppression (Arnold 1994).

• Drug treatment programs must become a priority. Countless women have been held back from treatment because programs have not been designed with women who are the primary caretakers of their children in mind. Programs for women, whether residential or outpatient, must also take their children into account. Residential programs will have to accommodate children, as well as provide services for women who are pregnant and women who are HIV positive (Bagley and Merlo 1995). Funding needs to be available for poor women, who are in desperate need of these services. Only about one-third of federal drug funding is allotted to prevention and treatment (Mauer and Huling 1995).

Given that 70 percent of the crimes committed by the Black Mountain women involved drugs in some way, and that women enter prison with more serious drug histories than men and have associated difficulties such as unemployment, low self-esteem, health problems, and emotional problems, drug treatment for them is an absolute prevention priority (Mauer and Huling 1995). There is "no mystery," according to Chesney-Lind (1997, 177), as to "why adult women use drugs." They are medicating themselves, selling drugs for economic survival, or both. Many incarcerated women have been through drug treatment programs before their imprisonment. Acknowledging the interrelated problems surrounding drug abuse reminds us that treatment alone may not be enough to halt addiction. All of the issues must be addressed in a multipronged manner.

• A study by Cathy Widom revealed that girls who had been abused or neglected had a 77 percent greater chance of being arrested as adults than girls who were not abused in childhood. They were more likely to be arrested for property, drug, and other misdemeanor crimes (1992, 2; Widom 1995). Studies of women in prisons across the country show a high rate of childhood abuse. There is absolutely no question that we need to strengthen child abuse laws and prevention programs.

• Virtually all women in prison have been battered in an adult relationship, affecting their physical well-being, their self-esteem, and even their prospects of holding a job or finishing an educational program. Psychologically, these women suffer from chronic fear and stress. We must strengthen domestic violence laws, holding batterers accountable, and stop treating these assaults as "communications problems" or "lovers' quarrels." Women who want to leave abusive relationships need short-term shelter, longer-term transitional housing, and assistance in putting their lives back together. Both the mothers involved and their children need counseling. Police need to make protecting the victims the first priority, and courts need to back up police actions with prosecutions. Both these levels of the criminal justice system have been woefully inadequate in dealing with battering.

• We are now in the midst of national public debate about the significant personal and social costs of racism. President Clinton has called for our energy, our ideas, and our personal commitment to challenge entrenched racism in America. Women of color are not simply "more" disadvantaged than white women. They are oppressed in a qualitatively different manner. This is based on different historical experiences, different controlling images in the media, and institutional racism (Rice 1990, 64). Many of the aforementioned recommendations address issues that overlap with race in significant ways (e.g., poverty and the disproportionate number of poor people of color).

Coramae Mann (1995, 132–33) suggests some changes needed within the criminal justice system, that although they are not prevention measures per se they are anti-racism measures. She proposes a study of the criminal justice system's treatment of women of color to provide the factual basis for policy changes; cultural sensitivity training of law enforcement personnel; intensive police training in gender, race, and minority-community relations; releasing poor women arrested for less-serious offenses on their own recognizance or on very low bail; decriminalizing prostitution or applying the laws more equitably to include customers; drug treatment for female addicts; appointing more judges from minority groups; and pursuing programs to strengthen family ties of women of color.

Programs Inside Prison

According to Barbara Bloom, gender-specific programming takes into account what we know about female offenders—greater levels of physical, sexual, and emotional abuse as children and of battering as adults; higher likelihood of drug dependency than male offenders; economic marginalization; and being the primary caretakers of their children (in Immarigeon 1997, 65, 76). Both juvenile corrections and adult corrections need to focus on a gender-specific, culturally sensitive approach to meeting the needs of female offenders. This course of action received more support when the Juvenile Justice and Delinquency Prevention Act of 1974 was reauthorized in 1992; it requires states to take an inventory of their female-specific programming.

• Programs for inmate mothers and their children are needed not only at Black Mountain. This is a vital factor for all mothers in prisons and jails. According to the Family Resource Coalition (1986, 14), three critical needs must be met in order to maintain parent-child bonds and ensure the well-being of children: contact visiting, community services for the children on the outside and the mother on the inside, and educational programs to help the mother better understand her children and gain parenting skills. Mothers should be placed as close as possible to where their sons and daughters live. If children are in state custody, attempts should be made to place them with foster parents close to the prison. Ideally, transportation should be provided for youngsters to visit their mothers. Efforts should be made to allow women to be at school meetings, court hearings, or counseling sessions with their children (Barry 1985, Henriques 1996).

Chances for successful reunions of inmate mothers with their children would be enhanced if the women had programs that allowed them to continue their relationships as they gained parenting and other life skills. In addition, since most incarcerated women have children and will return to them in a primary parenting role, job and vocational skills training are absolutely necessary so that they can support themselves and their daughters and sons.

A variety of courses, from parenting to nutrition to child psychology, could empower inmate mothers. Child development classes held at the prison could help them understand and evaluate the appropriateness of their children's behavior and aid in their interactions and judgments (Fogel and Martin 1992). A range of model programs are scattered across the country. Some focus on retreats or overnight time together, some have developed innovative visiting arrangements, and others involve babies born during incarceration living with their mothers in prison (Family Resource Coalition 1986). Prison administrators would do well to examine these programs and to contact some of the national agencies that can provide information and consultation (e.g., Family Resource Coalition, Chicago; Legal Services to Prisoners with Children, San Francisco; Family and Corrections Network, Palmyra, Virginia; and the Osborne Association, New York City).

• Prison has become a primary setting for drug treatment, increasingly important for the drug-addicted women who are now incarcerated. Off-site treatment like that offered for Black Mountain inmates at the Blue Ridge Center seems ideal, but in many cases inmates are in a maximum security facility and the unit is self-contained. Drug treatment for women is most effective when it is combined with treatment for the other chronic needs in their lives: abuse counseling, parenting skills, educational opportunities, and job training.

• Jean Harris (1988, 212) reminds us that some inmates serve sentences that extend well beyond the positive impact of incarceration. They "languish in prison long after they should be at home." Several women in the study felt that after five to seven years they had rehabilitated themselves and had changed all they were going to. Further incarceration was making them bitter. If women must be sentenced to prison, terms should be shorter or early parole should be earnestly considered.

The United States uses longer sentences than most other industrialized countries. The prison superintendent Elaine Lord (1995, 265) points out that we must reexamine "how punitive we really are and come to some decisions as a society in terms of what we want." Do lengthy sentences accomplish our goals, or do these sentences come at too high a cost?

• There is a serious need to reexamine probation and parole violations that result in incarceration. There were twenty-nine such violations by eighteen of the inmates in the study (45 percent). Fifteen inmates had new charges, some along with other violations. Among them were missed appointments, dirty urine, behind in restitution, behind in community service hours, moved without telling the officer, did not return to school as ordered, did not do drug treatment as ordered, and missed curfew. Chesney-Lind (1995) reports that in Hawaii half of the women in prison were returned there for failing drug tests while on parole. As one Black Mountain volunteer noted earlier, women released from prison have a long list of "dos and don'ts" to follow and it is difficult to do parole. Faith (1993, 169) remarks, "Few women are so consciously deliberate in their resolve to return to prison when the going gets rough, but the odds of surviving inevitable obstacles in the outside world are slender." I think we need to ask ourselves if those women who did not have new charges truly need to be incarcerated again. Is it "judicially appropriate," Charlotte Nesbitt (1995, 5) wonders, to return women to prison for breaking noncriminagenic parole conditions? Furthermore, is it cost-effective to the taxpayer, when keeping women in their communities and with their children would cost less?

• Several recommendations that came out of the interviews relate specifically to Black Mountain. For example, participation in AA and NA should be voluntary. Inmates overwhelmingly felt that those women who did not want to be there ruined it for those who did; they did not follow the twelve-step guidelines and turned the meetings into bull sessions. However, if inmates were to lose CV passes or home passes for not attending, clearly they were going to go, regardless of their sincerity. There is a strong need for more exercise in addition to walking. Aerobics would offer the best option and can be done at different skill levels. More exercise would decrease some of the tension and women might feel better about themselves physically.

Given the overwhelming predominance of church members in the base of volunteers, the Resource Council might consider running public service announcements on radio and notices in the newspaper to draw in other members of the public. This would increase the range of interests and ages of the volunteers. Several inmates mentioned they would like the superintendent to have more contact with them, perhaps walking out in the yard to chat or speaking with them at times other than when business was being conducted.

An abuse group is clearly needed. Inmates expressed a strong interest in having abuse counseling, both group and individual. The administration should look into several different options to address this chronic need and provide the women with means to deal with these issues affecting their lives. Other types of groups that would be helpful include anger management and stress reduction (for guards as well as inmates).

Among other programs, more for mothers and children are definitely required. The overnight retreats are the only ones offered, and those are infrequent and limited in the number of inmates who can participate. There was interest in the Mother Read program, where inmates read books on tape for their children. Events for families through the year, such as picnics, are another possibility. And making toys and games available during regular visiting could increase the bonding of women and their children, and provide some fun as well.

Alternatives to Incarceration

Chesney-Lind (1997, 172) suggests that "we know what to do about crime, particularly crime committed by women. Any review of the backgrounds of women in prison immediately suggests better ways to address their needs." Imprisonment should be the "absolute last resort—for use when all else has failed and when there is concern for the safety of others" (Lord 1995, 260). Separating women from their children, with attendant family dysfunction and increased risk of cycles of criminality, creates more problems than it solves (Albor 1995). Female offenders need viable options in their lives to change their patterns; otherwise the cycle will continue (Chesney-Lind 1995, Singer 1995).

One compelling reason to commit our society to community-based alternatives to incarceration is that imprisoning more and more people is expensive and counterproductive (Bloom et al. 1994). Putting women in prison is not stopping their drug addiction and the nonviolent criminal behavior that surrounds it. In fact, the reverse is true. By criminalizing these women, their chronic problems are not addressed and their options for change are diminished. Separation from their families and economic marginalization create a cycle of criminal justice interventions without transformation.

Women are especially appropriate for community-based alternatives because they are overwhelmingly incarcerated for nonviolent offenses, they are the primary caretakers of their children, they have medical needs for drug treatment, and they have psychological needs for abuse counseling. All of these services can be provided, and provided well, in the community without risk to the community. Alternatives to sentencing should include individual and group counseling, day care for their children, job placement assistance, restitution, community service, drug treatment, and case management supervision. Russ Immarigeon and Meda Chesney-Lind (1992, 10) suggest that "[c]entral to the success of these plans is an assessment of these women's needs, monitoring of their program, and aftercare services."

   • One of the most unusual alternatives to incarceration for women convicted of nonviolent felonies is the residential program at Summit House. With facilities in three cities in North Carolina (Charlotte, Greensboro, and Raleigh), as well as a day reporting center for women in Greensboro, Summit

House opened its doors in 1987 and lodges women and their children. The focus is on strengthening the mother-child bond, and they provide close supervision, group and individual counseling, substance abuse counseling, and twelve-step programs. Residents learn parenting skills and financial management, earn a GED or attend college or job training, and acquire other skills to strengthen their families and gain independence. Women and their children live at Summit House for from one to two years. This rehabilitation approach focuses on "treatment of offenders as women and mothers within larger systems of family and community" (Chapple et al. 1997, 88).

The North Carolina Department of Correction estimates that the average daily cost per inmate for the fiscal year ending June 30, 1997, was $63.27, or $23,093.55 per inmate for the year. Summit House reports that in the first quarter of fiscal year 1997–98 they served nineteen mothers and twenty-eight children, saving 1,214 potential prison days and 1,932 potential foster care days. Total program expenses were $472,684, the money being spent to maintain the families within the community and provide extensive treatment and rehabilitation.

Women at Risk, sponsored by Western Carolinians for Criminal Justice in Asheville, is a sixteen-week community-based treatment program serving female offenders as a condition of their regular or intensive probation. The program keeps women within the community, with their families, and provides intensive group sessions, intensive individual case management, and court advocacy. The goal is to reduce recidivism and enhance women's ability to lead productive, noncriminal lives.

In the first quarter of fiscal year 1997–98, Women at Risk served forty clients. Their operating budget is $153,726. Eighty-five percent of their graduates stay out of trouble for at least a year on average, and this model program addresses drug addiction, abuse histories, parenting skills, and referrals for job and education skill development. In fiscal year 1996–97, Women at Risk served sixty-seven clients and saved the taxpayers well over a million dollars in incarceration expenses. This demonstrates the huge financial incentive we have in funding alternatives to incarceration, in addition to supporting the programs that address specific needs of individual women.

• Homelessness and affordable housing are often serious problems for women facing a prison sentence or recently released, and a network of halfway houses in every state would support them as they work through their community-based programs. Living in halfway houses with their children would emphasize and reinforce the women's roles as mothers and family members. In addition to halfway houses, Pat Carlen (1990) recommends shelters for women to go to in times of crisis, and groups in the community that serve as support systems in which to share experiences and ideas.

• Drug treatment programs need to be expanded to include women with children and pregnant women. If the treatment is outpatient programming, there needs to be child care to free women up to attend sessions; if it is residential, children need to be living with their mothers. Michael Prender-gast et al. (1995) recommend a system-oriented approach that links criminal justice agencies, drug treatment programs, and social service agencies to provide the optimal network for women involved in drug treatment. We know that women bound for or coming out of prisons need services related to physical and sexual abuse, mental health, physical health, educational and job training, and parenting. Other problems that hinder successful community drug treatment include transportation and housing. Linkages between agencies should help coordinate and deliver these essential services.

Treatment services are available to only approximately 30 percent of offenders (male and female) on supervised probation, yet we know the need is greater. We spend about $45 million for 32,477 offenders in programs ranging from substance abuse halfway houses to mental health substance abuse centers to drug and alcohol education traffic schools. Drug and alcohol treatment may be the single most important aspect of crime prevention, and it is less costly to address it as prevention than within prison or even as an alternative to incarceration.

Concluding Comments

Jim Austin et al. (1992, 32–33) stress the importance of programs providing "the supervision necessary to foster both accountability and responsible, law-abiding behavior." The goal of alternatives to incarceration is to provide the most compassionate and rational system that reduces law-breaking behavior and at the same time addresses the underlying problems women in society face.

We have successful models. What we clearly need is the commitment to a new vision. A focus on "crime" takes us further from the real issues in our society. Building more prisons does not solve the problems of sexism, poverty, racism, economic marginalization, or abuse. We need to shift our focus from exclusively one on dysfunctional families and individuals to include analysis of our dysfunctional culture (Pipher 1984). A community-centered approach works on all aspects of these problems through face-to-face personal relationships, through building community networks, and through holding people and institutions accountable for their behavior.

Community-based programs save taxpayers money with a higher yield on investment. This investment is in human beings, and it must reflect the best we have to offer those in need, not what is most punitive. Pervasive distrust and shame-based punishment is contrary to our need to address the painful unfinished business in our lives. The various strands of the life stories of inmates, family members, community volunteers, and program providers contribute to our understanding of the networks that both hinder and support us. Now is the time to acknowledge that healing is done in a community that embodies equality, dignity, and justice. These women are not "other." They are us.

References

Albor, T. (1995, February 20). The women get chains . . . *The Nation,* 234–37.

Arnold, R. (1994). Black women in prison: The price of resistance. In M. Baca Zinn and B. Dill, eds., *Women of color in U.S. society,* 171–84. Philadelphia: Temple University Press.

Austin, J., B. Bloom, and T. Donahue. (1992, September). *Female offenders in the community: An analysis of innovative strategies and programs.* San Francisco: National Council on Crime and Delinquency.

Bagley, K., and A. Merlo. (1995). Controlling women's bodies. In A. Merlo and J. Pollock, eds., *Women, law, and social control,* 135–53. Boston: Allyn and Bacon.

Barry, E. (1985, July–August). Reunification difficult for incarcerated parents and their children. *Youth Law News,* 14–16.

Baunach, P. (1985). *Mothers in prison.* New Brunswick, N.J.: Transaction Books.

Belknap, J. (1996). *The invisible woman: Gender, crime, and justice.* Belmont, Calif.: Wadsworth Publishing.

Bergsmann, I. (1989, March). The forgotten few: Juvenile female offenders. *Federal Probation* 53: 73–78.

Bloom, B., M. Chesney-Lind, and B. Owen. (1994, May). Women in California prisons: Hidden victims of the war on drugs. *Report,* 1–10. San Francisco: Center on Juvenile and Criminal Justice.

Carlen, P. (1990). *Alternatives to incarceration.* Philadelphia: Open University Press.

Chapple, K., E. Cox, and J. MacDonald-Furches. (1997, September–October). Summit House: Alternative to prison for mothers, better future for kids. *Community Corrections Report* 4 (6): 85–86, 88.

Chesler, P. (1994). *Patriarchy: Notes of an expert witness*. Monroe, Maine: Common Courage Press.

Chesney-Lind, M. (1995). Rethinking women's imprisonment: A critical examination of trends in female incarceration. In B. Price and N. Sokoloff, eds., *The criminal justice system and women: Offenders, victims, and workers*, 2d ed., 105–17. New York: McGraw-Hill.

———. (1997). *The female offender: Girls, women, and crime*. Thousand Oaks, Calif.: Sage Publications.

Cressey, D. (1965). Prison organizations. In J. March, ed., *Handbook of organizations*, 1023–70. Chicago: Rand McNally.

Faith, K. (1993). *Unruly women: The politics of confinement and resistance*. Vancouver, Canada: Press Gang Publishers.

Family Resource Coalition. (1986). Programs and resources for inmate parents and their children. *FRC Report* (1), 14–16.

Fogel, C., and S. Martin. (1992, February). The mental health of incarcerated women. *Western Journal of Nursing Research* 14 (1): 30–40.

Greenberg-Lake Analysis Group. (1990). *Shortchanging girls, shortchanging America*. Washington: American Association of University Women.

Harris, J. (1988). *"They always call us ladies": Stories from prison*. New York: Charles Scribner's Sons.

Henriques, Z. (1996). Imprisoned mothers and their children: Separation-reunion syndrome. *Women and Criminal Justice* 8 (1): 77–95.

Immarigeon, R. (1997, July–August). Gender-specific programming for female offenders. *Community Corrections Report on Law and Corrections Practice* 4 (5): 65–80.

Immarigeon, R., and M. Chesney-Lind (1992). *Women's prisons: Overcrowded and overused*. San Francisco: National Council on Crime and Delinquency.

Jones, M., and B. Sims. (1997, September). Recidivism of offenders released from prison in North Carolina: A gender comparison. *Prison Journal* 77 (3): 335–48.

Lord, E. (1995, June). A prison superintendent's perspective on women in prison. *Prison Journal* 75 (2): 257–69.

Mann, C. (1995). Women of color and the criminal justice system. In B. Price and N. Sokoloff, eds., *The criminal justice system and women: Offenders, victims, and workers*, 2d ed., 118–35. New York: McGraw-Hill.

Mauer, M., and T. Huling. (1995, October). *Young black Americans and the criminal justice system: Five years later*. Washington: Sentencing Project.

Merlo, A. (1995). Female criminality in the 1990s. In A. Merlo and J. Pollock, eds., *Women, law, and social control*, 119–34. Boston: Allyn and Bacon.

Morgan-Sharpe, E. (1992, Winter). Gender, race, and the law: Elements of injustice. *Justice Professional* 6: 86–93.

Naffine, N. (1989). Towards justice for girls: Rhetoric and practice in the treatment of status offenders. *Women and Criminal Justice* 1 (1): 3–19.

Nesbitt, C. (1995). *The female offender in the 1990s is getting an overdose of parity.* Nashville: Association on Programs for Female Offenders.

Pipher, M. (1984). *Reviving Ophelia: Saving the selves of adolescent girls.* New York: G. P. Putnam's Sons.

Prendergast, M., J. Wellisch, and G. Falkin. (1995, June). Assessment of services for substance-abusing women offenders in community and correctional settings. *Prison Journal* 75 (2): 240–56.

Rice, M. (1990). Challenging orthodoxies in feminist theory: A black feminist critique. In L. Gelsthorpe and A. Morris, eds., *Feminist perspectives in criminology*, 57–69. Philadelphia: Open University Press.

Richie, B. (1996). *Compelled to crime: The gender entrapment of battered black women.* New York: Routledge.

Schur, E. (1983). *Labeling women deviant: Gender, stigma, and social control.* Philadelphia: Temple University Press.

Sidel, R. (1996). *Keeping women and children last: America's war on the poor.* New York: Penguin Books.

Singer, M. (1995, January). The psychosocial issues of women serving time in jail. *Social Work* 40 (1): 103–13.

Sokoloff, N., and B. Price. (1995). The criminal law and women. In B. Price and N. Sokoloff, eds., *The criminal justice system and women: Offenders, victims, and workers*, 2d ed., 11–29. New York: McGraw-Hill.

Tonry, M. (1995). *Malign neglect: Race, crime, and punishment in America.* Oxford: Oxford University Press.

Van Voorhis, P., S. Browning, M. Simon, and J. Gordon. (1997, June). The meaning of punishment: Inmates' orientation to the prison experience. *Prison Journal* 77 (2): 135–67.

Widom, C. (1992). *The cycle of violence.* Research in Brief, 1–6. Washington: U.S. Government Printing Office, National Institute of Justice.

———. (1995, March). *Victims of childhood sexual abuse—Later criminal consequences.* Research in Brief. Washington: U.S. Government Printing Office, U.S. Department of Justice.

Wilson, W. (1987). *The truly disadvantaged: The inner city, the underclass, and public policy.* Chicago: University of Chicago Press.

INDEX